ISLAM & ECONOMICS

Shah Wali-Allah's Approach

ABDUL AZIM ISLAHI

THE ISLAMIC FOUNDATION

Islam and Economics: Shah Wali-Allah's Approach

First published in England by

THE ISLAMIC FOUNDATION

Markfield Conference Centre,
Ratby Lane, Markfield, Leicester, LE67 9SY United Kingdom
Tel: +44 (0) 1530 249230
E-mail: info@islamic-foundation.org.uk
Website: www.islamic-foundation.org.uk

Quran House,
PO Box 30611, Kenya
P.M.B 3193 Kano, Nigeria

Cataloguing in-Publication Data is available from the British Library

ISBN Paperback 978-0-86037-851-8
ISBN Ebook 978-0-86037-856-3

Cover Design: Nasir Cadir
Cover Artwork: Urdu calligraphy – Wikimedia Commons – Yethrosh, Madrassa illustration: Iman Anwar
Typesetting: Litebook Prepress Services

Dedication

Dedicated to my parents

'My Lord! Have mercy on them both as they did care for me when I was little.'(al-Isra 17:24)

Contents

Introduction

Islamic Economics is a nascent, still evolving, social discipline. It is an effort to weave together the Islamic teachings about the principles, values, and institutions of economics, in order to develop a *new* paradigm of economics, and not merely adding one more wing, sub-set or branch to the contemporary science of economics as development in the West in the post-Adam Smith period till today, as has been the case with respect to welfare economics, behavioral economics, evolutionary economics, home economics, environmental economics etc.

The whole fabric of contemporary economics is built around the concept of separation of science from ethics and religion. As such economics, despite being a social science, was cast into the moulds of a natural science with the result that it not only relied mainly on tools of abstraction and selectivity, but it has also gradually disengaged itself from the society and humanity. Consequently the market occupied the centre space in decision-making. The whole economic paradigm hovered around a unidimensional concept of man, motivated by self-interest and motivated by profit. This has resulted in a diabolic situation as, on the one hand, the West has achieved stupendous development in production and wealth creation, and on the other, has led to the establishment of an economy and society where mal-distribution of wealth and wide-spread economic injustices prevail. They have torn the society into haves and have-nots and consequently engaged peoples, nations, and countries against each other, threatening the very survival of mankind. According to the UN Food Summit (Sept. 23, 2021), 768 million people of the world are facing hunger in 2020, up some 118 million from the previous year. Some 274 million people worldwide need some form of emergency assistance to survive. Today the richest 1 percent of the world has twice as much wealth as 6.9 billion people of the world. In the United States, 3 richest persons have wealth equal to the bottom 160 million people.

America is one of the richest countries of the world. With 5 percent of the world population, it has over 20 percent of the world's gross production. Yet 20 percent of American families have no assets at all. The situation of the Black American families is worse as 37 percent of them do not have any assets. The difference between the salaries of a middle executive and the top corporate executive in the US was 20 times in 1950's but now it is 400 times.

The Pandemic has further wreaked havoc. Almost 89 million American have lost jobs, over 44.9 million have been sickened by the virus, and over 724,000 have died from it. Yet, American billionaires, particularly those with investment in pharmaceutical industries are greedy beneficiaries; 45 billionaires are reported to have grown $ 2.1 trillion riches during these two years of global disaster. According to Forbes data analysed by "Americans for Tax Fairness (AFT), and the Institute for Policy Studies Program on Inequality (IPS), their collective wealth increased by 70 percent; from $ 3 trillion at the start of the COVID virus on March 18, 2020, to over $ 5 trillion by October 15, 2021.

The fact is that today the world economy, as well as the science of economics both are in a state of crisis. Profs Abhijit V. Banerjee and Esther Duflu, have, in their book '*Good Economies for Hard Times*' (2019) produced a valuable critique of contemporary economics, differentiating between good economics and bad economics and lamenting the distrust which common people have about economics. They also show how separation between economics and ethics have led to the production of a society that lacks justice and well-being of all its members. This is so because, in the words of the authors, "there is plenty of bad economics around".

The authors sum up the failure of economics by focusing on the faulty starting point of economics in the West.

> "Economists have a tendency to adopt a notion of well-being that is often too narrow, some version of income or material consumption. And yet all of us need much more than that to have a fulfilling life: the respect of the community, the comforts of family and friends, dignity, lightness, pleasure. The focus on income alone is not just a convenient shortcut. It is a distorting lens, that often has led the smartest economists down the wrong path, policy makers to the wrong decisions, and all too many of us to the wrong obsessions."

Their critique of modern economics is very succinct.

> "Bad economics underpinned the grand giveaway to the rich and squeezing of welfare programs, sold the idea that the state is impotent and corrupt and the poor are lazy, and paved the way to the current stalemate of exploding inequality and angry inertia. Blinkered economies told us trade is good for everyone, and faster growth is everywhere. Blind economics missed the explosion in inequality all over the world, the increasing social fragmentations that come with it, and the impending environmental disaster, delaying action, perhaps irrevocably."[1]

Search for good economics is the cry of the hour. Efforts to develop Islamic economics are a positive contribution in that direction. The thoughts of Shah Wali-Allah are a valuable source of light and guidance in this respect.

Shah Wali-Allah of Delhi (1703-1762) was one of the most profound, innovative and outstanding scholars and reformers of Islamic history. The Mughal empire (1526 – mid 1857), after a glorious sway, had

[1] Abhijit V. Banerjee and Esther Duflo, *Good Economics for Hard Times: Better Answers to our Biggest Problems*, Penguin Books, UK, 2019.

sunk into the throes of a crisis. Shah Wali-Allah was deeply concerned over the intellectual poverty, sectarian divide, political instability, internal dissentions and external threats to the Muslim empire.

He was not a political activist. He never associated himself with the princely powers. Yet his wide ranging contributions in the expositions and reconstruction of Islamic thought, his unceasing efforts to promote education and social reform and his thoughtful criticism of Muslim political, social and religious leadership played an important role in preserving and promoting Islamic values, thought and culture. He presented Islamic theology, philosophy, history, sufism, jurisprudence and socio-political thought with clarity, comprehension and applicability to his own times. In an era when involvement with fiqh had become so overwhelming that direct access to the original sources and inferences from the Qur'an and Sunnah had become few and far between, he re-emphasized the need to recourse first and foremost to the Qur'an and Sunnah, both in intellectual reconstruction and in the promotion of education, life and society. He translated the Qur'an in Persian to open up the meaning of the Book to the Persian speaking people of his country. He wrote extensively on different aspects of Islamic thought and history and presented Islam as a comprehensive and superior world-view and a complete code of life, providing guidance in matters of faith, character, family, economy, society, law and state, judiciary and national and international affairs. His *magnum opus* the *Hujjat Allah al-Balighah* is a masterpiece of scholarship and insightful understanding of the Islamic code of life, rightly described by Sayyid Abdul Hasan Nadvi as "a comprehensive and cogent work presenting a synthesis of the Islamic creed, devotion, transactions, morals, social philosophy, statecraft and spirituality."

He authored some eighty books covering almost every aspect of Islamic thought and culture. His thoughts and contributions in respect of economic issues are also extremely perceptive, penetrating and have a flavour of originality. He has not expressed his views in the manner they are presented in a textbook. Yet he has covered a wide range of issues and problems related to all the five areas that go to make up the modern science of economics: economic philosophy, economic analysis, economic institutions , economic policies, and economic history. Major economic issues he has covered include classification of wants, consumption, production, exchange, trade, property, business ethics, money and interest, labour and variety of occupations, division of labour, market mechanism and its imperfections, just price and market management, waqf, public goods and property, role of the state in the economy, taxation and public finance and historical trends in socio-economic development of mankind.

It is very interesting to note that in respect of money, consumption, prohibition of interest, taxations and its need, are limitations, as also its impact both positive and negative, he has not only expounded the Islamic position but also undertaken its analysis and consequences, as is done in modern economic analysis. His overall emphasis is not only on *efficient production* but also on *just distribution*, emphasizing that the purpose of all economic activity is not merely personal satisfaction, but need fulfilment in respect of all members of the society and their social well-being and development. 'Sustainable development' is a modern concept, first propounded in 1987, and developed during 1992-2015 and finally formulated in the form of the "17 Sustainable Development Goals" in 2015. It seems to be a modern statement of what Shah Wali-Allah said in the mid 18th century.

Similarly his exposition of the four stage socio-economic development of human society, from primitive family to city-state, national empire and finally global Khilafat is a highly perceptive exposition of history, more comprehensive and realistic than that of Ibn Khaldun and a forerunner to formulation of theories of stages of historical growth in the 20th century, from Arnold Toynbee to W. Rostowe and others. He is a pioneer in all these respects.

We are grateful to Dr. Abdul Azim Islahi for producing this well-researched and well-written introduction to the economic ideas and teachings of Shah Wali-Allah of Delhi. Dr. Islahi has done justice to Shah Wali-Allah and the value of his work has increased by the contextualization of Shah Wali-Allah's thoughts and contribution both in the historical context of the sub-continent and the deeper stream of Islamic thought from Abu Yusuf and Farabi to Ibn Taymiyyah and Ibn Khaldun.

This is an invaluable source book for all students and scholars of Islamic economics. This is a companion volume to his earlier study of Ibn-Taymiyyah[2] and these two books are a must read for all those who are engaged in the study of Islamic economics. I hope Dr. Islahi or some researcher may also undertake a comparative study of Shah Wali-Allah and his contemporary in Britain Adam Smith (1723-90), who is one of the key founders of modern economics.

It is interesting that Adam Smith was a professor of philosophy and his book *'Theory of Moral Sentiments'* (1759) emphasized the relevance of ethics to economic behavior. He emphasized in this book that personal interest and gain is only one aspect of human character. Self-utilization and self-formulations must be accompanied by ethics of sympathy, passion, concern for others, and desire to be recognized and accepted by others. Unfortunately he moved towards a rather uni-dimensional character of man and society in his other and more influential work, *'The Wealth of Nations'* (1776). Later developments of economics drew on *The Wealth of Nations* and that is how what could have been 'good economics' ended up as 'bad and poor economics'. That is why humanity is searching today for an economic order that may ensure expanding production and sustained development along with well-being of *all* members of the human society, resulting in the establishment of a just socio-economic order and not an economy resulting in the enrichment of a few and the impoverishment of the many.

Khurshid Ahmad
May 2022

---

2 Abdul Azim Islahi *'Economic Concepts of Ibn Taymiyyah'*, The Islamic Foundation, Leicester, 1996

Preface

Shah Wali-Allah Dihlawi was a profound thinker, brilliant scholar and versatile genius. He contributed immensely to various branches of Islamic learning in a period of waning Islamic culture and Shariah sciences all over the world, and particularly, during the declining phase of Mughal rule in India. That is why his birth is considered by many scholars no less than a miracle.

In fact, for many centuries before Shah Wali-Allah the world had not seen a great Muslim scholar who could match the towering personalities of al-Ghazali, Ibn Taymiyyah, Ibn Rushd and Ibn Khaldun in radical thinking and original ideas. Essentially, he brought about a revolution in Muslim minds by his writings on various branches of Shariah sciences. His ideas have relentlessly inspired his readers till this date.

Shah Wali-Allah's contributions include commentaries on the Qur'an and Hadith, principles of their interpretation, fiqh, principles of jurisprudence, dialecticism (*'ilm al-kalām*), wisdom (*ḥikmah*) and the philosophy of the Shariah, biography of the Prophet Muhammad and his Caliphs, *taṣawwuf* and related disciplines, Arabic poetry and grammar. He also wrote in the areas of sociology, politics, psychology, education, ethical philosophy and economy. When comparing his contributions in various branches of knowledge, he was the Abu Yusuf of his time, a replica of al-Ghazali and parallel to Ibn Taymiyyah. His magnum opus *Ḥujjat Allāh al-Bālighah*, one of the most powerful works of Islamic scholarship, bears resemblance with Ibn Khaldun's *Muqaddimah* in rendering difficult scientific ideas into Arabic. He appears to be like al-Farabi while discussing the concept of *al-millat al-quṣwā* (the perfect nation) in his work *Al-Budūr al-Bāzighah*, and is comparable with Ibn Rushd in his jurisprudential discourses. In many cases he surpassed his predecessors in depth of thought and clarity of ideas, which is why hardly any other scholar of the later centuries attracted as much attention of writers and researchers as he did.

In 2011 the present author published his work *Islamic Economic Thinking in the 12th AH/18th CE Century with Special Reference to Shah Wali-Allah al-Dihlawi* from the King Abdulaziz University, Jeddah, with the Turkish Translation published in Istanbul by IKAM/ILKE in 2018. Therein three scholars were selected, namely, Muhammad ibn Abd al-Wahhab, Uthman dan Fodio and Shah Wali-Allah Dihlawi, to study their economic thoughts. These scholars were born into three different regions of the Muslim world and brought about a revolution in thinking and action. While investigating the economic ideas of Muslim scholars of the twelfth century AH/eighteenth century CE, the focus was on the economic thought of Shah Wali-Allah as he had considerably more to offer in this area. His contribution is much wider in scope and deeper in analysis than his two contemporary scholars, being far ahead of his contemporaries on economic issues as well. In fact, after Ibn Khaldun the Islamic world has not seen such a great writer on socio-economic problems. In this respect, Shah Wali-Allah not only revived the economic ideas of past Muslim scholars but also made his own original contributions.

After the appearance of the above-mentioned work, a few readers observed that Shah Wali-Allah Dihlawi deserved exclusive and separate treatment. Convinced by their suggestions, I decided to improve and expand the chapters related to Shah Wali-Allah's life and add some new chapters on his economic ideas. Thus, the first chapter of this book provides some background knowledge of the world and the Muslim situation at the time of Shah Wali-Allah, followed by a chapter detailing his life and the environment in which he lived. The third chapter describes his intellectual and academic heritage with an introduction to his major works and a comprehensive list of his writings collected from various sources. Strictly Islamic in scope, Shah Wali-Allah's economic concerns revolved around a classification of wants, business ethics, prohibited and promoted contracts, cooperation and division of labour, opportunity cost, property rights, money and interest, and a balanced variety of occupations. He also discussed issues relating to public finance and mankind's socio-economic development. In the previous work, there were only four chapters on Shah Wali-Allah. The present study constitutes nine chapters, including the conclusion. The present work contains transliteration with diacritical marks as well as two separate indexes—names and subjects—to make it more user-friendly. Humbly, I feel that this book is a modest but significant addition to the works on Shah Wali-Allah Dihlawi.

I would like to express my thanks to my learned colleague Dr Ali Ahmad Nadwi at the Islamic Economics Institute, a fan of Shah Wali-Allah in his own right. He was first to draw my attention to undertake this project and showed interest in its completion.

My thanks are also due to our very much-loved Dean, Dr Abdullah Qurban Turkistani, who has provided us a peaceful congenial research atmosphere at the Islamic Economics Institute of King Abdulaziz University.

Last but not least, I am deeply indebted to Prof Khurshid Ahmad, one of the oldest surviving pioneers of Islamic Economics, who has been kind enough to grant a precious introduction to this work.

Finally, I must inscribe as Shah Wali-Allah Dihlawi used to write at the end of his works:

Al-ḥamdu li-llāh awwalan wa ākhiran wa ẓāhiran wa bāṭinā

Abdul Azim Islahi
Jeddah
4 Shaban 1443 / 08. 03. 2021

1

Overview of the Muslim Situation during Shah Wali-Allah's Time

Shah Wali-Allah Dihlawi lived in the eighteenth century (corresponding to the twelfth century After Hijra). During this century, decaying forces in the great Muslim civilization sped up and the Western colonization of Muslim lands began. At the same time, some sort of awakening, soul-searching, and efforts at renovation by Islamic thinkers were also initiated. Shah Wali-Allah was part of this eighteenth-century trend. To gain a proper perspective, a general historical overview of the time period including shedding light on the major aspects of awakening and their various manifestations would be in order.

1.1 The World and the Muslim situation in 12th c. AH/18th c. CE

The world in the twelfth/eighteenth century was full of important events. It saw war and peace,[1] decay and the fall of empires and the rise of new states.[2] It was the century of American independence[3] and the French Revolution.[4] Scientific inventions marked the Industrial Revolution.[5]

Furthermore, the frequent occurrence of epidemics and famines wiped out a substantial part of many populations.[6] In many countries, slavery was abolished.[7] This same century also produced eminent philosophers, scientists and thinkers.[8] In the field of economics, mercantilism was replaced by physiocracy at the hands of François Quesnay (1694–1774),[9] which, in turn, was dethroned by Adam Smith (1723–90), the Scottish economist, philosopher, and the founder of the modern science of economics.

Colonization of Muslim countries by westerns powers also began during this century. Russia occupied the Crimean Khanate, Bonaparte invaded Egypt, and the West continued its occupation of Indonesia. The British East India Company, after consolidating its power in Madras and Calcutta, started extending its rule into neighbouring states. This period also marked the beginning of modernization, intellectual awakening, and religious revival among Muslims after a long time of stagnation and blind imitation. According to Hodgson, 'By the end of the eighteenth century, the number of earnest reform movements being launched surely exceeded the average.'[10] He enumerates upon the chiliastic Shi'ism in the Safavid realm and the revivers of Sirhindi's Shariah-minded Sufism in India, at the top of which, no doubt, was Shah Wali-Allah of Delhi. In addition, revivalist movements were also started in the Arabian Peninsula by Muhammad ibn Abd al-Wahhab (1115–1206/1703–92) and in West Africa by Uthman dan Fodio (1167–1233/1754–1817). The following is a somewhat detailed picture of the Muslim situation during the eighteenth century.

1.2 Important Muslim regions

Based on regions of mass Muslim population and their governments in the eighteenth century, the following six broad categories of importance can be delineated: (a) Ottomans and the Arab Peninsula; (b) North African States and Bilad al-Sudan; (c) Safavids and Afghans; (d) the Indian Subcontinent; (e) Khanates in Central Asia; and (f) Muslim states in Far East Asia.

1.2.1 Ottomans and the Arab Peninsula

The signs of decadence in the Ottoman rule set in within the sixteenth century when the empire reached its zenith at the hands of Sultan Suleiman the Magnificent (926–74/1520–66). They became more visible in the subsequent centuries. During the eighteenth century, the Ottomans were exploited by European powers. Although conquests and defeats continued during this time, as a whole, the Ottoman territories contracted. After the end of the great struggle against Russia and Austria in 1739, the Ottomans entered a long period of peace on their western frontier. This ended in 1768 when the Ottomans went to war against Russia. Finally, peace was arranged at Kuchuk Kainarji or *Küçük Kaynarca* in July 1774 after a treaty between Turkey and Russia in which the latter emerged victorious from this war.

Between 1739 and 1798, the empire enjoyed peaceful relations with major European governments, which, in turn, benefitted it in consolidating its position and allowing attention to be paid to learning about European war techniques.

During this period, the Ottomans' hold on Arab regions was loosened. In 1798, Bonaparte occupied Egypt without any significant resistance. Although he was forced to withdraw as a result of British intervention, the impact on Muslim society and culture was nonetheless far-reaching. During this period, the Ottomans were also engaged in military confrontation with the Persian ruler Karim Khan Zand (d. 1779), in which the latter occupied parts of the Ottoman territory of Iraq. The Hijaz, however, remained under the protection of the Ottomans throughout these years. Yemen already had independent rule. Omar and the Saidi dynasty ruled Oman,[11] and Banu Khalid ruled al-Ahsa.[12] In 1795, al-Khalidi rule was put to an end by Āl Saūd.[13] In the *Waqā'i'-i Manāzil-i Rūm*, an eighteenth-century diary of an ambassador, we find the 'picture of the corruption and inefficiency of the Ottoman government of Basrah, the insecurity of roads in Iraq and of the rebellion of Shaykh Suwaini in the Basrah area and of Sulaiman al-Shawi in the neighborhood of Baghdad.[14]

1.2.2 North African States and Bilad al-Sudan[15]

For some time the Ottomans maintained their three regencies of North African Algeria, Tunis and Tripoli. The Moroccans generally kept their kingdom independent. Against North Africa, South and West Africa did not attract the attention of the Ottomans, nor for that matter did their North African suzerainties. There are reports of trade relations and scholarly exchanges between the two parts, but there was an absence of political contacts. This part of the African continent occupied great importance during the eighteenth and subsequent centuries. Muslim leaders of Hausaland especially played a significant role in Western Sudan.[16] Indeed, the great African Muslim leader Shehu Uthman dan Fodio carried his reviving campaign into Hausaland, thereby influencing the whole region.

In Bilad al-Sudan or Sudanic lands, as the region was generally called, a Western presence was not a serious factor during the eighteenth century. In the Niger, Sudan Muslims were on the defensive against a revival of pagan power: 'But it was a time of patient scholarship, intent on spelling out for the ruler and the city population what was meant by justice and proper living, in the Islamic sense, in a Sudanic condition. The most prominent scholar of the time was writing long-cherished studies in which he taught not only the details of the law, but the broader principles of fair dealing in commerce, in government, and in courts of justice.'[17]

1.2.3 Safavids and Afghans

In Iran, the Safavid Kingdom was brought to an end by Nadir Shah in 1722. Nadir Shah himself was assassinated in 1747, yet this did not end the glory of Iran. It remained a power to be reckoned with within West Asia up to the end of the Zand dynasty in 1794. Iranian rulers, however, did not take any notice of developments and advancements being made in Europe.

In the Safavid regime of the eighteenth century, political disorder and economic depression were severe; in essence, they suffered a dispersal of power. In 1722, the Afghans occupied Isfahan and put an end to the

Safavid regime. They could not, however, establish a dynasty there. Nadir Shah (d. 1747) reorganized the Safavid forces and expelled the Afghans, and in 1736 he proclaimed himself as the King of Persia, founding the Afsharid dynasty (1736–96). The next year he extended his rule to Afghanistan by capturing Kandahar. He invaded India in 1739 and ransacked Delhi, thereby ruining the city.[18] Nadir Shah also occupied Oman which was fast becoming the centre of the reviving Arab mercantile power in the Indian Ocean.[19]

Nadir faced almost continuous rebellions towards the end of his reign, which only multiplied his atrocities by way of response. When at last he was killed, his family held power for only a matter of months.[20] After him, Karim Khan Zand, an Iranian general, reinstalled a Safavid survivor as king and unsuccessfully tried to restore the Safavid dynasty. In 1753, he proclaimed himself as King of Iran and ruled till 1779. His descendants were then set aside by the Qajar tribe and a new dynasty was established to rule up to 1925; all in all, an uneventful rule. Thus, in the eighteenth century, Iran was ruled by four dynasties—a sign of a power struggle that left little scope for healthy construction and socio-economic development.

It may be noted that after the death of Nadir Shah, Afghans declared their independence from Iran and declared Ahmad Shah Abdali (d. 1186/1772) as their king. Abdali began his career as a young soldier in the military of the Afsharid kingdom where he was brought as a prisoner of war. With his abilities he had gained the confidence of Nadir Shah and soon rose to become a commander of the Abdali Regiment, a cavalry of four thousand Abdali Pashtun soldiers. He belonged to the Durrani branch of the Abdali tribe of Afghanistan and established the Durrani Kingdom (1747–1826). He is regarded as the founder of the modern state of Afghanistan. Abdali's successors proved to be incompetent and governed so ineffectually that within fifty years of his death, the Durrani dynasty came to an end.

1.3 Mughals and the emerging Indian Sultanates

The last great Mughal emperor, Aurangzeb Alamgir, died in 1119/1707 after fifty years of rule, leaving behind, in terms of area, the largest empire in the whole of Indian history. Adversary forces quickly arose from each corner as if they had been waiting for the emperor's departure. Although the Mughal dynasty survived for another 150 years, it was all to no avail. One weak puppet ruler followed another. In the previous century, only three rulers had been in power. The eighteenth century saw about a dozen of them,[21] a clear sign of destabilization and anarchism. India was also attacked by the Iranian king Nadir Shah in 1739 and the capital, Delhi, was looted and plundered for several days. Ahmad Shah Abdali (r. 1747–72) attacked India several times. His last assault came in 1761 when he defeated the ambitious Marathas, a regional force approaching Delhi so as to take over Delhi's rule. But the Mughal ruler had no courage nor guts to stabilize his forces and restore Mughal power and prestige.

Finding the Mughal ruler weak and unable to control the Empire, many ambitious governors and commanders declared their own rules in their states—Najib al-Dawlah (d. 1770) in Rohilkhand, Sa'adat Ali Khan (d. 1739) in Oudh, Murshid Quli Khan (d. 1727) in Bengal, Nizam al-Mulk Asif Jah (d. 1748) in Hyderabad Deccan and Haydar Ali (d. 1782) in Mysore. The Sikhs also saw in the troubles of the empire a chance to establish their own dominion, at least in the Punjab. The Marathas, who were active in southern India since Aurangzeb's time, advanced toward Delhi to establish their hegemony over the central region. The English East India Company also expanded its political, economic, and military powers, so much so that the survival of new emerging states depended on its support and sympathy.[22] The Company was well-equipped with the latest European warfare techniques and the most effective modern weaponry. Nawwab Siraj al-Dawlah challenged the Company, but his 120,000 Bengali army was defeated by 3,000 English forces in 1757. The treachery of Mir Ja'far (d. 1765)—a confidante of the Nawwab—also played a crucial role in this defeat at Plassey. Thereafter, English influence increased at a pace.

Another able and enlightened ruler who challenged the increasing power of the East India Company was Tipu Sultan of the Mysore Kingdom. He refused to compromise with English forces and fought a daring war in 1799. The same story of Siraj al-Dawlah was repeated here too; Tipu was killed while fighting bravely in the midst of his troops. The British forces surrounded his capital Srirangapatna and tried to persuade him to surrender. He rejected this offer contemptuously and fiercely fought on, saying that: 'One day's life of a lion is preferable to hundred years' existence of a jackal.'[23] Tipu Sultan's martyrdom in 1799 removed a huge obstacle in the way of the English East India Company, enabling it to extend its influence and occupation of southern India.

1.4 Khanates in Central Asia

Central Asia had many small Muslim states which were ruled by Mongol Khanates. During the eighteenth century, these states faced advancing Russian forces who, in 1783, annexed the Crimea. According to Lewis: 'This was the first cession of old Muslim territory inhabited by Muslim people.'[24] Imam Shaykh Mansur, a Chechen warrior and Muslim mystic, led a coalition of Muslim Caucasian tribes from throughout the Caucasus in a holy war against the Russian invaders during 1785 to 1791.

In the previous centuries, there had been many wars between Uzbeks and Iranians, but during the eighteenth century they kept themselves away from Iranian affairs. The Khanates of Khivah, Bukhara and Khoqand were all independent Muslim powers, but their economic and military strengths were much-reduced during this time. Around the mid-eighteenth century, the Chinese Empire occupied the Muslim state of Kashgharia in the upper Tarim basin. Thus, the northern Khanates were divided between the Russian and Chinese Empires. This occupation expanded in the century that followed, although not without resistance.

1.5 Muslim states in Far East Asia

The Dutch ruled Malacca from 1641 to 1824 (with a brief period of British rule during the Napoleonic Wars), but they were not interested in developing it as a trading centre, instead placing greater importance on Batavia (Jakarta). Indonesia was a colony of the Netherlands from the seventeenth century until the end of World War II. Shaykh Yusuf (1626–99), a Madinah-trained scholar, led a holy war against the Dutch in Indonesia and was later exiled to South Africa,[25] where he continued his teaching, preaching and reforms. He is considered by Greyling as the founder of Islam in South Africa.[26]

1.6 The economic front

Muslim states faced difficult times during the period under study, not only in the political arena but in the economic field as well. Capitulation granted to European traders in Muslim lands put the local population at a competitive disadvantage and soon removed almost the whole of the trading class from the Ottomans to privileged foreign jurisdiction. Thus, the loss of power to effectively regulate or to tax the increasing commerce was disastrous. Lewis writes: 'By the later eighteenth century, the balance of trade had changed decisively in favour of European and against the Islamic lands of the Middle East and North Africa.'[27] During the eighteenth century, the economic weakness of Muslim governments as contrasted with Europe became so overwhelming that it paved the way for the latter to dominate the former politically and militarily in the century that followed.[28] In essence, the Dutch and British powers, who had replaced the Portuguese in eastern trade, became stronger and stronger.

Commenting on this economic condition, Lewis says: 'Despite some occasional successes, the eighteenth century was on a whole a bad time for the Islamic states and the awareness of Muslims of their changed position is indicated in a number of ways.'[29] Some of the factors that brought about this change include the increasing cost of armaments and war, the adverse effects of rising prices on trade and the general economic condition, technological backwardness, and a lack of progress in agriculture, industry and transport within Muslim countries.

An eighteenth-century diary shows that in Iraq, 'the Jewish community was commercially very prosperous, and one of its members named Abdullah was not only a rich merchant, but exercised considerable political influence in Basra.'[30]

Tipu Sultan tried to develop a kind of mercantilism. He placed a number of restrictions on European traders while encouraging the indigenous Arab and Indian traders.[31] The embassy sent by him to the Ottoman sultan sheds light on 'Tipu's commercial ambition in the Persian Gulf and on certain aspects of his administration. It also describes the position of the Indian merchants in the Persian Gulf and the part they played in its economic life. It further throws light that, in spite of the efforts of Haydar Ali (r. 1761–82), Tipu's father the founder of Mysorian sultanate, and Tipu Sultan to build a mercantile marine and a navy, the Mysorians were still lagging far behind the Europeans in the technique of shipbuilding and the art of navigation.'[32] Hodgson observes: 'What was decisive in Muslim lands at this time was especially one feature: The West's tremendous expansion of commercial power.'[33] Tipu Sultan of the Mysore Kingdom well realized this but was unsuccessful in his efforts to keep it in check.

1.7 Awakening among the Ottomans

1.7.1 Military modernization efforts of Ottoman Sultans

In 1734, Ahmad, originally a Frenchman who embraced Islam, was assigned to establish a school of military engineering. Another modernizing step was taken in 1773 when a school of naval engineering was opened. French and other European military instructors were hired to train Turkish officers in the new art of warfare.[34]

The Treaty of Kuchuk Kainarji, concluded in 1774, in which the Ottomans lost the Crimea, shook the Ottomans out of their complacency. They realized that for the empire to continue to exist, it had to overhaul its military apparatus. Sultan Salim III (1761–1808) undertook the necessary reforms. In 1792–93, he promulgated 'a series of regulations designed to restructure the state's administration and military organization.' His far-reaching programme was known as the New Order.[35] An Institute of Language Instruction was opened where some European languages were taught to foreign service officials. Permanent diplomatic missions were opened in the main capitals of Europe and ambassadors were appointed. As a result, Sultan Salim III's regime stands midway between an old traditional empire and a newly emerging entity.[36] The French Revolution also affected Muslim thinking and was perhaps the first movement of ideas in Europe to break through the barrier that separated the two worlds of the Christian West and Muslim East.

1.7.2 Intellectual initiatives

This manifestation of an intellectual and scientific awakening among the Ottomans could be discerned from the early eighteenth century. Lewis reports that, in 1704, Umar Shifa'i authored a tract on the application of chemistry for medical purposes. Shifa'i presents it as a translation from Paracelsus. Another book on medical treatment was translated by Nuh bin Abd al-Mannan about the same period. A third physician, Sha'ban Shifa'i, wrote a book on conception and birth, including antenatal and postnatal care.[37]

In 1727, the Turkish printing press[38] was introduced for the first time in Istanbul by Ibrahim Mutafarriqah (d. 1745), a German Christian who had embraced Islam. He laboured for about eight years to achieve this goal. During this time, he published four maps. In 1726, he authored a treatise on 'print media' and its usefulness so as to convince people to welcome this innovation. He obtained a fatwa from the grand mufti and a royal decree (*farmān*) from Sultan Ahmad III in its favour, which was granted on condition that he would not publish religious works on fiqh, hadith, *tafsīr* and *kalām* (dialectic theology). He published his memorandum in 1731. The book is divided into three sections. The first looks at the importance of a well-ordered system of government in which he mentions some good systems existing in Europe. In the second section, he discusses the importance of the knowledge of geography. In the third, he reviews the military condition of France and its supremacy in war craft. Indeed, so impressed was he with the French system that he advised the Ottomans to imitate it.[39] Ibrahim published seventeen books up to 1743, after which he fell sick and died two years later in 1745.[40] Printing stopped after his death only to be restarted fifty years later in 1795.

It may be noted that in the Ottoman territory, the first newspaper was published in the 1790s in French and under French auspices.[41] Bonaparte, who invaded Egypt and took control over it for a while, introduced an Arabic and French printing press in Cairo in 1798.[42] Perhaps the first Arabic newspaper, *al-Tanbīh*, was launched in 1800, but was of short-lived duration.[43]

The innovation of the printing press, however, did play a revolutionary role in Turko-Arab society as it represented the success of new ideas over the closed, traditional mind. It prepared the Muslims to be ready to face and exchange new ideas. It also opened the door to the translation of Arabic, Turkish and Persian works into European languages and vice versa.

In the opinion of Ihsanoglu, the Ottomans did not close their eyes to whatever developments were taking place in Europe in the fields of science, technology, invention, medicine, geography, etc.[44] However, they did not borrow or copy everything. Their stance was rather eclectic, picking and choosing what to emulate. Thus, they borrowed their knowledge of medicine, geography, astronomy, war technology, etc. but refused to acquire European art and culture. Ihsanoglu presents various examples of the Ottoman's adoption of Western science and technology at this time.

During the twelfth/eighteenth century, ninety-four books were written in mathematics, out of which eighty-one were in Arabic and thirteen in the Turkish language. Ihsanoglu gives some detailed accounts of a few important works on the subject of mathematics.[45] He also noted some valuable works in astronomy, modern medicine, surgery, and geography, which were originally written or translated from European languages to Turkish and Arabic languages during the eighteenth century.[46] Perhaps up to the end of the eighteenth century at least, attention was not paid to the progress that Europe had made in other sciences, such as political economy and others.[47]

What the Ottomans lacked

From the foregoing account, it is clear that whatever awakening was found among the Ottomans was mainly among the ruling class. In many cases, they faced opposition from ignorant janissaries[48] and officials towards these selected Western sciences. As for the ulama and commoners, they were still strictly attached to their traditional patterns.[49]

While Ottoman scholars were the first to pay attention to modern sciences, their ulama were still far away from the intellectual awakening that was taking place in other parts of the Muslim world; instead, they opposed it.

1.8 India of Shah Wali-Allah's time

European forces started reaching India from the fifteenth century onwards—first the Portuguese, then the Dutch, and thereafter the French and British. Their power and authority increased with time. However, no record is available that suggests Indian rulers ever tried, at least up to the seventeenth century, to investigate the secret behind the Europeans strength. Perhaps the first time was when Tipu Sultan tried to establish contact with any European government. It is written that in 1787, 'Tipu Sultan of Mysore (r.1782–99) sent an embassy to Constantinople. This was required, in the first place, to establish commercial relations with the Ottoman Empire. In the second place, it was required to secure confirmation of Tipu's title to the throne of Mysore from the Caliph.'[50] To secure support against British forces and some native adversaries, he also sent messengers to the King of France, Louis XVI. However, the latter did not want to get entangled in Indian politics. According to Schimmel: 'Tipu Sultan even acknowledged the achievements of the French Revolution and called himself, in 1798, "Citizen Tipu."'[51] Tipu also tried to reform his administration in conformity with the Shariah. He organized trade and industry, had factories erected and the silk industry developed, and was one of few Indo-Muslim rulers who realized the importance of sea-power.[52] He also tried to modernize his army and invented the first missile in the eighteenth century.[53]

Later Mughal descendants failed to retain their traditional warfare apparatus, nor could they conceive of acquiring the latest European war technique, which any ruler should at least have taken notice of.

In this respect, they were nowhere in comparison to their contemporary Ottoman rulers. In this situation, they could not be expected to think about the modernization of their economy or of an educational system. Other regional states were also content to remain under British protection and use their arms and ammunition; they even sometimes used well-trained British soldiers. The deputation of Indian recruits and students to the West to acquire European sciences and training was perhaps beyond the imagination of the time. There is a report of a visit of only two Indians to Europe during this period; Shaykh I'tisam al-Din from Bengal in 1765, and Mirza Abu Talib Khan from Lucknow in 1799.[54] In their travel accounts, they described the manners and customs of the nations and countries they visited.

It was, however, left to the British, for their own benefit, to start the establishment of modern institutions. In 1781, Warren Hastings founded the Calcutta Madrasa, an educational institution on new patterns. In 1784, the Asiatic Society of Bengal was founded. Its library contained more than 6,000 valuable Arabic and Persian manuscripts. The translation of important works in oriental languages into English was initiated to acquaint the West with the heritage of the East. A more simplified Urdu prose, by eliminating difficult or pompous words of the Arabic and Persian languages and encouraging common local words in their place, was promoted to serve the purposes of the British Administration and its soldiers. A biased history was also written with the aim of creating hatred among Hindus and Muslims so as to divide and rule them comfortably.[55]

At Madras, which was an important seat of the East India Company since 1640, the British in the eighteenth century opened an Arabic madrasa. They also set up a printing press, where the first weekly appeared in 1785.[56] The first Persian weekly paper called *Mir'āt al-Akhbār* (the mirror of news) was issued by famous Hindu reformer Raja Rammohan Roy (1772–1833) from Calcutta on 12 April 1822. After a year, the first Urdu-Persian paper, a bilingual named *Shams al-Akhbār*, was started on 30 May 1823.[57]

The eighteenth century produced many great Muslim scholars, some of them developing religious studies like *tafsīr*, hadith and fiqh, while others excelled in philosophy and literature. According to Hodgson, 'By the eighteenth century, at least, Shar'ia work done in India was becoming influential in the Ottoman Empire: a collection of *fatāwā* decisions[58] made for Awrangzeb was honoured there (and Awrangzeb himself was honoured with the classical caliphal title of 'commander of the faithful' by an Ottoman author).'[59] Shah Wali-Allah—the tallest figure among them all, whose ideas we shall deal with in detail later—worked for overall reform and renovation. But surprisingly, he too takes no notice of the British danger. We also could not trace any discernible reaction in the sources, positive or negative, by the ulama of the eighteenth century against the British intruders. Theoretically, it is not possible that the ulama of Bengal and Mysore would have kept silent or remained indifferent against the British invaders. However, this has yet to be investigated.

1.9 Madinah, the City of the Prophet, becomes the foundation for revival and renovation

The so-called closure of the doors to ijtihad after the fourth/tenth century had a devastating effect not only on religious philosophy but intellectual growth as well. It discouraged original and creative thinking on religious issues, which unconsciously extended to social and scientific matters as well, so much so that after the ninth/fifteenth century one can hardly find a piece of work that matches the contribution of earlier periods. The sixteenth-century ulama discarded the use of analogy,[60] and prohibited a follower, for example, of Imam Shafi'i to give a fatwa according to the opinion of Imam Abu Hanifah.[61] Writing commentary and commentary-upon-commentary on earlier works, imitation and repetition became characteristic of our scholars.[62] It was not known how long such decline would continue. In referring to the eighteenth century, Zwemer, a zealous missionary and preacher of Christianity, writes that: 'The rise of innumerable heresies as the result of philosophical speculation, the spread of mysticism among the learned classes, and the return to many heathen superstitions on the part of the masses made Islam ripe for reform at the middle of the last century.'[63] Yet the eighteenth century did see a revival and awakening in various parts of the Muslim world. When one probes into the source of such inspiration, it would appear that it was the Prophet's city; directly or indirectly, all were inspired by the scholars of Madinah.

The eighteenth-century Madinah did not offer any material attraction; it was in fact the Prophet's neighbourhood that provided solace to restless hearts and agitated minds. Scholars from all over the Muslim world travelled to Hijaz, performed hajj, benefitted from the top ulama of the two holy cities, and returned home with religious enlightenment, new enthusiasm and fresh ideas. Some of them even settled there. Madinah, especially, became the station of great scholars who migrated from various regions. We find there the names of many famous scholars who originally belonged to the Najd in the Arabian Peninsula, Iraq, Central Asia, Iran, India, South West Africa, North Africa, Turkey, Bosnia, Egypt, Syria, Yemen, Hadramut, Daghistan, Uzbekistan, etc.[64] The most prominent among them was Muhammad Hayat al-Sindi who influenced almost all eighteenth-century revivalists.[65] These Medinan scholars did not launch any well-organized movement to bring about a revolution in thinking and change in the environment. Instead, they quietly inspired their students through their lectures and writings. Located in the spiritual centre of Islam, the scholarly community of Madinah, in general, was able to contact people from throughout the Muslim world because of the annual hajj gathering.[66] Thus, they had the opportunity to exercise some influence over the development of the Islamic movement in various parts of the world.

They exhorted their students to return to the basic sources of Islam—the Qur'an and the Sunnah— and to follow the practices of the Companions of the Prophet and to avoid blind following (*taqlīd*). This was a radical message in a period when people were completely divided on the basis of jurisprudential schools and any deviation from one's own school of jurisprudence was frowned upon. Actually, this revolutionary thinking in matters of jurisprudential practices also provided intellectual training that could be applied in other matters, particularly socio-economic and political. Its manifestations can be seen in the works and practices of all three great scholars of the century—Muhammad ibn Abd al-Wahhab, Shah Wali-Allah Dihlawi and Uthman dan Fodio.

It is worthwhile mentioning here a work that represents the new trend (in fact, it was also the earliest practice in Islam) that developed in eighteenth-century Madinah. Salih ibn Muhammad al-Umari al-Fullani (1166–1218/1751–1802), who originally belonged to the Fulani tribe[67] of West Africa but settled in Madinah, authored a work titled *Īqādh himām uli'l-abṣār li'l-iqtiḍā' bi Sayyid al-Muhājirīn wa'l-Anṣār wa taḥdhīrihim 'an al-ibtidā' al-sha'i' fi'l-qurā wa'l-amṣār min taqlīd al-madhāhib ma'al-ḥamiyyah wa'l-'aṣabiyyah bayn fuqahā' al-a'ṣār*. This work is translated as 'Awakening the fervor of those who have insight to follow the Leader (i.e. the Prophet) of Migrants and Helpers and warning them from common bad innovations existing in towns and cities regarding blindly following their respective jurisprudential schools with biased support and the defense of past jurists'. This long title suffices any further comment.

In this work, al-Fullani quotes Muhammad Ḥayat al-Sindi, the teacher of his teachers, saying that: 'It is obligatory for every Muslim to make an effort to understand the meaning of the Qur'an and to follow the *aḥādīth*, to know their meanings and to infer the rules. If he cannot, then he should follow the 'ulamā, without sticking to a particular school because it would be as if one were treating the *imām* as a prophet ... It is sheer ignorance, heresy and violation that people in our time make it compulsory to follow specific schools of jurisprudence and they do not permit, nor do they consider it valid to shift from one way to another way.'[68] Commenting on al-Sindi's statement, al-Fullani says that following a particular imam blindly is similar to equating him as one's Lord. This is what the Qur'an charged the People of the Book with.[69] In fact, these brain-and heart-storming ideas of the Medinan scholars marked the foundation of the modern period in Islamic history, the forerunners of which are Shaykh Muhammad ibn Abd al-Wahhab, Shah Wali-Allah Dihlawi and Shehu Uthman dan Fodio.

In the opinion of Hodgson, 'Though the eighteenth century was not without its interesting and creative figures, it was probably the least notable of all in achievement of high-cultural excellence; the relative barrenness was practically universal in Muslim lands.'[70] Hodgson's statement may be true to the political situation but not to the intellectual field. The eighteenth century is distinguished from its preceding two centuries in the sense that reformation and revival movements first started in this century. It produced great scholars in various parts of the Muslim world, such as

Shaykh Muhammad ibn Abd al-Wahhab in the Arabian Peninsula, Shah Wali-Allah of Delhi in the Indian Subcontinent and Shehu Uthman dan Fodio in West Africa, each of whom brought about a revolution in intellectual thinking and religious puritanism that marked the beginning of the modern period in the Muslim world.[71] Our aim in this work is to study the life and contributions of Shah Wali-Allah Dihlawi, especially his economic ideas.

Some authors think that the eighteenth-century reformative movements led by Shah Wali-Allah Dihlawi in India and Shehu Uthman dan Fodio in West Africa were influenced by Muhammad ibn Abd al-Wahhab's movement. This is, however, incorrect. When Dihlawi visited Hijaz in the year 1143 AH, Ibn Abd al-Wahhab was engaged in Basrah. His movement had not yet stabilized even in the areas of Najd. Uthman dan Fodio's visit to Arabia is not reported in the sources dealing with his life and work. Although he was trained by some teachers who had been to Islam's Holy places, they were too old to be aware of or affected by Ibn Abd al-Wahhab's movement. In fact, all these reformers were influenced by the same original sources, the Qur'an and the Sunnah, as well as the intellectual and religious network of Madinah. The following statement by Mawlana Sayyid Abul Hasan Ali Nadwi supports our claim:

> The thought and convictions of Shah Waliullah and Shaykh Muhammad b. Abdul Wahhab in regard to Divine Unicity, its elaboration in the light of the Qur'anic verses and the distinction between Divine Unity and Divine Providence indicate a great deal of similarity. It was because both had delved deep into the Qur'an and the Sunnah.[72]

Notes and References

1. Such as The Seven Years' War fought among European powers in various theatres around the world during 1756–63. Namely, the Russo-Turkish War 1768–74; the Russo-Turkish War 1787–92; the American Civil War 1775–83; when the Russian Empire annexed the Crimean Khanate in 1783; the Battle of Plassey which

signalled the beginning of British rule in India in 1757; the First Anglo-Maratha War 1775–82; and the Anglo-Mysore Wars during 1766–99.

2. For example, the Afghans conquered Iran, ending the Safavid dynasty in 1722; Nadir Shah assumed the title of Shah of Persia and founded the Afsharid dynasty in 1736. He ruled until his death in 1747. Ahmad Shah Abdali founded the Durrani Empire in modern day Afghanistan in 1747. A number of new regional kingships emerged in India. The first Saudi Government was founded by Muhammad ibn Saud in 1744.
3. In 1789, George Washington was elected President of the United States; he served until 1797.
4. The French Revolution of 1789–99.
5. In 1712, the steam engine was invented by Thomas Newcomen. In 1765, James Watt enhanced Newcomen's steam engine, allowing new steel technologies. The Spinning Jenny created by James Hargreaves in 1764 brought on the Industrial Revolution.
6. For example, with the 1738–56 famine across the Sahel, half of the population of Timbuktu died; the famine of 1740-41 in Ireland killed ten per cent of the population; the Bengal famine of 1770 killed one third of the Bengal population; a famine in Czech lands during 1770–71 killed hundreds of thousands; in 1783, a famine in Iceland was caused by the Laki volcanic eruption; in 1793, the largest yellow fever epidemic in American history killed as many as 5,000 people in Philadelphia—roughly ten per cent of the population.
7. Russia abolished slavery in 1723. Peter the Great converted his household slaves into house serfs; the Austrian monarchy abolished serfdom in 1781–85 as a first step with a second step taken in 1848, and Upper Canada banned slavery in 1793.
8. Such as Benjamin Franklin (1705–90), the founding father of the United States of America. Immanuel Kant (1724–1804), an eighteenth-century German philosopher, David Hume (1711–76), the Scottish philosopher; John Law (1671–1729), the Scottish economist; Jean-Jacques Rousseau, the French writer and philosopher, etc.
9. François Quesnay (1694–1774) was a French economist of the Physiocratic School. The founding document of the Physiocratic system was François Quesnay's *Économique* (1759).
10. Hodgson, *The Venture of Islam*, p. 159.
11. Muḥibbul-Hasan, *Waqā'i'-i Manāzil-i Rūm*, p. 16.
12. Ibid., p. 17.

13. Ibid.
14. Ibid., p. 3.
15. *Bilad al-Sudan* is the name early Muslim historians gave to the vast region of savanna grassland sandwiched by the Sahara and the dense forest stretching from the shores of the Atlantic in the west to the Nile in the east.
16. Hausaland, in the period under study, comprised the Zaria-Kano-Kodsina axis, with the three other kingdoms of Gobir, Zamfara and Kebbi as the Western axis. The Fulani people were widespread throughout the western Sudan.
17. Hodgson, *The Venture of Islam*, p. 158.
18. Rizvi, *Shah Wali-Allah and his Times*, 145.
19. Hodgson, *The Venture of Islam*, p. 153.
20. Ibid., p. 154.
21. The following is a list of eighteenth-century Mughal rulers of Delhi:
    a. Bahadur Shah I (Shah Alam I), b. 14 October 1643, ruled 1707–12, d. February 1712;
    b. Jahandar Shah, b. 1664, ruled 1712–13, d. 11 February 1713 in Delhi;
    c. Furrukhsiyar, b. 1683, ruled 1713-19, d. 1719 in Delhi;
    d. Rafi al-Darajat, ruled 1719, d. 1719 in Delhi;
    e. Rafi al-Dawlah (Shah Jahan II), ruled 1719, d. 1719 in Delhi;
    f. Nikusiyar, ruled 1719, d. 1719 in Delhi;
    g. Muhammad Ibrahim, ruled 1720, d. 1720 in Delhi;
    h. Muhammad Shah, b. 1702, ruled 1719–48, d. 26 April 1748 in Delhi;
    i. Ahmad Shah Bahadur, b. 1725, ruled 1748-54, d. January 1775 in Delhi;
    j. Alamgir II, b. 1699, ruled 1754–59, d. 1759;
    k. Shah Alam II, b. 1728, ruled 1759–1806, d. 1806.
22. The East India Company began its long history in 1600 with 281 shareholders' (Flinn, *An Economic and Social History of Britain 1066-1939*, p. 62). It was formed for the exploitation of trade with East and Southeast Asia and India as a monopolistic trading body. It established its hegemony over India in 1757, which continued for a century. After the mutiny of 1857, the British Government founded its own rule in India.
23. Bhatt, and Bhargava (eds,), *Land and people*, 13:28.
24. Lewis, *The Muslim Discovery of Europe*, p. 51.
25. Voll, 'Muhammad Hayya al-Sindi', p. 39.
26. Greyling, 'Schech Yusuf, the founder of Islam in South Africa', *Religion in South Africa*, 1/1 (1980), pp. 9–22.

27. Lewis, *The Muslim Discovery of Europe*, p. 195.
28. Ibid., p. 196.
29. Ibid., p. 199
30. Muḥibbul-Hasan, *Waqā'i'-i Manāzil-i Rūm*, p. 3.
31. Ibid., pp. 13–15.
32. Ibid., p. 2.
33. Hodgson, *The Venture of Islam*, p. 137.
34. Lewis, *The Muslim Discovery of Europe*, pp. 49–50.
35. Itzkowitz, *Ottoman Empire and Islamic Tradition*, p. 109.
36. Ibid.
37. Lewis, *The Muslim Discovery of Europe*, p. 230.
38. The eighteenth century is marked for the introduction of the Turkish printing press. Spanish Jewish refugees at the end of the fifteenth century were first responsible for bringing with them the printing techniques of Europe, being allowed to print their religious books. It was, however, prohibited for them to publish any Turkish or Arabic books. Later, the Armenians and Greeks also established printing presses to publish their religious scriptures. It took almost two and half a centuries to permit its use for Muslims. When this was established by 1727, only non-religious material was permissible for print. The Press was forcibly closed in 1742 only to reopen in 1784, after which it spread throughout Ottoman territories. In the first round, only seventeen books could be printed on the subjects of history, geography and language (cf. Lewis, *The Muslim Discovery of Europe*, p. 50).
39. Lewis, *The Muslim Discovery of Europe*, p. 49.
40. Ihsanoglu, *al-Dawlat al-'Uthmāniyah-Tārikh wa Hadārah*, 2: pp. 81–2.
41. Lewis, *The Muslim Discovery of Europe*, p. 304.
42. Ibid.
43. Ibid.
44. Ihsanoglu, *al-Dawlat al-'Uthmāniyah-Tārikh wa Hadārah*, 2: 496.
45. Ibid., pp. 665–68.
46. Ibid.
47. Ottoman visitors to Europe, as their travel accounts reveal, were very much impressed by the industrial and economic progress of the West (Lewis, *The Muslim Discovery of Europe*, pp. 197–99). But the Ottoman Turks who established intellectual contact with Europe paid no attention to the West's economic literature. There is no report of the translation of any work of economics into Arabic, Turkish, Persian or Urdu before the nineteenth century.
48. It may be noted that the Ottomans invented a unique kind of tax called *devsherme*, a term applied to the compulsory levy in the form

of a child on Christians of conqured land for training and eventual employment in the civil and military service of the Empire. It was forbidden to take an only son. When they had learned Turkish and had became familiar with Muslim ways, which may have taken as long as ten years, they were admitted to the *yenicer* (new troops), anglicized as 'janissary', and in Arabic '*inkishariyah*' (Lewis, G. *Turkey*, p. 29).

49. According to Lewis (*The Muslim Discovery of Europe*, p. 240), the ulama did not look favourably on anything other than purely religious sciences. In 1716, the grand vizier Damad Ali Pasha died, leaving a rich library. The chief mufti opposed its annexation as a *waqf* because it contained books on worldly sciences and literature.
50. Muḥibbul-Hasan, *Waqāʿiʿ-i Manāzil-i Rūm*, p. 1.
51. Schimmel, *Islam in the Indian Subcontinent*, p. 168)
52. Ibid.
53. Durant, Frederick C. 'Rocket and missile system', Britannica [Website] https://www.britannica.com/technology/rocket-and-missile-system accessed 31 July 2021
54. Lewis, *The Muslim Discovery of Europe*, p. 131.
55. Schimmel, *Islam in the Indian Subcontinent*, pp. 177–78. Some British laws replaced Sḥariah rules. Institutions were established to impart a Christian education. All those measures adversely affected the social situation of the Muslim population. According to Schimmel (*Islam in the Indian Subcontinent*, p. 178): 'the revenue organization known as Permanent Settlement which was enforced upon the landlords and peasants in Bengal in 1793 reduced the Muslim peasantry practically to the status of serfdom.'
56. Ibid., p. 167.
57. Bhatnagar, *Rise and Growth of Hindi Journalism*, p. 82.
58. Perhaps this is a reference to *fatāwā-i-ʿAlamgīrī* (*al-Fatāwā al-Hindiyyah*).
59. Hodgson, *The Venture of Islam*, p. 82.
60. Allamah ibn Nujaym (d. 970/1563) stated that the door to analogical reasoning was closed during his age. The role of the ulama was only to report the opinions of past scholars of their school of thought (Ibn Nujaym, *Rasāʾil Ibn Nujaym*, p. 87).
61. Allamah ibn Hajar al-Haytami (d. 973/1566) says: 'It is not permissible for anyone to pronounce a judgement against his school of jurisprudence. If they do, it is void because the capacity for ijtihad was missing from the people of this age' (al-Haytami, *al-Fatāwā al-Kubrā al-Fiqhiyyah*, 2: 213).
62. Study of *shurūḥ* (notes and commentaries) and the writing of such commentaries and sometimes commentary over commentary was

the pattern of scholarship (al-Muhibbi, *Khulāṣat al-Athār*, 2: 122; 3:89, 123; Islahi, *A Study of Muslim Economic Thinking in the 11th AH / 17th CE Century*, p. 31).

63. Zwemer, 'The Wahabis: Their Origin, History, Tenets, and Influence', p. 311.
64. For details, one may refer to al-Tunji, Muhammad (ed.), *Tarājim A'yān al-Madīnat al-Munawwarah fi'l-Qarn al-Thānī 'Ashar al-Hijrī* (Biographies of the Elites of Madinah in the twelfth-century Hijrah), (Jeddah, Dar al-Shuruq, 1984).
65. Voll, 'Muhammad Hayya al-Sindi', p. 32.
66. Ibid., p. 35.
67. The Fulani tribe had migrated from Senegal and settled in Kawani in the Hausa city state of Gobir, in the northern part of present Nigeria.
68. al-Fullani, *Īqādh Himām Uli'l-Abṣār*, p. 72.
69. Ibid., p. 73. His remark is with reference to *al-Tawba* 9: 31.
70. Hodgson, *The Venture of Islam*, p. 134.
71. Hodgson (*The Venture of Islam*, p. 136) is not correct when he says that among Muslims, the eighteenth century was a relatively 'sterile' time.
72. Nadwi, *Tārīkh-i Dāwat -o- Azīmat*, 5: 396.

2

Shah Wali-Allah Dihlawi: Life and Times

2.1 Social and political background

Shah Wali-Allah Dihlawi (1114–74AH/1703–62CE), son of Shah Abd al-Rahim, was born in Phulat, a small town in Muzaffarnagar (a district in north India), and lived and died in Dehli (anglicized as Delhi) hence the attribution of Dihlawi (also written as Dehlawi or Dehlavi). At that time, India was passing through a period of extreme unrest and chaos. After the death of Mughal Emperor Aurangzeb (d. 1118/1707), during a time span of just sixty years, ten rulers came to the throne of Delhi, yet none could restore or arrest the deteriorating power and prestige of the Mughal Empire.[1] Ghulam Husayn Tabatabai, a historian of the period, stated that after Aurangzeb, 'thoughtless and feeble-minded rulers and ignorant but proud nobles came to power, and all sense of justice completely vanished, so that there was no way out of impasse. The whole country was ruined and the people were left with no love for life and in an exceedingly miserable condition.'[2] The country lacked political stability, peace and security. Regional forces like Maratha, Jats, Sikhs, etc. from all over India were on the path of revolt; their aim was an invasion of the capital city of Delhi to gain hold of the country and establish their own hegemony. Eventually, being unable to defeat these uprisings, the Mughal Empire was confined to Delhi's Red Fort and its adjoining areas. The king, despite his image as the rightful emperor of India, was helpless. Furthermore, the army—the empire's backbone—was highly inefficient and demoralized.[3]

Some of the European countries had already increased their influence in various parts of India, but the eighteenth-century Indian Muslims had paid no attention to the land, language and progress of European countries. Nor did the Mughal rulers, who were losing their territories to these foreign intruders, initiate any effort to establish the secrets of their power and progress. Essentially, they learned no lessons from the growing power and influence of the British East India Company. Indeed, hardly any sign of awakening or modernization can be discerned among the eighteenth-century Mughal rulers of India, efforts which find their counterparts among the Ottoman Turks. Instead, the descendants of the great Mughal Emperor Aurangzeb squandered the wealth amassed by their forefathers on luxurious living. In a situation where they were unable to cope with the problems arising at their door due to invasions and the uprising of internal forces, it was unthinkable that they would pay attention to external and distant enemies. Their economic condition was terrible. The Mughal Empire reeled under severe spells of drought, poverty, hunger, and hopelessness. The character of the people had fallen to the lowest levels of civilized behaviour. Looting, plundering, fighting and feuds were common scenes. From the religious point of view, the condition of the Muslims was highly deplorable.[4]

2.2 Life

Shah Wali-Allah Dihlawi's full name is Qutb al-Din Ahmad, but he is popularly known by his first name Wali-Allah.[5] He was born on Wednesday, 4 Shawwal 1114 (21 February, 1702). His genealogy can be traced back to the second caliph of Islam, Umar al-Faruq, from his paternal side and to Musa Kazim[6] from his maternal side.[7] His grandfather, Shaykh Wajih al-Din, known for his piety and knowledge of the spiritual sciences, was an important officer in the army of Mughal Emperors Shah Jahan and

Aurangzeb. He had three sons: Abu al-Rida Muhammad, Abd al-Rahim and Abd al-Hakim. They did not engage themselves in military profession and instead adopted Sufism.[8] Shah Abd al-Rahim (1054-1131/1644-1718), the father of Shah Wali-Allah, became a great scholar of the Prophetic tradition (*muḥaddith*) and established the Madrasa Rahimiyah in Delhi for the promotion of Hadith studies and other Islamic sciences. He participated for a short time in the compilation of *al- Fatāwā al-ʿAlamgiriyyah*[9] also known as *al-Fatāwā al-Hindiyyah*.[10] Shah Abd al-Rahim died on 29 Muharram 1131, corresponding to 23 December 1718, at the age of seventy-seven. At that time, Shah Wali-Allah was seventeen years old.

Shah Wali-Allah Dihlawi's birth was no less than a miracle for many of those who had noticed the steady dissipation of science and original thinking among the Muslims for centuries, especially during the declining period of the great Mughal dynasty of Babar in India. Allamah Shibli Nuʿmani has rightly observed that due to the intellectual decline, which started since the time of Ibn Taymiyyah and Ibn Rushd, no one expected that a genius would be born again who would be able to arrest this continuous degeneration. By the grace of the Almighty, in the declining phase of Islamic culture, a person like Shah Wali-Allah was born whose subtle arguments eclipsed the academic accomplishments of al-Ghazali, Razi and Ibn Rushd.[11]

2.2.1 Education

Shah Wali-Allah Dihlawi has given an account of his early education and the advanced religious studies in his two works *al-Juzaʾ al-Laṭīf fi Tarjamat al-ʿAbd al-Ḍaʿīf* and *Anfās al-ʿĀrifīn*. At the age of five, he began his education under the supervision of his father when he was admitted into the primary religious school (*maktab*). He completed his first recitation of the Qur'an at the age of seven. After that, he was admitted to his father's seminary, Madrasa Rahimiyah, where he started taking introductory lessons in Persian and Arabic and completed them in one year.

After finishing the preliminary textbooks, he started the higher syllabus and studied the *Kāfiyah* (Arabic grammar) of Ibn al-*Ḥ*ājib. At the age of ten, he began to study the *Sharḥ Mullā Jāmi* (commentary on *Kāfiyah*) and very soon developed the ability to go through other books by himself. He studied parts of *Tafsīr al-Bayḍāwī* when he was fourteen. At the age of fifteen, he completed his study of the then prevalent curriculum. He studied under his father volumes of Hadith works like *Mishkāt al-Maṣābīḥ,* a part of Bukhārī's *Al-Jāmi' al-Ṣaḥīḥ* , *Shamā'il al-Tirmidhī,* and works of *tafsīr* like *Tafsīr Madārik al-Tanzīl* and *Tafsīr al-Bayḍāwī.* He attended his father's lectures on the exegesis of the Qur'an, which helped him to understand the Qur'an in depth. He also acquired knowledge of philosophy, logic, jurisprudence, *ṭibb* (Eastern medicine), algebra, mathematics, and oratory from his father. Shah Wali-Allah received from his father *ijāzah* (permission or certificate) for teaching and guiding in religious matters.

2.2.2 Teaching career

When Shah Wali-Allah completed his studies at Madrasa Rahimiyah at the age of fifteen, he started teaching in the same institution. Two years later, when his father died, Shah Wali-Allah succeeded his chair and became the principal of this renowned seminary. A large number of students were attracted to this institution so much that the existing space could not accommodate their increasing number. Impressed by Shah Wali-Allah's educational activities, the Mughal Emperor Muhammad Shah (r. 1719–48) granted a spacious site for Madrasa Rahimiyah in the nearby locality of Shahjahanabad.[12] Shah Wali-Allah taught there for about twelve years before he went on the pilgrimage to the two holy places of Islam, Makkah and Madinah. According to Jalbani, 'The real purpose of his going to the holy land, besides the performance of hajj, was to make there an exhaustive and critical study of Tradition and Jurisprudence.'[13] Here he would study under the famous teachers of these subjects at that time. He did not only satisfy his spiritual hunger and thirst for knowledge but also intellectually equipped himself with the spirit of revival and renovation which existed in the City of the Prophet at that time, as we noted in the previous chapter. This same spirit also prepared his two contemporaries, Muhammad ibn Abd al-Wahhab and Uthman dan Fodio through his Madinah-trained teachers.[14]

2.2.3 Pilgrimage to Makkah

In the year 1143/1730, Shah Wali-Allah decided to perform the pilgrimage to Makkah al-Mukarramah. Despite the perils that lay ahead on the journey, he reached the holy city of Makkah on 14 Dhū al-Qa'dah 1143 AH and performed hajj. He then went to the City of the Prophet, may Allah bless him and give him peace, al-Madīnah al-Munawwarah. Incidentally, this was at the same time as when Ibn Abd al-Wahhab was carrying out his revolutionary reforms in the Najd region of the Arabian Peninsula.[15] However, they did not have the opportunity to meet each other because, at that time, Ibn Abd al-Wahhab was in Basrah.

During his stay in Hijaz, Shah Wali-Allah studied under Shaykh Wafd-Allah ibn Muhammad al-Maghribi al-Maliki (d. 1110 AH), Abu Tahir Muhammad ibn Ibrahim al-Kurdi al-Shafi'i (d. 1145/1733), Taj al-Din al-Qala'i al-Hanafi (d. 1144/1733), Umar ibn Ahmad al-Basri and Abd al-Rahman ibn Ahmad al-Nakhli. Shah Wali-Allah has given account of his Arab teachers in his work *Fuyūḍ al-Ḥaramayn*.[16] His stay in Madinah filled him with a revolutionary spirit and reformative zeal.[17] In particular, Shaykh Abu Tahir had a great impact on Shah Wali-Allah in shaping his future career in India.[18]

According to Schimmel, his teachers were mainly the same as those of Ibn Abd al-Wahhab. Most outstanding among them was Muhammad Hayat al-Sindi.[19] However, it may be noted that other sources do not mention al-Sindi as Wali-Allah's teacher.

During his stay Hijaz, Shah Wali-Allah came across the works of many great Muslim scholars such as al-Khaṯṯabi (319–388/931–98), Abu Hamid al-Ghazali (450–505/1058–1111), Izz al-Din ibn Abd al-Salam (577–660/1181–1262), Ibn Taymiyyah (661–728/1263–1328), Ibn al-Qayyim (691–751/1292–1350), etc. He benefitted from their works in his writings. Like Ibn Abd al-Wahhab, he was clearly influenced by the works of Ibn Taymiyyah.[20] The father of Shah Wali-Allah's teacher Abu Tahir al-Kurdi was a fan of Ibn Taymiyyah, thus Ibrahim Kawrani (1025–1101 AH) had a rich collection of Ibn Taymiyyah's works. There are proofs that Shah Wali-Allah had benefitted from his collection. Sayyid Abul Hasan Ali Nadwi writes: 'The advocacy and acclamation of

Shaykh al-Islam Ibn Taymiyyah in the writing of Shah Waliullah should have come from the influence of Shaykh Abu Tahir and his father Shaykh Ibrahim Kawrani just as he is more often inclined to adopt a conciliatory attitude in some other matters like his father.'[21]

The Baghdadi scholar al-Alusi in his work *Jalā' al-Aynayn* reports with reference to *al-Tafhīmāt al-Ilāhiyyah* that Shah Wali-Allah paid a glowing tribute to Ibn Taymiyyah as he said: 'We investigated the matter and found that he [Ibn Taymiyyah] had thorough knowledge of the Qur'an and Sunnah. He was an expert of Arabic language and its grammar. He was an authority on the Hanblite school of fiqh. He was highly brilliant, very clear and outspoken in defence of the Sunnah and its followers. No blunder or heresy has ever been attributed to him. ... Nothing in his writings is unsupported by textual authority from the Book of Allah and the Sunnah or the practice of the earliest Muslims. He was a scholar of exceptional abilities. Is there anybody who can be compared with him either in speech or writing? Those who have decried him do not possess even one-tenth of his talents.'[22]

Not only were there scholars from the Hijaz, for during the twelfth century, Yemen was also an important centre of Hadith works. According to Nadwi, 'Shah Waliullah's presence in the neighbouring Hijaz must have afforded him an opportunity to study the writings of Yemeni scholars.'[23]

After staying for fourteen months in Arabia—performing the hajj twice and also learning books of Hadith from scholars of the holy cities—Shah Wali-Allah finally returned to Delhi on 16 Rajab 1145 AH (2 January 1733).

2.2.4 Revival and renovation—the effect of Madinah training

Shah Wali-Allah was different after returning from the Ḥaramayn (the two Holy places). As Sayyid Nadwi observes, 'The Shah's journey for the pilgrimage and stay in Hijaz is a landmark of crucial importance, in his subsequent intellectual and reformative endeavour. During his stay in Hijaz which extended to a period of more than a year, he equipped himself thoughtfully in a way that was scarcely possible in India.'[24] After returning from the holy cities of Makkah and Madinah the miserable condition of Indian Muslims compelled Shah Wali-Allah to work for their reform, tone up their morale, and inculcate a feeling of selflessness and love in them for their fellows. He started training the scholars in different branches of knowledge and filled them with the missionary zeal to enlighten people with the true Islamic manners and etiquettes. He began the task of reforming various sections of the society. For this purpose he produced a number of authentic works on Qur'anic teachings, the Prophet's traditions, and many other branches of Islamic learning.

2.2.5 Aspects of his reform

Shah Wali-Allah strived to bring about reform in every sector of society. In his work *al-Tafhīmāt al-Ilāhiyyah*, he especially addressed these various elements, warning them of the consequences of their errant behaviours. He pointed out their faults and explained to them the way of rectification. In view of its importance, we reproduce below a few parts of his address:

Descendants of Sufis and spiritual guides

Eighteenth-century India had various cults of Sufism. In most cases, it was used to obtain honour, position and prestige as if a family business. Since Shah Wali-Allah wanted to bring reform in the system, he questioned the descendants of sufis and spiritual guides who were unjustly sticking to the customs of their forefathers, 'Why have you divided yourselves into groups and factions following your prejudices and whims? Why have you all abandoned the Way which was ordained and taught by Allah through His Apostle Muhammad (may Allah's peace be upon him) and elevated yourselves to the position of guides, inviting the people to join your own order?'

He exposed them by saying, 'Each one of you considers himself as rightly-guided and capable of guiding others although he has himself lost the Right Way and is misguided. We cannot approve of the behaviour and attitude of those who seek to enlist the allegiance of the people simply for financial gains, or who acquire knowledge in order to fulfil and meet their worldly objectives, to serve their lust and selfishness. They pretend to show themselves as pious and guided as they know very well that they cannot get wealth and position without it. Nor do I support those who ask people to follow and love them instead of Allah and His Prophet. They are indeed all dacoits and impostors and liars; they have deceived themselves and are now deceiving others.' He advises people to be careful of them: 'Never follow except one who calls towards the Book of Allah and Traditions of His Apostle, not to himself.'

He made it clear that he would not approve the prattle about esoteric practices of Sufis in public gatherings, as the ultimate goal of mysticism is the attainment of *iḥsān*.[25] He asked: 'Have you not learned lesson from the Quranic verse "This is My straight path, so follow it. Follow not other ways, let ye be parted from His way" (the Qur'an 6: 153)'.[26]

The ulama and scholars

Shah Wali-Allah addressed the religious scholars and warned them not to forget the difference between what is real knowledge and what is the instrument to it. He spoke frankly: 'I say to these seekers after knowledge, O blockheads! You are pleased to be called the *'ulamā* while you have got yourselves entangled in the so-called Greek sciences and grammar and syntax, and thought it was true knowledge. The true knowledge, as you must know, is the clear and precise verses of the Book of Allah, or the Sunnah of the Holy Prophet.' He then reminded them, 'You have become unduly absorbed in the legal preferences and details worked out by the early jurists. But is it not a fact that only that command has a legal sanction which has been ordained by Allah and His Apostle? Most of you are such that if a *ḥadīth* from the Holy Prophet reaches one of you, he does not act on it, but says that he follows such and such an *imām* and not the *ḥadīth*.' Then he justifies his stance by saying: 'The appreciation of the *aḥādīth* and taking decisions in accordance with them were reserved for the great scholars of *ḥadīth*.

It is improbable that the Tradition in question escaped their notice, but they must have rejected it for sound reasons.' He cautions: 'Be aware that this is not the way of true Faith. If you sincerely believe in your Prophet, you must follow him whether it goes in favor of your School of thought or against it.'[27]

Shah Wali-Allah made it clear that the things in which they engaged themselves had nothing to do with the disciplines that will benefit them in the Hereafter. These are all mundane sciences. The sciences which are means and instruments should remain as they are; they should not take the position of the ultimate goal.[28]

Mystic preachers and worshippers:

Pointing out misdeeds of mystic preachers, worshippers and dwellers of monasteries, Shah Wali-Allah said, 'O you who lay a claim to piety, went astray into all the valleys and believed in all kinds of bogus stories. You called the people to fabrications and false idols making the life of people difficult and burdensome. You, in fact, had been appointed to facilitate life for them and not to make it difficult. You tell them stories current about the self-absorbed lovers for guidance and instruction; whereas these things are not fit to be circulated, they should rather be buried deep and disposed of forever. You have suspicion and overconcern and consider it as precautions. You had only to ask the people to attain the stage of *iḥsān* with its two ingredients—belief and action.' He asks them: 'Do you not know that the greatest blessing and guidance is what you have received through the Prophet Muhammad, peace be upon him. Can you then affirm whatever you are doing today conforms to the practice of the Prophet and his Companions?'[29]

The kings

Addressing the kings, Shah Wali-Allah says: 'O Kings, pleased by *al-mala' al-a'lā* (the celestial sphere), I urge you to unsheathe your swords and do not put them back in the scabbards again until Allah has separated the Muslims from the polytheists and the rebellious disbelievers and sinners are pushed back to their weak companions, and can do nothing that sort of thing again for themselves. "And fight them until persecution is no more, and religion is for Allah."[30] When the difference between infidelity and Islam become marked and clear, then the celestial sphere (*al-mala' al-a'lā*) would be pleased with you to appoint commanders at a distance of three and four days' journey. The men appointed should be upright and just and strong who may be able to give back the weak and oppressed his right, enforce the Divine commandments and, at the same time, are vigilant enough to curb any rebellion in future. They should not allow the contumacious elements to regroup themselves again for waging war, nor to apostatize, nor yet to commit any major sin. Islam's teachings should be preached openly and everybody should perform the prescribed duties. The administrator of each city ought to have adequate power at his disposal to improve affairs of the city under his control. At the same time nobody should be allowed to become powerful enough to have designs for personal benefit and challenge the authority of the government.[31]

It is necessary for larger regions within the dominion that such governors should be appointed who have the experience of conducting warfare. Such governors should be allowed to have an army consisting of twelve thousand combatants, but only those should be recruited who possess the zeal to fight for the cause of Allah, fearing not the blame of any blamer, be willing to fight every person unruly and disobedient and be also capable of it. ... O King, when this is realized, the Divine will shall require you, to pay attention to home affairs and related contracts, and see that no dispute arises that contravenes the Sharī'ah. Only then people can enjoy full peace and security.'[32]

The nobles and governors

Shah Wali-Allah awakens the rulers and governors by asking them: 'Don't you have any fear of God? You are getting mesmerized by the transient pleasures and have completely forgotten your subjects so that they eat up each other. Drinking has become a common thing but you do not stop it;

adultery and gambling are rampant but you do not eradicate them. Is it not true that in the major towns the Shari'ah punishment has been meted out for the last six hundred years? You eat up when you find a weak offender but spare and let go the powerful. Pleasures of the delicious victuals, coquetry and flirtations of women, fine clothes and artistic dwelling places have absorbed your attention. You never bow down to Allah. You mention His name in your table talk and stories.'[33] He warns them of the bad consequences of forgetting Allah.

Army and soldiers

Shah Wali-Allah was worried about the growing bad habits among the soldiers. Addressing them, he said,'O fighting personnel: Allah made you soldiers so that you might fight for His cause, propagate the true message and wipe out polytheism and the power of polytheists. But you have abandoned your real object for which you have been created and took to horse-riding and armour-equipment to amass wealth, not to fight in the Way of Allah. You indulge in wine and other kinds of intoxications; shave your beards and grow moustaches; you oppress the innocent people and never care how you earn your living. By God, you have to leave this world one day; then Allah will tell you what you had been doing. Allah wants of you to adopt dress and manners of pious fighters, keep the beards and trim the moustaches, perform the five daily prayers, fear Allah and take not people's goods by unfair means and remain firm in the battle field.'[34] In fact, in between the lines of this address one can read the Mughal army's moral and martial condition, the reason for their defeats at different occasions, and the remedy to improve the situation.

Artisans and craftsmen

In every economy, the producing units play a very important role in the socio-economic development of the country. Shah Wali-Allah was not happy with the artisans and craftsmen of his time. Not only were they not very serious in production activities, their moral and religious lives were also deplorable. He advised them to reform their condition, to give up the wastage of resources and immoral lifestyle. Addressing such artisans and craftsmen, he frankly said, 'You have lost the sense of responsibility and honest work and given up the worship of your Lord. You are holding associates with Him, offering sacrifices for others than Allah and go for pilgrimage to the graves of chiefs and saints. That is the worst you could do. If one of you becomes prosperous he begins living beyond his means, thus depriving his near and dear ones: or he wastes his worldly means and ruins his hereafter in drinking and prostitute. Thus they ruin themselves in this life and the Hereafter. Allah has created innumerable sources to earn livelihood sufficient for you and your dependents if you adopt moderate living and contend with the earning for virtuous living. But you have become ungrateful to the favor of Allah and adopted unfair means to manage things. Do you not fear the torment of the Hell and the worst abode?'[35]

Shah Wali-Allah suggested to them the remedy: 'Spend your morning and evening in remembrance of Allah, the day in economic activities, and the night living with your wives.' He advised them to adopt the golden economic rule: 'Spend less than what you earn and keep the saving for helping the wayfarer and the poor and keep also something as precautionary measures for meeting emerging and unforeseen needs.' He warns them that if they do not follow this course, their entire efforts will be liable to failure and corruption. [36]

His call to all sections

Shah Wali-Allah knew that there was a need to bring over total reform in the whole society. Therefore, after addressing various sections of society separately, Shah Wali-Allah addressed the whole population together and called them to reform themselves: 'O children of Adam: your sense of morality has become dormant; greed and avarice have overpowered you and the devil has dominated you... Do not spend on living and clothing beyond your resources ... Do not make your life too hard for it would eventually lead you to wrongdoing ... Allah wants that the concession given by Him should be enjoyed as well as His commandments should be followed in more meticulous manner. Satisfy your hunger with foods you have and earn resources sufficient for your needs. Do not depend on people as you ask them and they refuse. Similarly do not become parasite on kings and governors. It is desired from you to earn your living by your own hands. O children of Adam, if Allah has favoured anyone of you with a house where he can live, drink to quench his thirst, food sufficient to satisfy his hunger, cloth enough to cover his body, and a wife chaste and helpful in maintaining the household, he should be thankful to Allah for he has everything he needs in this world. He should adopt a source of earning that may be sufficient for him. He should be content and moderate in living and he should spend the spare time in worship and remembrance of Allah.'[37] (Ibid., pp. 217–18)

Shah Wali-Allah asks people to abandon such vicious customs that have corrupted true faith. For instance, gathering together on the tenth of Muharram and behaving in an unbecoming way, spending too much on feasts, wasting time and money on indecorous conventions and rituals at the cost of healthy practice. Similar is the case of behaving and indulging in frivolous acts like the ignorant communities on the occasion of Shab-i-Barat (a night of prayer). He says, 'A section of the people among you thinks that on this day plenty of food should be sent to the dead. Do you have any authority for such ideas and acts? Then you have adopted such customs as have made your lives difficult for you, for instance, expending beyond means on marriage ceremonies, holding divorce as prohibited, keeping widows back from re-marriage, and such other things in which you have imposed undue restrictions on yourselves in clear contravention of the right Guidance. The right course would have been that you adopted the customs which facilitated your lives instead of restraining them. Then you have turned the events of death and mourning into occasions for eating and rejoicing, as if it had been made obligatory on you that you must feed your relatives and near ones, and feed them well, on such occasions. You have become neglectful of prayers, some of you do not find time for prayers because they are engrossed in their business; others forget offering prayers because they were having a good time with their friends.'[38] He suggests that people can correct their behaviour with a little change in their course of action and intention, for example, they have become unmindful of zakah although there is no rich man who is not feeding a number of relatives with him, but he does not do so with the intention of paying zakah. If he could do so with the intention of paying zakah, he would have well discharged his obligation due to the poor. There are many who have become a burden on the government and completely depend on the ruler's stipends, but when he finds that his revenue resources are not rich enough to sustain you, he begins taxing his poor subjects. What a bad state your performance is![39]

These excerpts can help the reader form a general overview of how thoroughly Shah Wali-Allah examined the past and the present of the Muslims and how sharply he has criticised their notions and institutions in an effort to bring about a comprehensive reform.

2.3 Areas of major contributions

2.3.1 Dissemination of Qur'anic knowledge

Shah Wali-Allah believed that the reform of the Muslim society and the reconstruction of Islamic sciences is not possible without knowledge of the Qur'an. Thus, the motive behind his translation of the Qur'an was to popularize its understanding among both the intelligentsia and the masses to enable them to clearly perceive the message of their Lord. He translated the Qur'an in the Persian language as that was the official language of the country at that time. It was also the language of the ulama and scholars. Although he started the translation of the Qur'an before he travelled to Hijaz for pilgrimage, after his return, he felt a pressing need to continue it. He completed it in 1151/1738. It should be noted that Shah Wali-Allah was not the first to translate the Qur'an into the Persian language. A few translations were already existing at the time, but their language and style were outdated. There was a need for a fresh Persian translation of the Qur'an that the masses could understand properly and easily. Since then, his work has been published and republished several times. Despite the passing of more than 275 years, the language and meanings are so accurate and perfect that Saudi Arabia's Qur'an Complex could not find a better translation than this to publish. Therefore, it is considered as one of the most outstanding contributions of Shah Wali-Allah.

Shah Wali-Allah's method of teaching the Qur'an was direct without the use of any commentary. It was through this method that he himself was taught by his father Shah Abd al-Rahim. Describing the disadvantage of using commentaries for teaching the Qur'an, Jalbani has rightly observed:

> It generally happens that by consulting the commentaries, the attention of the student is diverted from the Word of God to the comments made by other persons of the same stock to which he belonged. The result is that the whole of his time is taken away in solving the difficulties of the commentators themselves. He, thus, gets no time to devote to understanding the Holy Qur'an independently. If the Holy Qur'an is read with some attention, many wonderful ideas, hitherto unknown, are suggested.[40]

Shah Wali-Allah stressed that success lies in following the teachings of the Qur'an and Sunnah. He criticized scholars and students for paying undue attention to Greek philosophy and other tools of language. He writes that real knowledge comes through the study of the Book of Allah and traditions of His Prophet, may Allah bless him and give him peace.[41] The Qur'an is the real science as it fulfils the criterion of a true science which meets the requirements of the time. The Qur'an is always apace with the time and was revealed to respond to its call provided that attention is paid to its obvious meaning, keeping away as far as possible from the time bound interpretations.

Shah Wali-Allah also authored books entitled *al-Fawz al-Kabīr* and *Fatḥ al-Khabīr* on the principle of exegesis and methods of interpretation to guide students and teachers of the Qur'an. He was of the view that as soon as a child learns the Persian language and develops the capacity of understanding written materials, he should first be taught the translation of the Qur'an before other subjects. This is because it is not guaranteed whether he would complete his study, therefore, the first thing to enter his heart and mind should be the words of the Almighty Allah. He advised those who were busy in their economic pursuits to sit down in groups during the time of leisure to read and listen to the commandments of their Creator. This was the practice of the Prophet's Companions as well.

2.3.2 Propagation of the Prophet's Traditions

Hadith or traditions of the Prophet are the second most important source of Islam. According to Wali-Allah, the science of Hadith is the crown of all infallible knowledge and the source and foundation of religious branches of learning.[42] This was a neglected subject in the period in which Shah Wali-Allah was born as people were fascinated with the sayings of Sufis and saints. Shah Wali-Allah's father, Shah Abd al-Rahim, realized this deficiency of the education system. He was the first to introduce Hadith as the subject of study in Madrasa Rahimiyah, training his son to carry on this mission. To equip himself better, Shah Wali-Allah travelled to the Holy places of Islam, Makkah and Madinah, to perform hajj and to study Hadith under the learned scholars of hadith in those two cities. He adequately quenched his thirst for gaining complete knowledge of the Prophet's traditions while staying in the Prophet's city.[43]

After returning from the Hijaz to India, Shah Wali-Allah devoted himself to the promotion of hadith studies in the country. Very soon, Madrasa Rahimiyah became a well-known center for hadith studies, and a large number of students from far off places reached Delhi to study under Shah Wali-Allah. In addition to his son Shah Abd al-Aziz, he trained many scholars of repute, such as Sayyid Murta*ḍ*a Bilgarami al- Zabidi (1145–1205/1732–91), Qa*ḍ*i Thana-Allah Panipati (d. 1225/1713), and Mirza Mazhar Jan-i Janan (1111–95/1699–1781), to name a few.

Along with teaching, Shah Wali-Allah enriched hadith literature by writing a number of works on hadith and related subjects. He wrote a commentary in Persian on the *Muwaṭṭa*ʾ of Imam Malik ibn Anas (d. 179/795) entitled *al-Muṣaffā*, which reflects the depth of his knowledge and insight into the science of hadith. It represents Shah Wali-Allah's methodology in teaching hadith. He prepared another version of *Muwaṭṭa*ʾ entitled *Musawwā*. This work contained a selection of hadiths from the *Muwaṭṭa*ʾ arranged with a more scientific pattern. He dropped those sayings of Imam Malik that are not shared by the other three great imams—Abu Hanifah, al-Shafi'i and Ahmad ibn Hanbal. He has also added verses of the Qur'an in support of the hadith. From these two works one can clearly observe the depth of his knowledge and insight into hadith and fiqh. According to Ubaid-Allah Sindhi, after the Qur'an he finds Wali-Allah's *Musawwā* sufficient for the knowledge of hadith and fiqh.[44]

It may be noted that among the hadith collections, Shah Wali-Allah gave Imam Malik's *al-Muwaṭṭa*ʾ the highest place as it combined both hadith and fiqh and was the earliest compilation of hadith, the most authentic and trustworthy. In his opinion, when the student has learned the Arabic language and developed to understand Arabic books, the *Muwaṭṭa*ʾ should first be taught. He ranked the collections of Hadith somewhat differently, putting at the top the *Muwaṭṭa*ʾ of Imam Malik, then *Ṣaḥīḥ Bukhārī* and *Ṣaḥīḥ Muslim*. His other works on Hadith are: *Sharḥ Tarājim Abwāb Ṣaḥīḥ Bukhārī, Majmūʿah Rasāʾil Arbaʿah* (a collection of four short tracts), *al-Faḍl al-Mubīn fi'l-Musalsal min Ḥadīth al-Nabiy al-Amīn, al-Nawādir min Ḥadīth Sayyid al-Awāʾil wa'l-Awākhir* and *al-Durr al-Thamīn fi Mubashshirāt al-Nabiy al-Amīn*. A brief introduction to these works will be provided in the next chapter.

2.3.3 Jurisprudence

In the field of jurisprudence, Shah Wali-Allah had a remarkable ability to reconcile diverse opinions found in different schools of fiqh and explain them with reference to the basic principles that may be deduced from the Qur'an and be plausible on rational grounds. He considered *ijtihad* (original thinking) as the socially obligatory duty (*farḍ kifāyah*) of Muslim scholars and ulama in every age. He lamented the fact that the simple-minded people of his time were too ignorant to attach due importance to this.[45] However, Rudolph Peters finds Shah Wali-Allah's views on ijtihad to be more conservative than the comparable but later works of al-Shawkani (1760–1832) and al-Sanusi (1787–1859).[46]

According to Mawlana Nadwi, Shah Wali-Allah had already made up his mind to strive for bringing about a greater conformity between hadith and the fiqh, and it was for this reason that he had started giving preference to the juristic opinions of the hadith scholars over those of different schools of jurisprudence. He had written in *al-Juz' al-Laṭīf fi-Tarjamat al-ʿAbd al-Ḍaʿīf*: 'A study of the four juristic schools and their principles of jurisprudence as well as the *aḥādīth* on which they base their arguments has led me to prefer the juristic findings of the *ḥ*adīth scholars- This inclination was backed by divine influence. Thereafter, I was seized with a longing to make the pilgrimage to the two sacred Mosques.'[47] The Shah also writes in his *Waṣīyat Namah*, 'Scholars who are well-versed both in fiqh and *ḥadīth* should be followed in petty matters, but the major Juristic issues should be constantly checked with the Book of God and *ḥadīth* of the Prophet (peace be upon him).' Acknowledging its merits, he wrote on different occasions that owing to various historical, intellectual, political and cultural developments, the Hanafi (as well as Shafi'i) fiqh had come to receive greater attention; it was more polished and had a unified sequence, more commentaries on it were written, and better exposition of its principles was made than could be claimed for any other juristic system.[48]

2.3.4 Exposition of the wisdom and rationale of Shariah provisions

One of the most important contributions of Shah Wali-Allah is his exposition of the wisdom and rationale of Shariah rules occurring in the Qur'an and Hadith. He gave it the name of *ʿIlm Asrār al-Dīn* (The Science of the Secrets of Religion). He devoted his complete work *Ḥujjat Allāh al-Bālighah* to this new branch of knowledge. The book is rightly considered as the magnum opus of the author. Mawlana Nadwi remarks:

> Few works can compare the compendious yet clear and cohesive exposition attempted in the *Ḥujjat Allah al-Bālighah*, which laid the foundation of a new dialectical theology for the modern age of reason. It is thus a work which can satisfy any truehearted man endowed with common sense, provided,

of course, he can appreciate and ponder over the profound investigations of the Shah.[49]

Thus, Shah Wali-Allah has mentioned the endeavours made by earlier scholars but these were, in his view, meagre and inconsiderable. He writes in the introduction to *Ḥujjat Allah al-Bālighah*: 'The scholars of old had tried to expound the rationale which have been given due consideration in legal matters. Those who delved into them later on have hinted at some very profound reasons, but these are also scanty. To delineate these issues now will not mean going against the consensus as nobody has left any full fledged work on this subject nor laid down the norms and corollaries in a systematic manner.'[50] The Shah has referred to the writings of Imam al-Ghazali, al-Khattabi and Shaykh al-Islam Izz al-Dīn ibn 'Abd al-Salam which allude, at places, to the wisdom of the Shariah.[51]

He has refuted the view that the prescriptive directions of the Shariah need not have any design and goal or that there was no relationship between the actions and their retribution. He based his arguments on the Qur'anic verses and hadith in which such a relationship has been spelt out, or the merit or demerit of any deed has been explained.

As we shall see in the next chapter, *Al-Budūr al-Bāzighah* is the second most important contribution of the author after *Ḥujjat Allāh al-Bālighah*, addressing the wisdom and rationale of Shariah provisions and a philosophical and rational interpretation of Islam.

2.3.5 Philosophy

In India, Islam came through Iran, Turkistan and Afghanistan, mixed with the elements of Greek and Persian philosophy. In this long journey, it lost much of its strength and vigour. Those who brought Islam to India were not totally free from their racial and national tendencies. For a long time, instead of re-establishing its link directly with the Qur'an and the Sunnah, Muslim scholars in India had paid more attention to Greco-Persian thought and philosophy due to the domination of Iranian intellectual traditions. Since rationalism and philosophy had a profound impact on the people, doubts were created in their minds regarding the truth of religion. Everything was tested at the touchstone of reason. Shah Wali-Allah, like Ibn Taymiyyah, has convincingly shown that all Islamic teachings fulfil the criteria of rationality. He argued and successfully demonstrated that 'proper philosophy is one which is enshrined in the teachings of the Prophets'.[52]

In the opinion of Mawlana Mawdudi, Shah Wali-Allah is:

> ... the first scholar in our history laying down the foundations of the Philosophy of Islam. Before him all that had been written in the name of philosophy by the Muslims has been wrongly and ignorantly called "the philosophy of the Muslims" which had been derived and imported from Greece and Rome, Iran and India. The real Islamic philosophy was actually started and propounded by this great Shaykh of Delhi, though he wrote in the language and terminology of the same classical philosophy, scholasticism and philosophic mysticism, and has unwittingly incorporated many of their ideas also, as is natural for anyone who breaks new ground. But in spite of that it cannot be gainsaid that his has been a major effort to open new vistas of research, especially in an age of decline and disintegration of the worst type. The appearance of a man with such intellectual and rational powers in such an age is all the more amazing.[53]

In his work *Al-Budūr al-Bāzighah* (The Bright Moons), Shah Wali-Allah employs philosophical terminology in discussing human nature and social behaviour. It presents a philosophical and rational interpretation of Islam. His book *al-Khayr al-Kathīr* is on the philosophy of religion. It elucidates the concept of gnosis (*ma'rifat*) (gnosis) and the wisdom of the Divine Names (*al-Asmā' al-Ḥusnā*), revelation, etc. He has also discussed, from a philosophical angle, matters like *waḥdat al-wujūd* (unity of being), *'arsh* (empyrean), *zamān wa makān* (time and space), *aflāk wa 'anāṣir* (vault of heaven and the constituent matters), *ma'dan* (minerals), *nabāt* (vegetation), *ḥaywān* (animal life), *al-a'yān al-thābitah* (prototypes of things), *'alam al-mithāl* (sphere of similitude) etc.[54]

Shah Wali-Allah was against any concentration on philosophy per se. To him, 'true scholarship, *'ilm*, means to ponder the verses of the Holy Book or the tradition of the Prophet'.[55] His other books which have philosophical discussions include *Sata'at* (Illuminations), *The Radd (refutation) of the Gawhar-i Murād*, etc.

2.3.6 *Taṣawwuf*

In the opinion of Schimmel, 'in spite of his own exalted spiritual claims, Shah Wali-Allah was most critical of the mystics of his time. What he abhorred most—quite in tone with his Wahhabi colleagues in Arabia—was the veneration of saints and tomb worship'.[56] He explains that, 'Sufis who talked in terms which are not based on the Koran. Particularly concerning *tawhid*, were the object of his blame.'[57] Shah Wali-Allah criticized the ignorant Sufis and foolish practitioners of *taṣawwuf*, describing them as robbers and thieves of religion, and warning others to be aware of them.[58] He condemned those Sufi practices that were in contravention of the basic sources of Islam—the Qur'an and Sunnah. His call was to believe in a pure and unmixed *tawhid* and to shun all kinds of un-Islamic innovations, polytheism and bad practices.[59]

According to Siddiqi, Shah Wali-Allah made an effort to purify *taṣawwuf* from un-Islamic elements by combing out 'all unhealthy foreign influences, such as a morbid kind of neo-Platonism and *Vedantism*'.[60] ... 'He stressed that genuine mysticism, as distinguished from pseudo-mysticism, encourages an active way of life which assures progress and prosperity in this world and salvation in the hereafter.'[61] It was due to this conviction that, in spite of his mystic training, he involved himself in the social, political, economic and intellectual reform and development of the Muslims. Shah Wali-Allah built a bridge between Sufis and the ulama (Islamic scholars). The same kind of bridge he built between theology and mysticism as well. This is obvious, for instance, from his synthesized version of the doctrines of *waḥdat al-wujūd* (unity of existence) and *waḥdat al-shuhūd* (unity of manifestation). In other words, he tried to reconcile the well-known doctrine of *waḥdat al-wujūd* of Ibn 'Arabi[62] and *waḥdat al-shuhūd* (unity of manifestation), which was put forward by Ahmad Sirhindi.[63] Shah Wali-Allah maintained that there was no significant difference between the two ideas; it is only a problem of semantics. In his opinion, ultimately both arrived at the same conclusion.

Shah Wali-Allah's critical approach to the issue is clear from the following passage extracted from his book *Shifā al-'Alīl*:

> 'I declare that one should not keep company of illiterate sufis, nor of illiterate men of piety, nor of the legists going by the letter of the law, nor of the scholastics who rely exclusively on their own reason and reject everything transmitted from the scholars of old. A seeker after truth ought to be a learned mystic, inclined to renunciation of worldly desires, always immersed in the remembrance of Allah and ever inclined to follow the practice of the Prophet as well as keen to learn more about *ḥadīth* and lives of the Prophet's Companions. He ought to be desirous of being enlightened by legists predisposed to *ḥadīth* and by scholars who are not opinionated but place reliance on the *sunnah* in the matters of creed.'[64]

It may be noted that Shah Wali-Allah's inclination towards harmonization and reconciliation (which was his inherited trait) is evident in his work *Shifā al-'Alīl*. He did not favour giving preference to any one of the juristic schools over another and argued that the principles enunciated by all these schools should be accepted in principle, but in the case of specific issues only the juristic opinion nearest to a well-known Sunnah should be followed.[65]

2.4 Political role

Shah Wali-Allah took part in politics to restore the vanishing power of the Muslim State. He was extremely worried about the increasing strength of the Marathas, the helpless position of the Delhi ruler, and the disunity among the Muslims. He wrote a letter to the Afghan ruler Ahmad Shah Abdali (d. 1187/1773) to come to the rescue of Delhi's emperor. Abdali responded to his call and dealt a crushing defeat on the Marathas, thereby turning their tide from north India and confining them to their own region, namely south west India. In fact, as Nizami writes, 'Neither the Maratha, nor Jat, nor yet Sikh stirring were broad based and catholic enough to think of maintaining the unity and integrity of the country. Shah Wali-Allah wanted under the new set up conceived by him, to restore the central power of the days of Akbar, Jahangir, Shahjahan and Awrangzeb and the sovereignty of the Empire based on justice but not ruled by autocratic kings.'[66] After the victory of the Panipat war, Ahmad Shah Abdali came to Delhi. At that moment, Shah Alam, the Mughal king, was not at Delhi. Abdali tried his best to recall Shah Alam to Delhi and restore his rule. However, the Mughal king was unable to avail himself of this opportunity to strengthen his rule. In the opinion of Nizami, 'the Mughal empire was, in fact, like a body without life and the benefit accruing from the battle of Panipat was availed of by the victors of Plassey.'[67]

Shah Wali-Allah was extremely worried about the terrible condition of the Muslims.'[68] He sided with the Rohilla chief, Najib al-Dawlah, because he found him to be the best among the newly emerging powers. Essentially, he wanted the Muslim society to return to the Prophet's era with its political unity of Muslim rulers. Thus, Rizvi is not correct when he says that 'the basis of Shah Wali-Allah's political thought was the "Perso-Islamic theory of kingship" discussed in the Arabic-Persian "Mirror for Princes" particularly in the works of Ghazali and Tusi.'[69]

2.5 His death and resting place

After a lifetime devoted to teaching and writing about Islam, Shah Wali-Allah died on Saturday 29 Muharram 1176 (21 August 1762) at the age of sixty-one years and four months, according to the Hijri calender. He was buried next to his father in Mehdiyan, a famous graveyard in Delhi. After his death, his son, Shah Abd al-Aziz, along with his followers and generations of successors, continued his reformatory mission to regenerate the Muslim faith. However, in the political arena Shah Abd al-Aziz diverted his endeavours against the hegemony of the British East India Company that had by that time become the greatest danger to the sovereignty and independence of India.

Shedding light on his character, Jalbani observes:

> Shah Waliyullah, by nature was free from prejudice and his visitors holding different religious views generally returned satisfied or at least contended. He was an embodiment of magnanimity, tolerance and sympathy for the whole of mankind. This is the reason why he always tolerated the critical remarks of those who differed with [a] smile.[70]

2.6 Impact of Shah Wali-Allah

The birth of Shah Wali-Allah during the declining phase of Mughal rule in India is considered by many as a miracle. For centuries before Shah Wali-Allah, the world had not seen a great Muslim scholar who could match the towering personalities of al-Ghazali, Ibn Taymiyyah and Ibn Khaldun, etc. in radical thinking and original ideas. Essentially, he brought about a revolution in Muslim minds by his writings on various branches of Shariah science, ideas that have relentlessly inspired his readers to this date.

Siddiq Hasan Khan al-Qannuji (d. 1307/1889) observed that if Shah Wali-Allah had lived in the early centuries of Islam, he would have been regarded as a great imam and crown of original thinkers (*mujtahidīn*). Shah Wali-Allah stands in the history of the Indian subcontinent as a link between medieval and modern Islamic thought. Ghazi considers him as 'a bridge between the medieval and the modern periods in the religio-intellectual history' of Muslim South Asia.[71] Moinul-Haq also expressed a similar view: 'Shah Wali-Allah was a versatile genius. He was undoubtedly the greatest Muslim thinker of the Subcontinent; his philosophy provides a connecting link between medieval Islamic thought and trends of modern interpretation of the fundamental teaching of Islam.'[72] According to Schimmel, Imam Dihlawi was 'a most unusual personality among the mystically trained thinkers of the 18th century, he was ahead of his time in many respects, combining sublime mystical speculations, rationalism, prophetic energy and common sense in a strange way.'[73] His noble students, fortunately the most important of them being his sons, Shah Abd al-Aziz,[74] Shah Abd al-Qadir,[75] Shah Rafi' al-Dīn,[76] Shah Abd al-Ghani,[77] and his grandson Shah Isma'il Shahid,[78] carried on his message. Dār al-'Ulūm Deoband in the district of Saharanpur in India is considered a descendant of the Madrasa Rahimiyah. Amongst those who were very much influenced by Shah Wali-Allah was the famous scholar Muhammad Siddiq Hasan Khan al-Qannuji (d. 1307/1889), as well as noted reformer of the nineteenth century Sir Sayyid Ahmad Khan (d. 1316/1898), the founder of Mohammedan Anglo-Oriental College, which later became the Aligarh Muslim University. The profound influence of his writings can also be seen on the great lights of the twentieth century, namely, Allamah Shibli Nu'mani (d. 1332/1914), Dr. Muhammad Iqbal (d. 1357/1938), Mawlana Ashraf Ali Thanawi (d. 1362/1943), Mawlana Abu'l-A'la Mawdudi (d. 1399/1979), Mawlana Abu'l-Hasan Ali Nadwi (d. 1419/1999), etc. Mawlana Obaydullah Sindhi (d. 1364/1944) made it his life-long mission to propound and propagate the revolutionary ideas of Shah Wali-Allah Dihlawi. Imam Hamiduddin Farahi (1863–1930) was profoundly influenced by Shah Wali-Allah's educational ideas. He introduced *Ḥujjat Allāh al-Bālighah* in the study course of Madrasat al-Islah, a noted seat of Islamic learning in India of which he was a director. Like Shah Wali-Allah, he also ranked the *Muwaṭṭa*' of Imam Malik as the first place in all collections of Hadith and made it part of al-Islah's syllabus. As Shah Wali-Allah suggested in his syllabus, *Muwaṭṭa*' is the first collection of hadith which the students are taught after learning Arabic grammar and developing an understanding of the language. The emphasis is to teach Islamic fiqh instead of any particular school of fiqh. Again, Allamah Farahi seems to be influenced by Imam Dihlawi's idea that the students of the Qur'an should not be taught with the help of a *tafsīr* book. Thus, he did not prescribe any book of *tafsīr* for the study course in Madrasa al-Islah. Like Shah Wali-Allah, he also believed that one part of the Qur'an interprets another part of it (*al-Qur'an yufassiru ba'ḍuhu ba'ḍa*). Last but not least, Farahi wrote some instructions entitled *Aṣl al-funūn* for the teachers and suggested that it should be studied along with Shah Wali-Allah's treatise called *Risālah-i Dānishmandī*.[79]

2.7 Shah Wali-Allah—a parallel to Ibn Taymiyyah

Shah Wali-Allah Dihlawi's reformative endeavours resemble those of Ibn Taymiyyah in both their conviction and methodology; both were based on the Qur'an, Sunnah and pattern of the early righteous people. Siddiqi considers Shah Wali-Allah a parallel to Ibn Taymiyyah.[80] Both Shah Wali-Allah and Ibn Taymiyyah were the great imams (leaders) of their time who strived to bring reform in education, politics, and the religious life of people. Ibn Taymiyyah virtually participated in jihad against the Mongols in 801 AH/1301 CE.[81] Shah Wali-Allah had no such occasion, but he was ready to do so if the need arose. In his work *al-Tafhīmāt,* he writes that if the circumstances demanded, he would have taken up arms, led the war and practically endeavoured to reform the conditions.[82] According to Sayyid Abul Hasan Ali,'Among those who have devoted their lives to the reform and revivification of Islam, only Ibn Taymiyyah can be compared with the Shah who urged the Syrian Muslims in 700/1301 to stand up against the Mongols.'[83] Like Ibn Taymiyyah, Shah Wali-Allah also had a lasting impact on the generations that followed, especially in the Indian subcontinent.

Notes and References

1. Rizvi, in the "Introduction" of his work *Shah Wali-Allah and his Times* pp. 2-21, gives a detailed account of the period.
2. Tabatabai, *Siyar al-Muta'akhkhirin,* 2: 529, cited in Rizvi, *Shah Wali-Allah and his Times,* p. 7.
3. For more details one may refer to the "Introduction" by K.A. Nizami to the collection of Shah Wali-Allah Dihlawi's letters entitled *Shah Wali-Allah ke Siyāsi Maktūbāt.*
4. al-Siyalkoti, *al-Shāh Walī-Allāh al-Dihlawī,* pp. 13–14.
5. Shah Wali-Allah wrote in his work *al-Tafhīmāt al-Ilāhiyyah* (2: 154) that his father had been foretold of his birth in a dream

by Khawaja Qutb-al-Dīn Bakhtiyar Kaki (d. 634/1236), who also asked his father to give his name to the baby. However, Shah 'Abd al-Rahim forgot about the instruction of the Khawaja and thus he was given the name of Wali-Allah. Later on when his father recalled it to his memory, he was renamed as Qutb al-Dīn Ahmad.

6. In one of his works, he writes: 'We are Arab people whose fathers have fallen in exile (*ghurbah*) in the country of Hindustan, and Arabic genealogy and Arabic language are our pride' (Dihlawi, *al-Tafhīmāt*, 2: 296).
7. al-Siyalkoti, *al-Shāh Walī-Allāh al-Dihlawī*, p. 17.
8. Rizvi, *Shah Wali-Allah and his Times*, pp. 204, 206.
9. *Al- Fatāwā al-Hindiyyah*, also known as *fatāwā-i 'Alamgiri* or *al-Fatāwā al-'Alamkiriyyah*, was compiled in Arabic at Aurangzeb Alamgir's orders by a committee of eminent jurists under the supervision of Shaykh Nizam al-Dīn Burhanpuri (d.1092/1680). Consisting of five volumes, it is a collection of authentic, accepted and preferred rules and opinions in the Hanafi jurisprudence. It is an extract of more than one hundred past works of fiqh and fatwas, arranged in the pattern of fiqh books. It took eight years to complete and was started at around 1050/1640 before finally being completed in 1058/1648 (Nadwi, *Fatāwā-i Ālamgirī aur uske Mu'allifin*, pp.6–7).
10. Nadwi, *Tārīkh-i Dāwat -o- Azīmat*, 5: 84.
11. Numani, *Ilm al-kalam*, p.96.
12. Ahmad, *Waqiat-e Dar al-Hukumat-e Dihli*, 2: 173–74.
13. Jalbani, 'Shah Waliyullah of Delhi', p. 23.
14. Islahi, *Islamic Economic Thinking in the 12th AH and 18th CE Century*, p. 38.
15. It may be noted that before Shah Wali-Allah's visit to Madinah, Ibn Abd al-Wahhab also spent four years studying in Madinah from 1128/1715 to 1132/1719 (Ibn Bishr, *'Unwān al-Majd fi Tārīkh Najd*, p. 21). Thus, both had studied in the same environment and mostly under the same scholars.
16. The title of the book *Fuyūḍ al-Ḥaramayn* (The Emanations of the Two Holy Cities) reveals that he received a great deal from his stay in Islam's two holy cities.
17. al-Siyalkoti, *al-Shāh Walī-Allāh al-Dihlawī*, p. 32.
18. Dihlawi, *Anfās al-'Ārifīn*, pp.191-03, 197–200.
19. Schimmel, *Islam in the Indian Subcontinent*, p. 153.
20. al-Siyalkoti, *al-Shāh Walī-Allāh al-Dihlawī*, pp. 59, 126.
21. Nadwi, *Tārīkh-i Dāwat -o- Azīmat*, 5: 112.
22. al-A'lusi, *Jalā' al-'Aynayn fi Muḥākamat Aḥmadayn*, 1: 59–60. It may be noted that scholars like Sayyid Ali Nadwi (2006, 5: 168)

and Uwais Nagrami (1359/1941, p. 349) stated this with the same reference to *Jala' al-Ainayn* without details of Shah Wali-Allah's work *al-Tafhīmāt*. However, the present author had tried to check it by going trough *al-Tafhīmāt*, but could not trace it. There may be some errors in al-Alusi's reference if he had not missed it. This remains to be verified.

23. Nadwi, *Tārīkh-i Dāwat -o- Azīmat*, 5: 25.
24. Ibid., 5: 107.
25. *Iḥsān* is an Arabic term which means to obtain perfection or excellence in worship, such that a person should try to worship Allah as if he sees Him, and although he cannot see Him, the person must undoubtedly believe that He is constantly watching over him (al-Bukhārī, *al-Jāmi' al-Ṣaḥīḥ*, 1: 20. hadith no. 50.
26. Dihlawi, *al-Tafhīmāt al-Ilāhiyyah*, 1:. 214.
27. Ibid., 1: 214–15.
28. Ibid.
29. Ibid., p. 215.
30. The Qur'an. al-Baqarah 2: 193, and al-Anfal 8: 39.
31. Dihlawi, *al-Tafhīmāt al-Ilāhiyyah*, 1: 216.
32. Ibid.
33. Ibid.
34. Ibid., pp. 216–17.
35. Ibid., p. 117.
36. Ibid.
37. Ibid., pp. 217–18.
38. Ibid., p. 219.
39. Ibid.
40. Jalbani, 'Shah Waliyullah of Delhi', pp. 22-23.
41. Dihlawi, *al-Tafhīmāt al-Ilāhiyyah*, 1: 214, 215,
42. Dihlawi, *Ḥujjat Allah al-Bālighah*, 1: 2.
43. Jalbani, 'Shah Waliyullah of Delhi', p. 35.
44. Sindhi, 'Imām Wali-Allah ki ḥikmat ka ijmali ta'aruf', p. 287.
45. Dihlawi, *al-Muṣaffā*, p. 12.
46. Hermansen, *The Conclusive Argument from God*, p. xxxii.
47. *al-Juza' al-Laṭīf fi Tarjamat al-'Abd al-Da'īf* included in the *Anfās al-'Ārifīn*, Matba' Mujtaba'i, pp. 203–204, cited in Nadwi, *Tārīkh-i Dāwat -o- Azīmat*, 5: 141–142.
48. Nadwi, *Tārīkh-i Dāwat -o- Azīmat*, 5: 202.
49. Ibid., pp. 215–16)
50. Dihlawi, *Ḥujjat*, 1: 3.
51. Ibid., p. 6.
52. Jalbani, 'Shah Waliyullah of Delhi', p. 33.

53. Mawdudi, *Tajdīd -o- Ihyā'-i Dīn*, p. 103.
54. Nadwi, *Tārīkh-i Dāwat -o- Azīmat*, 5: 403–4.
55. Schimmel, *Islam in the Indian Subcontinent*, p. 158.
56. Ibid., p. 157.
57. Ibid., p. 158.
58. Dihlawi, *al-Tafhīmāt*, 2: 243.
59. Dihlawi. *Ḥujjat*, I: 59, 61–64; 2: 93.
60. Siddiqi, 'Renaissance in Indo-Pakistan: Shah Wali-Allah Dihlawi', p. 1577. *Vedantism* the Hindu form of mysticism, which is based on their religious books or *Vedas*.
61. Ibid.
62. Ibn 'Arabi (560–638/1165–1240), an Arab Andalusian scholar, mystic, poet, and philosopher. Propounder of the controversial theory of *waḥdat al-wujūd* (unity of being). His works have grown to be very influential beyond the Muslim world. His cosmological teachings became the dominant worldview in many parts of the Muslim world. His major works are the monumental *Al-Futūḥāt al-Makkiyyah* (The Makkan Revelations) and *Fuṣūṣ al-ḥikam* (The Bezels of Wisdom). The majority of Muslim scholars are opposed to his ideas. He should not be confused with the Malikite jurist scholar Ibn al-'Arabi (468–543/1076–1148). Many writers do not notice the difference between Ibn 'Arabi and Ibn *al-*'Arabi.
63. Ahmad b. Abd al-Ahad Sirhindi (972–1034/1564–1624) played a vital role in rejuvenating Islam and opposing the dissident opinions prevalent in the time of the Mughal Emperor Akbar. Hence he was called *mujaddid-i alf-i thānī* (the renovator who came at the beginning of the second millennium of Hijrah). He was an Islamic scholar, a Hanafi jurist, and a prominent member of the Naqshbandī Sufi order. As against Ibn 'Arabi's theory of *waḥdat al-wujūd* (unity of being), Sirhindi propounded the theory of *waḥdat al-shuhūd* (unity of manifestation). His most famous work is a compilation of his letters (*Maktūbāt*), written in Persian to his friends, containing his social and religious thought.
64. Dihlawi, *Shifā al-'Alīl*, pp. 116–17, cited in Nadwi, *Tārīkh-i Dāwat -o- Azīmat*, 5: 410.
65. Dihlawi, *Shifā al-'Alīl*, p. 117, cited in Nadwi, *Tārīkh-i Dāwat -o- Azīmat*, 5: 411.
66. Nizami, *Shāh Wali-Allāh ke Siyāsī Maktūbāt*, p. 45.
67. Ibid., p. 47.
68. al-Siyalkoti, *al-Shāh Walī-Allāh al-Dihlawī*, p. 35.
69. Rizvi, *Shah Wali-Allah and his Times*, p. 397.
70. Jalbani, 'Shah Waliyullah of Delhi', p. 20.

71. Ghazi *Islamic Renaissance in South Asia 1707-1867*, p. 133.
72. Moinul-Haq, *Islamic Thought and Movements*, p. 426.
73. Schimmel, *Islam in the Indian Subcontinent*, p. 159.
74. Shah Abd al-Aziz (1159–1239/1746–1824), the eldest son of Shah Wali-Allah, was still a student of Madrasa Rahimiyah when Shah Wali-Allah died. Having completed his necessary education, he assumed the responsibility of Madrasa Rahimiyah. He devoted his life to teaching, spiritual guidance, delivering sermons and writing books. *Tafsīr Fatḥ al-Aziz* (in Persian) and *Tuḥfah-i-Ithnā 'Ashariyyah* are among his well-known books. *Fatāwā 'Aziziyyah* is a collection of his opinions on various issues and queries addressed to him. Throughout his life, he was busy propagating the ideals and thought of his father, carrying on the mission started by his father.
75. Shah Rafi'al-Dīn (1163–1233/1750–1818) obtained primary instruction from his father and then completed his higher education under his elder brother, Shah Abd al-Aziz. Besides his skill in Islamic subjects, he was an unparalleled specialist in mathematics and rational sciences. After completing his education, he started teaching in Madrasah Rahimiyah and became of assistance to his brother, Shah Abd al-Aziz. He also looked after the administration of the Madrasah. He translated the Qur'an into Urdu and authored many other books in Persian and Urdu.
76. Shah 'Abd al-Qādir (1167–1228/1753-4–1813) was nine years old when his father Shah Wali-Allah died. He obtained an early education under his father, then studied under his elder brother, Shah Abdul Aziz and Muhammad Ashiq Phulati. After completing his education, he retired to a room attached to the Akbarabadi mosque in Delhi, south of the Red Fort, and spent his entire life there in study and writing. He translated the Qur'an in simple Urdu language with commentary named *Mūḍiḥ al-Qur'ān*. This name gives its date of completion i.e. 1205 AH (1791 CE). His translation is still considered among the best translations of the Qur'an in precision and accuracy. It enabled the Muslim masses to relate directly to teachings of the Qur'an.
77. Shah Abd al-Ghani (1171–1203/1758–1789) was the youngest of four brothers and the first to pass away. He was very similar to his father in appearance, nature, and dress. He was an accomplished Sufi. Due to his death at the early age of 32, he could not play a scholarly role like his other brothers. He had one son, Shah Muhammad Ismail, who earned the highest fame among the grand sons of Shah Wali-Allah Dihlawi. See the note below.

78. Shah Ismail Shahid (1193–1246/1779–1831) was son of Shah Abd al-Ghani, the youngest son of Shah Wali-Allah. Since his father died at an early age, he was brought up by Shah Abd al-Aziz, his eldest uncle. He displayed a remarkable ability to comprehend intricate treatises of theology and jurisprudence. He learned the rational sciences of logic, mathematics, systematic theology, and hermeneutics along with the traditional sciences. He accompanied Sayyid Ahmad Shahīd (1201–1246/1786–1831) to perform hajj in 1826. After they returned, both of them launched a campaign in order to reform Muslim society and inject in them the passion to regain their past prestige and position. In their drive for the administration of justice to Muslims, Shah Ismail and Sayyid Ahmad Berelvi lost their lives in the battlefield in Balakot on 6 May 1831 during a fierce battle against the army of Ranjit Singh (1780–1839), the ruler of the region at that time. *Taqwiyat al-Īmān* (Strengthening of the Faith), and *Ṣirāṭ al-Mustaqīm* (Right Path) are two important works of Shah Ismail Shahid. His intellectual contributions were overshadowed by his martyrdom.
79. Islahi, Ajmal, 'Tasānīf-e Farāhi Kā Ghair Matbuah Sarmāyah', p. 83, 85.
80. Professor Muhammad Nejatullah Siddiqi observed this in his "Introduction" to *Economic Concepts of Ibn Taimiyah* (Islahi, Abdul Azim, *Economic Concepts of Ibn Taimiyah*, p. 13).
81. Ibn Kathīr, *al-Bidāyah wa'l-Nihāyah*, vol. 14, pp. 22–5.
82. Dihlawi, *al-Tafhīmāt al-Ilāhiyyah*, vol. 1, 101.
83. Nadwi, *Tārīkh-i Dāwat -o- Azīmat*, 5: 294.

3

Intellectual and Academic Heritage of Shah Wali-Allah Dihlawi

Shah Wali-Allah Dihlawi was a prolific writer who wrote extensively on several Islamic subjects. His contributions include commentaries on the Qur'an and Ḥadith, their principles, fiqh, principles of jurisprudence, dialecticism ('ilm *al-kalām*), wisdom (*ḥikmah*), the philosophy of the Shariah, the biography of the Prophet and his Caliphs, biographies of his teachers and ancestors, his own biography, *taṣawwuf* and related disciplines, collections of his letters, Arabic poetry, and miscellaneous tracts. Wali-Allah also wrote in the areas of sociology, politics, psychology, education, and ethical philosophy. Although most of his work is in Persian, he had skill in both languages for his Arabic writings are like those of a native Arab, free from literary errors which are not only lucid, simple and direct, but also the most appropriate for literary creations and the expression of serious thoughts. His work *Ḥujjat Allāh al-Bālighah* bears resemblance with Ibn Khaldun's *Muqaddimah* in rendering difficult scientific ideas into Arabic. Many experts of Arabic and Islamic literature have acknowledged Shah Wali-Allah's excellence in this field. In the opinion of Nadwi, no writer after Ibn Khaldun could afford to bear comparison with the facile pen of Shah Wali-Allah.[1] Jalbani, an expert of Shah Wali-Allah's writing has rightly observed:

> He has explained every point, however difficult and obscure, very clearly and in the simplest possible way. His sayings, writings, and the style he employed were all above ambiguity and equivocation. He has taken care to avoid the use of unfamiliar words and phrases. His composition is strong and firm and at certain places there is a marked brevity in it, the words used are few and the meaning implied is abundant. This brevity is the chief characteristic of his work *Ta'wīl-al-Aḥādīth*. He has vividly expressed the varying sheds of emotions and the feelings of the hearts of people that one is surprised to see such tremendous power of his expression.[2]

While commenting on Shah Wali-Allah's contribution, Mawlana Mawdudi has remarked: 'One is simply amazed when one views the accomplishments of the Shah Sahib against the dark background of his time and wonders how the appearance of a man of such deep insight and vast intellect became possible in that age... Even while going through and turning the pages of his books one does not at all feel that these were written in a place surrounded on all sides by luxury and self-worship, killings and coercion, tyranny and chaos.'[3]

Among others, Wali-Allah's style of writing and method of argument are a major factor behind the popularity of his works. This same quality he tried to inculcate among his disciples and the students of Madrasah Rahimiyah.

3.1 Shah Wali-Allah's syllabus—an academic legacy

The educational syllabus before Shah Wali-Allah was one called *Dars-i Niẓāmī*, named after Mullah Nizam al-Dīn Sihalwi (d. 1161/1748), a leading scholar of rationalist disciplines such as philosophy and logic and a member of the Indian Farangī Maḥallī family of scholars.[4] This was a very lengthy syllabus; logic, philosophy, metaphysics, and dialectics were dominating subjects of Dars-i Niẓāmī. The portion dedicated to ḥadith was the minimum. Only one book, *Mishkāt al-Maṣābīḥ*, was prescribed.

The syllabus had 'five text each of mathematics and logic, in addition to three of the most advanced texts on natural philosophy and physics, two texts in Islamic jurisprudence and two on *'ilm al-kalām* or scholasticism'.[5] Shah Wali-Allah was against such an onerous, lengthy syllabus having so much emphasis on Greek logic, philosophy, metaphysics, etc.

In light of his own education and his experience while educating students in Madrasa Rahimiyah, Shah Wali-Allah prepared a very precise and intensive course of study in which he retained only a few necessary elements of Dars-i Niẓāmī and introduced some new subjects. According to him, 'to begin with, the students should be taught three or four tracts on Arabic grammar according to their respective grade and level of understanding. Then they should be taught a text book on history or practical philosophy in Arabic in such a way that they are trained to consult dictionaries and to resolve independently the difficult portions in the text. As soon as the students have acquired proficiency in Arabic they should be taught the *Muwaṭṭa'* as narrated by Yahya b. Yahya al-Masmudi (d 234/849).[6] This should in no case be interrupted for it contained the essence of Hadith and its study was full of blessings. It has reached us without interruptions. Later on, the translation of the Qur'an should be taught and not the commentary. The difficulties of grammar and syntax or the circumstances that occasioned the revelation of different verses should not be discussed during the course of the lesson on translation but should be taken up later. After completely learning the translation, lessons on *Tafsīr Jalālayn* should be started, for that method was also endowed with blessings. Then the following time-table should be adhered to. Different periods should be allotted to the study of the *Ṣaḥīḥ Bukhārī* and *Ṣaḥīḥ Muslim* and other books of hadith, to the books of fiqh, beliefs and Sufism. A period should be assigned for the study of the books of *dānishmandī* (logic and philosophy) such as *Sharḥ Mullā*,[7] the *Qutbi*,[8] and other similar works. If possible, the students should study a portion of the *Mishkāt al-Maṣābīḥ* and its commentary by Tibi[9] on alternative days. This would be very beneficial.'[10]

Strangely enough, Dār al-'Ulūm Deoband,[11] which is considered as the incarnation of Madrasa Rahimiyah, preferred to adopt Dars-i Niẓāmī—of course with certain partial modifications. For example, they increased the study of *Ṣiḥāḥ Sittah* (the six collections of the most correct hadith) as well as the study of a few *tafsīr* (exegesis of the Qur'an). Dār al-'Ulūm Nadwat al-'Ulamā, Lucknow, moved further towards Shah Wali-Allah's syllabus.[12] However, the institution which implemented Shah Wali-Allah's syllabus to the maximum extent perhaps could not attract the attention of his biographers. This institution is Madrasat al-Islah.[13] As Shah Wali-Allah suggested, the madrasa prescribed a few texts of Arabic grammar along with Arabic readers and classical Arabic poetry to master the language.[14] *Muwaṭṭa'* is introduced just after this stage. Only one text is prescribed for each subject of logic and philosophy to introduce these subjects to the students. In addition, prescribing the *Muqaddimah* of Ibn Khaldun fulfils many objectives. The teaching of the Qur'an is direct, without a commentary. Last but not least, it has also included *Ḥujjat Allāh al-Bālighah* in its study course, which is perhaps something that was not thought of by Shah Wali-Allah himself. Throughout their study, students are required to consult dictionaries to solve problems themselves instead of simply depending on the instructor, as was suggested by Shah Wali-Allah in his syllabus.

In this way, this compact syllabus creates among the students the ability to study thereafter any subject, read any book, and specialise in any branch of knowledge. They obtain the master key to open the doors of all sciences. However, by presenting this syllabus, Shah Wali-Allah did not aim to introduce something static and stagnant for all time to come. Obviously, there would be a need to adjust and improve the course of study to accommodate the requirements of the time and move along with the social and scientific advancements. However, there are certain elements that have to be retained at all costs. Shah Wali-Allah brought a change to the existing syllabus at that time and reformed it. Thus, change and reform are the very message of his endeavours.

3.2 Sources of Shah Wali-Allah's thought

Shah Wali-Allah's first and foremost source of thought is the Book of Almighty Allah (the Qur'an) and His Prophet's traditions (Hadith).

He depended on these two sources of Islam in his writings; this is more than obvious and needs not any proof or explanation. He was a versatile genius and a very great person in his thought and intellectual discourses in his own right, so much so that many scholars thought his birth during the decaying phase of the Mughal period was no less than a miracle. However, this does not mean that he did not benefit from scholars of the past. Greatness is not in ignoring the wisdom and intellectual achievements of humankind. Greatness lies in explicating and advancing past ideas. Since human beings are, by nature, moving forward in ideas and actions, Dihlawi never hesitated to benefit from the intellectual heritage of the various clusters of past thinkers, be it scholars, jurists, philosophers or Sufis, to advance it further.

Shah Wali-Allah held the early leaders of jurisprudence (*a'immah*) such as Malik, Abu Hanifah, Shafi'i, Abu Yusuf and Muhammad b. Hasan al-Shaybani in high esteem. Once, he suggested that the Shaf'i and Hanafi fiqh may be merged by retaining the most authentic rules of the two schools.[15]

In his philosophical discussions, Shah Wali-Allah seems to be highly influenced by Abu Nasr al-Farabi (d. 339/950). Although the former never refers to the latter, Muhammad Al-Ghazali presents strong evidences of this influence.[16] According to him: 'The effort to reconcile the rational with the traditional, so conspicuous in Farabi, is also evident, and in fact seems to have reached its culmination, in Shah Wali-Allah. The idea of integrating the institution of prophethood with cultural development in human society was first initiated by Farabi. This idea found its mature expression in Shah Wali-Allah's *Ḥujjat Allāh al-Bālighah*.'[17]

Shah Wali-Allah's discussion of *irtifāqāt* is similar to al-Farabi's classification of *al-ijtima'at al-insaniyyah* (human civilization) into perfect and deficient.[18] Again, Shah Wali-Allah's ideas about *millat quṣwā* (high people) and its *qayyim* (administrator) as discussed in *Al-Budūr al-Bāzighah* is similar to al-Farabi's *al-madīnat al-fādilah* (the perfect city) and its *al-ra'is al-ala* (the chief executive), which is in turn indicative of Plato's ideal state and its philosopher king.[19]

Jalal al-Dīn Dawwani (d. 1501) was in the chain of Shah Wali-Allah's teachers,[20] basing his ideas on Nasir al-Dīn Tusi and earlier *ḥukamā*

(Muslim philosophers) who learned Greek translations. *Tadbīr al-Manzil* is a good example of such influence.

In terms of *taṣawwuf*, Shah Wali-Allah was much influenced by his father Shah Abd al-Rahim. His efforts included trying to present a synthesis between Ibn Arabi's *waḥdat al-wujūd* (unity of being) and Ahmad Sirhindi's *waḥdat al-shuhūd* (unity of manifestation).

Shah Wali-Allah himself referred to al-Ghazal (d. 505/1111), al-Khattabi (d. 388/998), and Izz ibn Abd al-Salam (d. 660/1262) in the beginning of his master literary work, *Ḥujjat Allāh al-Bālighah* with respect to the wisdom and rationality behind various Shariah provisions. Shah Wali-Allah raised this branch of knowledge to the height of sky.

3.3 Influence of Ibn Taymiyyah and Ibn al-Qayyim

A major source of Shah Wali-Allah's inspiration was Ibn Taymiyyah, but a section of Shah Wali-Allah's admirers would not like to accept it. Therefore, this fact needs to be substantiated.

We have already noted in the previous chapter that during his stay in Hijaz, Wali-Allah came across the works of Ibn Taymiyyah through his teacher Abu Tahir al-Kurdi and his father Ibrahim Kawrani who, as a fan of Ibn Taymiyyah, had a rich collection of his books. Shah Wali-Allah must have read some of these works and benefitted from them as seen in his writings. Shah Wali-Allah's admirer Mawlana Ubaidullah Sindhi has also emphasized this.[21] Mawlana Sindhi points out that some important discussion in Dihlawi's work *Izālat al-Khafā 'an Khilāfat al-Khulafā'* seems to have been adopted from Ibn Taymiyyah's work *Minhāj al-Sunnat al-Nabawiyyah*.[22] Rizvi is also of the same opinion.[23] Shah Wali-Allah also has the same concept regarding the reason for revelation (*sabab nuzūl*) of the chapters of the Qur'an which Ibn Taymiyyah held before him.[24]

In fact, Ibn Taymiyyah's fame and influence extended well beyond the boundaries of Egypt and Syria during his own lifetime.[25] One of his disciples, Allama Abd al-'Aziz Ardabili, went from Damascus to the court of Sultan Muhammad Tughluq.[26] Prof. K. A. Nizami writes: 'Ibn Taimiyya's disciples reached India at a time when the country was in the grip of pantheistic doctrines. The policies of Sultan Muhammad bin Tughlaq and Firuz Shah seem to have been very greatly influenced by these tendencies of the age.'[27] No doubt, Ibn Taymiyyah's revolutionary ideas must not have been welcomed in India for many centuries to come and he might have been considered as a *persona non grata*. This may be the reason why Shah Wali-Allah does not mention him in his important works despite benefitting from him.[28] Nagrami proved that Shaykh al-Islam Ibn Taymiyyah was an important source for Shah Wali-Allah. Furthermore, Al-Sialkoti reproduces in his book a letter written by Shah Wali-Allah in reply to a query addressed to one of his disciples called Muhammad Amin al-Sindi in which he praised Ibn Taymiyyah's stances on various issues.[29] According to al-Sialkoti, Shah Wali-Allah in his Persian work *al-Balāgh al-Mubīn* has noted sections and chapters from Ibn Taymiyyah's *Iqtiḍā' al-Ṣirāṭ al-Mustaqīm* so much so that it looks like an abridged edition of said work.[30]

3.4 Introducing Shah Wali-Allah's works

3.4.1 His major works

Shah Wali-Allah was a prolific writer. In addition to several major works, he authored a number of treatises ranging from a few pages to a small tract. The following list of all his known works is arranged alphabetically. He wrote both in Arabic and Persian, and some of his works are partly in Arabic and partly in Persian. In the following lists, the letter A or P is written along with the title to indicate whether the work is Arabic or Persian.

1. *Al-Budūr al-Bāzighah* (A)

Al-Budūr al-Bāzighah (The Bright Moons) is a work on theology employing philosophical terminology in discussing human nature and social behaviour. It presents a philosophical and rational interpretation of Islam. It is the second most important contribution of the author on the topic after *Ḥujjat Allah al-Bālighah*. According to Mawlana Nadwi, 'The topics touched in this work are far in excess of those dealt with in the *Ḥujjat Allāh al- Bālighah* and it examines certain metaphysical and theological issues which have not been normally touched upon by other scholars. However, the *Ḥujjat* outshines this work because of the depth of knowledge and maturity of ideas as well as the Arabic idiom and diction displayed by Shah Wali-Allah in that work.'[31] In this work, Shah Wali-Allah deals with man's physical characteristics and ethical instincts and details practical wisdom to show what guidance the Shariah provides for the establishment of a moral-spiritual society. He examines in this work the basic characteristics of a Muslim umma as against the pre-Islamic nations.

2. *Fatḥ al-Raḥmān fi Tarjamat al-Qur'an* (P)

Shah Wali-Allah felt that only direct knowledge of the Qur'an would lead the umma to the right path. Therefore, he paid careful attention to translating the Qur'an into Persian, the official language of the Mughal court. He completed this in 1151/1738 under the title *Fatḥ al-Raḥmān fi Tarjamat al-Qur'an*. This is among the first popular renderings of the Qur'an into simple Persian language. It is considered as 'one of the most important contributions to the religious life of the Indian Muslims.'[32] According to Schimmel, 'he rightly felt that the Muslims would be more easily in a position to live in accordance with the Holy Writ if they could understand its text instead of relying solely upon commentaries and super commentaries which often obscured the original, living word.'[33] Although many good translations into the Persian language were available back then, the main characteristic of Shah Wali-Allah's translation was its simplicity. It was meant for common people and soldiers as earlier translations were delivered in a high-flown language intended for literary circles. Its popularity can be imagined from the fact that it was printed several times by Matba' Hashimi in Meerut (1254/1869); by Matba' Faruqi in Delhi (1294/1877) along with Shah Abdul Qadir's Urdu rendering of the Qur'an entitled *Mūḍiḥ al-Qur'an*; Lucknow (1902). It was also printed by Nur Muhammad Karkhana Tijarat-i Kutub in Karachi and by Taj Company in Lahore in 1986.

3. *al-Fawz al-Kabīr fi Ūṣūl al-Tafsīr* (A and P)

Al-Fawz al-Kabīr fi Ūṣūl al-Tafsīr (The Great Success) is a treatise on the principles of exegesis and Qur'anic interpretation. It followed the author's Persian translation of the Holy Qur'an. The main characteristic of this work is that it is a concise, but extremely valuable treatise on the principles of Qur'anic exegesis. It is among the most popular works of Shah Wali-Allah, which has made an outstanding contribution to the study and understanding of the Qur'an. This is clear from the fact that it has been translated into many languages. Furthermore, its full Arabic version has been prepared by several editors/translators.

4. *Ḥujjat Allāh al- Bālighah* (A)

Ḥujjat Allāh al-Bālighah (The Convincing Proofs of Allah) is the most important work of Shah Wali-Allah. After returning from his journey to the two holy cities of Islam in 1145/1732, he began writing this work and completed it in 1148/1735. It elucidates the inner meanings and the wisdom (*al-asrār wa'l-ḥikam*) of various Shariah provisions. According to Schimmel, this is the prescribed reading at al-Azhar University and is taught in many other seminaries. It is the *summa* (summary) of Shah Wali-Allah's thought and teachings, comprising theories of religion, economics, man's spiritual development, political philosophy, and so on.[34] In the opinion of Sayyid Nadwi, 'The *magnum opus* of Shah Waliullah, the *Ḥujjat Allah al-Bālighah*, is a comprehensive and cogent work presenting a synthesis of the Islamic creed, devotions, transactions, morals, social philosophy, statecraft and spirituality. All these have been balanced and integrated in such a perfect manner that they appear to be jewels of the same necklace or links of the same golden chain.'[35]

5. *al-Inṣāf fi Bayān Sabab al-Ikhtilāf* (A)

In *al-Inṣāf fi Bayān Sabab al-Ikhtilāf* (The Just Stand in dealing with Juridical Differences), Shah Wali-Allah discussed the history and nature of differences among various schools of jurisprudence. He suggested how to adopt a just and middle path through those differences. Basically, this work is a juridical discourse on the evolution of the different schools of jurisprudence. It also discusses the nature of disagreement among jurists and the principles to resolve various conflicting opinions. Some of its contents also form part of *Ḥujjat Allāh al-Bālighah*. The book has been published many times and its Urdu translation by Sadruddin Islahi (1916–1998) is also available.[36]

6. *Izālat al-Khafā ʿan Khilāfat al-Khulafāʾ* (P)

Izālat al-Khafā ʿan Khilāfat al-Khulafāʾ (Removal of doubts from the caliphate of the Caliphs) is another important work by Shah Wali-Allah. In this work, he presents guidelines to rulers, noblemen, soldiers and government officials. It is a good source for understanding the Islamic political system and the principles of an Islamic economy. Al-Hasani, the author of *Nuzhat al-Khawāṭir*, remarks that 'on its subject the book has no peer—neither before it, nor after it. It shows that its author is an ocean of knowledge that has no shore.'[37]

7. *al-Khayr al-Kathīr* (A)

Al-Khayr al-Kathīr (A Lot of Goodness) is on the philosophy of religion and elucidates the concept of *maʿrifat* (gnosis) as well as the wisdom of Divine Names, revelation, etc. Herein, he attempts to explain the fundamentals of faith with an approach to combining rational and traditional arguments. He has also discussed from a philosophical angle matters like *waḥdat al-wujūd* (unity of being), *ʿarsh* (empyrean), *zamān-o-makān* (time and space), *aflāk o ʿanāṣir* (vault of heaven and the constituent matters), *maʾdan* (minerals), *nabat* (vegetation), *ḥaywān* (animal life), *aʿyān-i-thābitah* (prototypes of things), *ʿalam al-mithāl* (sphere of similitude), etc.[38]

8. *Muṣaffā Sharḥ al-Muwaṭṭaʾ* (P)

Muṣaffā is a commentary in Persian on Imam Malik's *Muwaṭṭaʾ*. In this work, Shah Wali-Allah dealt with the opinions of the Hanafi and Shafiʿi schools, revealing his depth of knowledge and insight into the science of Hadith and fiqh. It was first published by Matba' Faruqi, Delhi, and then reprinted by Matba' Murtadawi, Delhi, in 1293/1876.

9. *Musawwā Sharḥ al-Muwaṭṭa'* (A)

Musawwā is another commentary on the *Muwaṭṭa'* of Imam Malik. This very concise and to-the-point work is in Arabic. It was lithographed on the margin of *Muṣaffā*, published by Faruqi Press, Delhi in 1293/1876. Thereafter it has been published several times from Delhi and abroad.

10. *al-Tafhīmāt al-Ilāhiyyah* (A and P)

Al-Tafhīmāt al-Ilāhiyyah (The Divine Explanation) is in two parts. It was written at different times on different topics and later collected. The book is a mystical work, partly in Arabic and partly in Persian, containing Wali-Allah's mystical experiences. It is like the author's diary in which he has noted down esoteric feelings. In it, he interprets subtle issues of rational and spiritual importance in light of personal revelations. Some of the sections also deal with social, ethical and political issues.

3.4.2 Shah Wali-Allah's other works

Shah Wali-Allah was actively engaged in writing on various subjects of his days. He had a capable team of disciples and followers who efficiently prepared and preserved copies of his manuscripts. In fact, it is not known if ever anything was lost. It is said that the number of his work reached over two hundred, however, the correct view is that it ranged between forty and seventy if we count all his works, which are sometimes as short as a few pages. Most of such works formed part of a volume but were sometimes published separately. In addition to the ten major works introduced above, we have attempted to provide a comprehensive list of Shah Wali-Allah's works from various sources. The total amounts to sixty works which can be seen listed below:

1. *Alṭāf al-Quds* or 'Blessings of the Sanctuary' (P) deals with the esoteric principles of mysticism. It was first published by Sayyid Zahir al-Dīn from Matba' Ahmadi, Delhi, in 1307 AH. There are several translations of the work in Urdu. The english translation by Jalbani, edited by Pendlbury, is entitled 'The Sacred knowledge of the Higher Functions of the Mind', published in 1982 by Octagon Press, London.
2. *Anfās al-'Ārifīn* (P) narrates the spiritual attainments of the author's forefathers and spiritual ancestors, published in 1335/1917 by the Mujtaba'i Press in Delhi. It consists of the following seven tracts, most of which have also been published separately as these titles have been mentioned again in this list.
   (a) *Bawāriq al-Wilāyah.*
   (b) *Shawāriq al-Ma'rifah.*
   (c) *al-lmdād fi Ma'āthir al-Ajdād.*
   (d) *al-Nubdhah al-lbrīziyyah fi al-Laṭīfah al-'Azīziyyah.*
   (e) *al-'Aṭiyyh al-Ṣamadiyah fi al-Anfās al-Muḥammadiyyah.*
   (f) *Insān al-'Ain fi-Mashā'ikh al-Ḥaramayn.*
   (g) *al-Juza' al-Laṭīf fi Tarjamat al-'Abd al-Ḍa'īf.*
3. *al-'Aqīdah al-Ḥasanah* or *Ḥusn al-'Aqīdah,* also known as 'Good Belief' (A), is a plain and rational presentation of the fundamental beliefs in Islam in light of the Qur'an and Sunnah. Mawlana Nagrami has written a commentary on this work under the title of *al-'Aqīdah al-Sunniyyah* published in 1962 by Nadwat al-'Ulamā, Lucknow.
4. *al-Arba'īn* otherwise known as 'The Forty Hadith' (A) is a collection of forty hadith which are brief yet of inclusive character. The collection was published by Matba' Anwar Ahmadi in Lucknow in the year 1319/1901. Its Urdu translation by the pen of Khalifa Sayyid 'Abdullah, a spiritual successor of Sayyid Ahmad Shahīd, was brought out in 554/1836 from Matba'-i Ahmadi, Calcutta. Later on, another rendering including short

comments by Mawlana 'Abdul Majid Daryabadi was published in 1387/1967 as *Chahl Ḥadīth Walī-Allāhī* or *Arba'īn Walī-Allāhī* by several publishers in India and Pakistan.

5. *al-'Aṭiyyh al-Ṣamadiyyah fi al-Anfās al-Muḥammadiyyah* (P) is a short treatise on the biography of Shaykh Muhammad Phulati, a Sufi and the maternal grand-father of Shah Wali-Allah. It is included both in the *Anfās al-'Ārifīn* and in the *Majmū'ah Khamsa Rasā'il*.
6. *Al-Balāgh al-Mubīn fi Aḥkām Rabb al-'Ālamīn wa Atbā' Khātam al-Nabiyyin* (P) is a tract refuting tomb-worshipping and rejecting heresy.
7. *Bawāriq al-Wilāyah* (P) is a tract forming part of the *Anfās al-'Ārifīn* in which Shah Wali-Allah has described the life and spiritual attainments of his father Shah Abd al-Rahim and conveyed some of his sayings and dictums.
8. *Dīwān Ash'ār* (A) is a collection of the Arabic poetry of Shah Wali-Allah, compiled by Shah 'Abd al-'Aziz and Shah Rafi' al-Dīn. The manuscript is available in the Dār al-'Ulūm Nadwat al-'Ulamā Library in Lucknow.
9. *al-Durr al-Thamīn fi-Mubbashsharāt al-Nabī al-Amīn* (A) is a collection of glad tidings that Shah Wali-Allah and his ancestors had from the Prophet, may Allah bless him and give him peace. It was published with Urdu translation and annotation by Matba' Ahmadi Delhi in 1899.
10. *al-Faḍl al-Mubīn fi al-Musalsal Min Ḥadīth al-Nabī al-Amīn* (A), also known as *Musalsalat*, is a work on hadith.
11. *Fatḥ al-Khabīr* (A) is a glossary of the intricate words of the Qur'an, included as an appendix to *al-Fawz al-Kabīr*. It aims to explain the difficult words used in the Qur'an.
12. *Fatḥ al-Wadūd-li-Ma'rifat al-Junūd* (A) is a work not listed by most authors, except for Rahim Bakhsh who authored a biography of Dihlawi entitled *Ḥayat-i Wali*. Herein, he mentioned that this work is related to ethics and mysticism.[39]
13. *Fuyūḍ al-Ḥaramayn* or 'The Emanations of the Two Holy Cities' (A), as can be deduced from the name, is a work in which the au-

thor narrates his experiences during his sojourn in Makkah and Madinah. Here he details the spiritual benefits received from his teachers at the two most holy mosques of Islam.

14. *Hama'āt* (A/P) is on the subject of Sufism. The book contains a history of different mystical orders. The author's description sheds light on the stages and development of mysticism, and discusses the faith of *waḥdat al-wujūd* (unity of being) as propounded by the famous Sufi, Muhi al-Dīn Ibn 'Arabi (560–638/1165–1240). In this book, Shah Wali-Allah appears to be an expert physician in the spiritual field. This was published in Lahore in the year 1941, edited by Ghulam Mustafa Qasimi.
15. *Hawāmi' Sharḥ-i-Ḥizb al-Baḥr* (P) is a translation of and commentary on the famous Arabic invocations named *Ḥizb al-Baḥr,* written by Shaykh Abul Hasan Shadhili. It was published in 1302 AH by Matba'Ahmadi, Delhi, and in 1350 AH by Matba' Mujtaba'i, Delhi.
16. *al-Imdād fi Ma'āthir al-Ajdād* (P) gives Shah Wali-Allah's genealogical table and contains a biographical account of some of the ancestors of the author. It forms part of *Anfās al-'Ārifin* as well as *Majmū'ah Khams Rasā'il Shāh Wali-Allāh.* It was published in 1335/1917 by the Mujtaba'i Press, Delhi.
17. *Insān al-'Ain fi Mashā'ikh al-Ḥaramayn* (P) was written by Shah Wali-Allah in memory of his teachers in the two sacred cities, Makkah and Madinah. It forms part both of *Anfās al-'Ārifin* and *Majmū'ah Khamsa Rasa'il Shah Wali-Allah* and was published with them.
18. *al-Intibāh fi Salāsil Awliā'-Allāh* (P) gives the history and a brief introduction of the different mystic orders. It was published by Sayyid Zahir al-Dīn along with its Urdu translation in 1311/1893 from Matba'Ahmadi.
19. *'Iqd al-Jīd fi Bayān Aḥkām al-Ijtihād wa'l-Taqlīd* or 'Dealing with the rules of independent decision-making and following others' (A) is a treatise. In this work, Wali-Allah discusses various dimensions of the issues involved in original thinking (*ijtihad*) and

imitating and following others (*taqlīd*), presenting a balanced view on this oft-discussed and much-debated subject.

20. *al-Irshād ilā Muhimmāt 'Ilm al-Isnād wa Asānīd Wārith Rasūl-Allāh* (A) is on the importance of the chain (*sanad*) of hadith and on the teachers of Shah Wali-Allah in the Hijaz from whom he transmitted the Hadith. It was published with his work *Tarājim al-Bukhārī* by Matba' Ahmadi, Delhi in 1307/1889.
21. *al-Juza' al-Laṭīf fi Tarjamat al-'Abd al-Ḍa'īf* (P) is a short autobiography of the author and contains some of his reminiscences. It forms a part of *Anfās al-'Ārifīn*, which has also been published separately with Shah Wali-Allah's work *Saṭa'āt* by Matba' Ahmadi, Delhi, undated.
22. *Kalimāt Ṭayyibāt* (A/P) is a collection of selected letters relating to mystical discussions which were sent by Shah Wali-Allah to Mirza Mazhar Jan-i Janan, Khawaja Muhammad Amin, Shah Abu Sa id and others. It has been published by Matba' Mujtaba'i in Delhi in 1891/1909, and by Abul Khair Academy, Delhi, in 1983.
23. *Kashf al-Ghayn fi Sharḥ al-Rubā'iyyatayn* (P) is a commentary on two *ruba'*īs or quatrains of Khwaja Baqi Billah, published by the Mujtaba'i Press, Delhi, in 1310/1892.
24. *Lama'āt* or 'Flashes of Lightening' (P) is an important work on Sufism. It had been published in Hyderabad, Sindh. It has also been translated into English.
25. *Lamaḥāt* (P) is a booklet dealing with being, reality, the holy circle (*Ḥaẓīrat al-Quds*) and the universe, etc. It was edited and published by Ghulam Mustafa Qasimi from Hyderabad, Sindh, undated. The Urdu translation by Muhammad Hasan is published by Idara Thaqafah Islamiyyah, Lahore, in 1966 and 1984. The English translation by G N Jalbani, from Hyderabad, Sindh was published in 1970. Another translation exists by Jalbani and D B. Fry entitled *Sufism and the Islamic Tradition.*
26. *al-Makātīb al-Madhkūrah fi Kitāb Kalimāt Ṭayyibāt* (P) printed.
27. *al-Maktūb al-Madani* (A) is a letter written to Shaykh Isma'il bin 'Abd-Allah Rumi comparing the concepts of *waḥdat al-wujūd* (Unity of Being) and *waḥdat al-shuhūd* (Unity of

Manifestation). It forms part of *al-Tafhīmāt al-Ilāhiyyah,*[40] and has also been published separately. The Urdu translation by Muhammad Hanif Nadwi is under the title *Maktūb Madani* published by Idara Thaqafa Islamiya in Lahore, 1965.

28. *Maktūbāt ma' Manāqib imām Bukhārī wa Faḍīlat-i Ibn-Taymiyyah* (P) is not a complete book, according to Mawlana Nadwi. The work brought out under this title by Mawlawi 'Abd al-Rauf of the Naziriah Library comprises two letters written by Shah Wali-Allah acclaiming Imam Bukhārī and Ibn Taymiyyah. It is also included in some of his other works.[41]
29. *al-Maqālah al-Waḍī'ah fi al-Naṣīḥah wa'l-Waṣiyyah* (P) is also known as the *Waṣiyyat-nāmah* and has been published several times. Qazi Thanaullah Panipati had annotated the work in light of Wali-Allah's book *Irshād al-Ṭālibīn,* which was published by Muti' al-Rahman Press, Delhi, in 1268/1852.
30. *Muqaddimah dar fann-i tarjamah-i Qur'an* or 'Rules for the guidance of the translation of the Qur'an' (P) is also published at the beginning of Wali-Allah's Persian translation of the Qur'an *Fatḥ al-Raḥmān* as *aI-Muqaddimah fi Qawānīn al-Tarjamah.*
31. *al-Muqaddimah al-Saniyyah fi Intiṣār al-Firqah al-Sunniyyah* (A) is a work at the request of Shaykh Abu Tahir al-Madani in which Shah Wali-Allah rendered Shaykh Ahmad Sirhindi's Persian treatise *Radd-i Rawāfiḍ* into Arabic with certain additions and comments. Manuscripts of this work are available in the libraries of Tonk and Bhopal. It has been published in Delhi by Mawlana Abul-Hasan Zayd Mujaddidi.
32. *al-Nawādir min Aḥādīth Saiyid al-Awā'il wa'l-Awākhir* (A) has been published with the *Musalsalat.*
33. *al-Nubdhah al-Ibrīziyyah fi'l-Laṭīfat al-'Azīziyyah* (P) has been brought out with the *Anfās al-'Ārifīn* as well as the *Majmū'ah Khamsa Rasā'il.* It gives a biographical account of Shaykh 'Abd al-'Aziz Dihlawi, the maternal great grandfather of Shah Wali-Allah, and is published with *Anfās al-'Ārifīn.*[42]
34. *Qaṣīdah Na'tiyyah Hamziyyah,* an Arabic ode on the Prophet Muhammad, may Allah bless him and give him peace, was written in 1151/1738–39.[43]

35. *al-Qawl al-Jamīl fi Bayān Sawā' al-Sabīl* or 'The beautiful statement about the Right Path' (A) discusses the legality of allegiance (*bay'at*). Shah Wali-Allah traced the practice to the time of the Prophet and the causes leading to its fall into disuse in the subsequent period. He also covers the necessity of its revival. He goes on further to throw light on the qualities required of mystic guides and he initiates, the content and method of mystical guidance, as well as the prerequisites of an effective sermon. According to Sayyid Ali Nadwi, 'The readers of the book will not find in it the logical and dialectical approach which characterises other important works of Shah Wali-Allah. Rather, a few of the passages in this work are hardly in conformity with his reformative attitude and scholarly style.'[44] In Nadwi's opinion, 'The apparent reason for proffering such views is that this book was written by the Shah before he set out for pilgrimage to the two holy cities, in 1143/1731.'[45] Mawlana Nadwi provides convincing reasons for his conclusion.
36. *Qurrat al-'Aynayn fi Tafḍīl al-Shaykhayn* (P) brings forward evidence to prove the superiority of the first two caliphs. It discusses the significant achievements of the first two caliphs and their superior place in Islam. The discussion is substantiated by verses of the Qur'an and the traditions of the Prophet. It has been reprinted several times.
37. *The Radd (refutation) of the Gawhar-i Murād* is a work by Mulla Abd al-Razzaq Lahiji (d. 1145/1661), a disciple of Mulla Sadra.
38. *Risālah* was written in reply to certain mystical issues raised by Shaykh 'Abd-Allah bin 'Abd al-Baqi, also known as Khwaja Khurd.
39. *Risālah Dānishmandi* (P) is a valuable tract containing detailed directions regarding the methodology of teaching. It was published by Matba' Ahmadi, Delhi, in 1321/1899, as well as in Lucknow in 1894 at the margin of the *Waṣiyyat-nāmah*. The Urdu translation by Muhammad Sarwar was published from Lahore in 1964, and also published in *al-Rahim* Journal, Vol. 2, No. 4, September, 1964. The Arabic translation by Muhammad Akram Nadwi, entitled *Ūṣūl al-dirāsah wa'l-ta'lim* was published in the journal *al-Ba'th al-Islāmi*, Lucknow, Vol 27, No 4, in October 1403/1982.

40. *Ṣarf-i Mīr* (P) is a rendering by Shah Wali-Allah of Mir Jurjani's work on morphology for the purpose of teaching his son, Shah Abd al-ʿAẓiz. It was published by Matba ʿ Muhammadi, Lahore, in 1293 AH.
41. *Saṭaʿāt* or 'Illuminations' is a tract that discusses issues related to faith, mysticism and dimensions of Divine theophany. It attempts to explain the nature of the abstract and material worlds and their respective characteristics. According to Jalbani, '*Saṭaʿāt* is one of the famous works of Shah Waliyullah on mystical philosophy. Though it is a small treatise, it throws sufficient light on the subject. ... What chiefly characterizes this treatise is the frequent quotations from the Qur'an in support of the argument the author has advanced.'[46] It was published by Sayyid Zahir al-Dīn Wali-Allah from Matba ʿ Ahmadi, Delhi in 1307 AH, reprinted from Baitul-Hikmah, Karachi in 1939. A second edition prepared by Ghulam Mustafa Qasimi was published by Shah Waliullah Academy, Hyderabad, in 1964. Also available is the Urdu translation by Muhammad Matin Hashmi published by Idarah Thaqafah Islamiyah in Lahore in 1986 and 1999, as well as the English translation by Jalbani from Shah Waliullah Academy in Hyderabad, Sindh in 1970.
42. *Sharḥ Tarājim Baʿḍ Abwāb al-Bukhārī* (A) is a treatise in which Shah Wali-Allah has discussed the wisdom of the topical headings adopted by Imam Bukhārī for different chapters of Hadith of this important compendium of traditions compiled by Imam Bukhārī (d. 256 AH). The work also includes the *Tarājim Abwāb al-Bukhārī* and was published by Da'irat al-Ma'arif, Hyderabad, in 1323/1905.
43. *Shawāriq al-Marifat* (P) deals with the biography and mystical views and practices of his uncle Shaykh Abu al-Rida Muhammad. It also forms part of the *Anfās al-ʿĀrifin*.
44. *al-Sirr al-Maktūm fi Asbāb Tadwīn al-Ulūm* (A) is on the reasons of recording knowledge. It was published in Delhi in 1321/1809. An Urdu translation by Imam Khan Nawshahravi has been published in *al-Rahim* Journal, Vol. 2, No. 2, June–July, 1964.

45. *Surūr al-Maḥzūn* is a concise rendering of Ibn Sayyid al-Nas' work *Nūr al-Uyūn fi Talkhīṣ Siyar al-Amīn al-Māmūn* which was authored by Shah Wali-Allah at the request of Mirza Mazhar Jan-i Janan (d. 1195/1781). It was published by Matba' Mujtaba'i, Delhi in 1308 AH. It has been rendered in Urdu by several translators.
46. *al-Tanbīh alā mā yaḥtāj ilayhi al-muḥaddith wa al-faqīh* (A/P). Al-Maktabah al-Salafiyah in Lahore published it under the title *Itḥaf al-Tanbīh fi mā yaḥtāj ilayhi al-muḥaddith wa al-faqīh* with notes by Ataullah Hanif Bhojiyani.
47. *Tarājim Abwāb al-Bukhārī* or 'Introductions to the Chapters of al-Bukhārī' (A) expounds upon those principles that would be found helpful in understanding certain difficult portions of *Ṣaḥīḥ al-Bukhārī*.
48. *Tāwīl al-Aḥādīth* (A) recounts the stories of different prophets mentioned in the Qur'an in order to draw out lessons and rules of Shariah from the Qur'anic descriptions. It has been translated into English under the title 'A Mystical Interpretation of Prophetic Tales' by an Indian Muslim named J.M.S. Baljon. The translation of the title indicates the content of the treatise. This is one of Wali-Allah's early writings 'dating from approximately the year 1735'.[47] The Urdu version of *Tāwīl al-Aḥādīth* is entitled *Qaṣaṣ-i anbiyā ke rumūz aur unki ḥikmaten*, published by the Shah Wali-Allah Academy in Hyderabad, Pakistan.
49. *Tuḥfat al-Muwaḥḥidīn* or 'Gift of the Monotheists' (P) explains the creed of *tawḥīd*. First published by Afzal-al-Matabe in Delhi, Mawlana Hafiz Rahim Bakhsh, the author of the *Hayat-i-Wali*, brought out its Urdu rendering from Maktabah Salafiyah, Lahore, in 1381/1952.[48]
50. *Zahrāwayn* is a commentary on *Surah al-Baqara* and *Surah Āl-Imrān*, the second and third chapters of the Qur'an.[49]

3.4.3 Miscellaneous books attributed to Wali-Allah

The following titles have been mentioned by some biographers as books by Shah Wali-Allah, but not much information is available about these books.. Most of them are in Persian. Their subject matter may be guessed from some of the titles. These works remained unpublished or they formed part of some other works. It is difficult to tell about the number of their pages. These books are listed here just for the record:

1. *Ajwibah 'an Thalāth Masā'il*
2. *al-Anwār al-Muḥammadiyah*
3. *Asrār-i Fiqh*
4. *Awārif*
5. *Fatḥ al-Islām*
6. *Ḥāshiyah Risālah Lubs Aḥmar*
7. *I'rāb al-Qurān*
8. *al-I'tṣām*
9. *Kashf al-Anwār*
10. *Manṣūr*
11. *Nihāyat al-Ūṣūl*
12. *al-Nukhbah fi Silsilat al-Ṣuḥbah,*
13. *Qaṣīdah Aṭyab al-Nagham fi Madḥ Sayyid al-'Arab wa'l-'Ajam*
14. *Risālah fi Taḥqīq Masā'il Shaykh 'Abd al-Bāqī al-Dihlawī*
15. *Risālah fi Mas'alah 'Ilm al-Wājib*
16. *Risālah-i Dihlawī*
17. *Shifā al-Qulūb*
18. *Wāridāt*
19. *Waṣiyyat Namāh Naẓm Kardah Sa'ādat Khan*
20. *al-Dhikr al-Maymūn*

In addition to the above mentioned works, there are some other titles which are either falsely attributed to Shah Wali-Allah or their authenticity is disputed. Such titles are ignored. There are, however, a few collections of his letters, some of them listed in preceding pages.

3.4.4 Number of Shah Wali-Allah's works

Hafiz Ibrahim Mir Sialkoti, a biographer of Shah Wali-Allah, claims that Wali-Allah wrote more than 200 books.[50] Most of the writers gave the number of his works at around fifty. The maximum number of titles are seventy-eight as mentioned by Nasim Faridi.[51] We have tried to present a comprehensive list, including titles of treatises with unknown details, and have also reached around the same number. There can never be a consensus as sometimes a few small tracts are published in a single volume and then they are published separately, resulting in multiple counting. Moreover, while giving the number, generally it is left undefined what is considered as a book. Sometimes an article of a few pages is also counted among the books. Some people think that the reason for not giving all the titles of Wali-Allah's book is that most of them were lost. In our humble opinion, this is not something convincing. Shah Wali-Allah had friends, students and relatives who were devoted to him and were fans of his writings. Madrasa Rahimiyah was also a source in preserving his works. Additionally, the printing press was soon introduced in Delhi after a few years, although not in his lifetime. All these factors must have protected his work from any harm or destruction. In fact, the greatness of a scholar depends on the quality of his work, not the quantity. Each one of the first ten works introduced at the beginning of this section is sufficient to give its author a distinguished place in Islamic scholarship.

3.5 The impact of Shah wali-Allah's ideas -factors that rapidly spread his work

Shah Wali-Allah Dihlawi brought about a revolution in Muslim minds by his writings on various Shariah sciences, and all of which have continued to inspire his readers to this date. Within a century some of his works reached Arabia and Turkey.

His work *Ḥujjat Allāh al- Bālighah* was published in Bulaq, Egypt, as early as 1877. It has influenced most of the great scholars of the modern period, such as Jamal al-Dīn al-Qasimi, Muhammad Zahid al-Kawthari, Muhibb al-Din al-Khatib, Abu Zahrah and Abd al-Mun'im al-Namir etc.[52]

Shah Wali-Allah is among the few prolific writers of the past whose writings attracted students and scholars; almost all of his important works are now available in print form, in addition to a large number of manuscripts in various libraries of India and abroad, some of them by the author's pen. Although he lived in a very disturbed period of Indian history, as noted above, his works remained protected from misplacement and annihilation. There are many factors responsible for that:

1. His learned sons and devoted students

   Shah Wali-Allah was fortunate to have a large number of devoted students and admirers as well as four noble sons who not only longed to have his original handwritten manuscripts but prepared several copies. These manuscripts are still preserved in the libraries of Delhi, Deoband, Saharanpur, Kandhla, Muzaffarnagar, Rampur, Lucknow, Patna, etc. During his lifetime, he also received queries from outside of India, to which he responded. Since such persons have tried to obtain copies of his works, some of his work has traveled abroad to the famous oriental libraries of the world.

2. Madrasah Rahimiyah

   Shah Wali-Allah used to teach students of the higher classes after his return from Pilgrimage. Here he remained busy most of the time in research and writing. This also facilitated the copying and dissemination of his works and ideas as Madrasah Rahimiyah was an educational lab for him where he made experiments of his pedagogical visions.

3. The printing press

   Although the printing press was already introduced in the first colonized cities of India like Goa, Bombay, Madras and Calcutta, it was delayed in reaching Delhi. But within less than a century, the printing press was established, which helped with the publicity and wide circulation of his works. His various books were the first to be published from among the works of the Indian ulama. One of the descendants of Shah Wali-Allah's family, Ahmad Zahir al-Dīn Wali-Allah, established a printing press in Delhi called Matba῾-i Ahmadi (Ahmadi Press) around 1884–5. This establishment specialised in the publication of Shah Wali-Allah's works in their original languages or as translations.

4. Academic and Research Institutions

   Many academic and research institutions have been established in the sub-continent that specialise in the research, editing and publication of Shah Wali-Allah's works, for example:

   (a) Sind Sagar Academy, Hyderabad, Pakistan.
   (b) Shah Wali-Allah Academy, New Delhi.
   (c) Mufti Ilahi-Bakhsh Academy, Kandhla, U.P, India.

All these factors helped to spread Shah Wali-Allah's works, influencing the thought and ideas of writers in the modern period, especially in South Asia.

Notes and References

1. Nadwi, *Tārīkh-i Dāwat -o- Azīmat*, 5: 285.
2. Jalbani, *Teaching of Shah Waliullah of Delhi*, p. 45.
3. Mawdudi, *Tajdid*, p. 83.
4. According to Rizvi, Dars-i Niẓāmī was originally developed by Mulla Fat'h-Allah Shirazi (d. 1589) (Rizvi, *Shah Wali-Allah and his Time*, p. 392).
5. Khan, 'The Awadh Scientific Renaissance and the Role of the French: C. 1750-1820', p. 283.
6. There are two famous versions of *Muwaṭṭa'*— one by Yahya b. Yahya al-Andalusi al-Masmudi and the other by Muhammad b. Hasan al-Shaybani. Shah-Wali-Allah recommended the one reported by Yahya for study purposes.
7. *al-Fawā'id al-Ḍiyā'iyyah* by Nur al-Dīn Jami (817–98/1414–92). It is a commentary on Ibn Ḥājib's work *al-Kāfiyah*.
8. *Taḥrīr al-Qawā'id al-Manṭiqiyyah fi Sharḥ al-Risālah al-Shamsiyyah* by Qutb al-Dīn Muhammad b. Muhammad al-Razi (d. 766/1364).
9. *al-Kāshif 'an Ḥaqā'iq al-Sunan* by al-Ḥusayn b. Abd-Allah Sharaf al-Dīn al-Ṭībī (d. 743/1342).
10. Dihlawi, *Wasiyat-namah*, pp. 6–7.
11. The foundation of Dār al-'Ulūm was laid down by some ulama headed by Mawlana Muhammad Qasim Nanautawi, Mawlana Rashid Ahmad Gangohi and Haji Muhammad Hussain Abid at Deoband in the district of Saharanpur on Thursday, 15 Muharram AH 1283 (30 May 1886).

12. Dār al-'Ulūm Nadwat al- 'Ulamā was established by a group of enlightened scholars at Lucknow in 1898.
13. Madrasat al-Islah was originally started at Sarai Mir, a town in the Azamgarh district of U.P. in 1908 as a movement called 'Anjuman Islah al-Muslimin' for the reform of the Muslim population living in the area.
14. It may be noted that Shah Wali-Allah included no textbook on Arabic literature.
15. Dihlawi, *al-Tafhīmāt*, 1:211–212.
16. al-Ghazali, Muhammad, *The Socio-Political Thought of Shah Wali-Allah*, pp. 38–41.
17. Ibid., p. 38.
18. al-Farabi, *al-Madīnat al-Fāḍilah wa Maḍāddātuhā*, pp. 69–70.
19. For details, see Fahd, *Islami Umraniyat*, pp. 172–3.
20. The chain of Shah Wali-Allah's teachers reaches to Jalal al-Dīn al-Dawwani (d. 907/1501) through his father Shah Abd al-Rahim who had studied under Mir Muhammad Zahid Hirawi (d. 1101/1689). The latter benefitted from al-Dawwani's works and his students.
21. Sindhi, *Shāh Waliullāh aur unki Siyāsi Tahrik*, 2, p. 129.
22. Ibid., p. 131.
23. Rizvi is also of the same opinion. See *Shah Wali-Allah and his Times*, p. 251.
24. Nagrami, '*Shah saheb ka yek Ilmī mākhaz*', p. 351.
25. Islahi, *Economic concepts of Ibn Taimiyah*, pp. 69–70.
26. Hasani, *Nuzhat al-Khawāṭir*, Vol. II, p. 69.
27. Nizami, *Some Aspect of Religion and Politics in India during the Thirteenth Century*, p. 56.
28. Nagrami, 'Shah saheb ka yek Ilmī mākhaz', pp. 348, 350.
    The following passage of Shah Wali-Allah's *Ḥujjat Allāh al- Bālighah* (vol. 1, p. 342) is the same as in *Majmū'Fatāwā Ibn Taymiyyah* (MFS, vol. 23, pp. 374–75):

    «وقد كان في الصحابة والتابعين ومن بعدهم من يقرأ البسملة ومنهم من لا يقرؤها ومنهم من يجهر بها ومنهم من لا يجهر بها وكان منهم من يقنت في الفجر ، ومنهم من لا يقنت في الفجر ، ومنهم من يتوضأ من الحجامة والرعاف والقيء ، ومنهم من لا يتوضأ من ذلك ، ومنهم من يتوضأ من مس الذكر ومس النساء بشهوة ، ومنهم من لا يتوضأ من ذلك ، ومنهم من يتوضأ مما مسته النار ، ومنهم من لا يتوضأ من ذلك ، ومنهم من يتوضأ من أكل لحم الإبل ، ومنهم من لا يتوضأ من ذلك . ما كان خلاف الأئمة تعصباً أعمى : ومع هذا فكان بعضهم يصلي خلف بعض مثل ما كان أبو حنيفة أو أصحابه والشافعي وغيرهم رضي الله عنهم يصلون خلف أئمة المدينة من المالكية وغيرهم وإن كانوا لا يقرؤون البسملة لا سراً ولا جهراً . وصلى الرشيد

إماما وقد احتجم ، فصلى الإمام أبو يوسف خلفه ولم يعد . وكان الإمام أحمد بن حنبل
يرى الوضوء من الرعاف والحجامة فقيل له : فإن كان الإمام قد خرج منه الدم ، ولم
يتوضأ هل تصلي خلفه ؟ فقال : كيف لا أصلي خلف الإمام مالك وسعيد بن المسيب»

29. al-Siyalkoti, *al-Shāh Walī-Allāh al-Dihlawī*, pp. 53–59.
30. Ibid., p. 59.
31. Nadwi, *Tārīkh-i Dāwat -o- Azīmat*, 5: 400–1.
32. Schimmel, *Islam in the Indian Subcontinent*, p. 157.
33. Ibid., p. 154.
34. Ibid., pp. 154, 155. A number of Urdu translations of *Ḥujjat Allāh al- Bālighah* have appeared. It has also been translated into English under the title 'The Conclusive Argument from God' by Marcia Hermansen. The first part of the translation has been published by E.J. Brill at Leiden in 1996. In the mid-text, wherever we benefitted from her translation we indicated it as Hermansen, tr.
35. Nadwi, *Tārīkh-i Dāwat -o- Azīmat*, 5: p. 215.
36. Its importance and advantage can be seen by the fact that the work has been published several times in India and abroad, and has been translated into other languages. For example, Matba' Siddiqi in Bareilly published it in 1307 AH; Matba' Mujtaba'i, Delhi, in 1308/1891; Al-Matba'ah al-Ilmiyah, Egypt, in 1327/1909; an edited version by Rashid Ahmad Jalndhari, Lahore, in 1971; another edited version by Muhibb al-Dīn al-Khatib, Cairo, in 1960. Shaykh Abd al-Fatthah Abu Guddah has also edited and published it from Beirut in 1397/1977. It has been translated into Urdu by Muhammad Abdullah Baliawi, entitled as *Kashshāf* and published from Lucknow in 1886; another Urdu translation by Abd al-Shakur Faruqi, entitled *Waṣṣāf*, was published by Umdatul-Matabi', Lucknow, in 1910, etc. An excellent Urdu translation has been done by Sadruddin Islahi under the title *Ikhtilāfi Masā'il mein I'tidāl ki Rāh* (The middle path in controversial issues), printed by Maktabah Jama'at Islami, Rampur, in 1952. Since then it has been published a number of times.
37. Al-Hasani, *Nuzhat al-Khawāṭir*, 6: 863.
38. Nadwi, *Tārīkh-i Dāwat -o- Azīmat* 6, 5: 403.
39. Ibid., 5: p. 407.
40. Dihlawi, *al-Tafhīmāt al-Ilāhiyyah*, 2: 216–36.
41. Nadwi, *Tārīkh-i Dāwat -o- Azīmat*, 5: 413.
42. Dihlawi, *Anfās al-'Ārifīn*, (Delhi, 1917, Matba' Mujtaba'i).
43. Rizvi, *Shah Wali-Allah and his Times*. p. 222.
44. Nadwi, *Tārīkh-i Dāwat -o- Azīmat*, 5: 408.
45. Ibid.

46. Jalbani, *An English Translation of Sata'at*, p. III.
47. Baljon, *A Mystical Interpretation of Prophetic Tales by an Indian Muslim*, P. VIII.
48. Nadwi, *Tārīkh-i Dāwat -o- Azīmat*, 5: 402.
49. Ibid. 405.
50. Sialkoti, *Tārikh Ahl-i Ḥadīth*, p. 463.
51. Faridi, *Nādir Maktubāt Shāh Wali-Allāh*, pp 78–90.
52. Siddiqi, 'Renaissance in Indo-Pakistan: Shah Wali-Allah Dihlawi', pp. 1576–77.

4

Economic Ideas of Shah Wali-Allah Dihlawi

4.1 Economic ideas in Shah Wali-Allah's works

Shah Wali-Allah was not a worldly philosopher to specifically author books on economic issues. Yet, he could not ignore these as to him economic matters were part of the reality of life. Thus the economic ideas of Shah Wali-Allah are fragmentary and scattered across his different works. Some of them are illustrated below:

1. *Ḥujjat Allāh al-Bālighah* (The Convincing Proofs of Allah), as we noted in Chapter 3, is the magnum opus of the author and constitutes a highly significant exposition of the Islamic worldview. It elucidates the wisdom and the inner meanings behind various Shariah provisions. This book is also a repository of Shah Wali-Allah's economic ideas. In addition to his major contributions to economic thought like the stages of socio-economic development, this work conveys his views on household management, money and interest, and public finance, which will be discussed in detail in the following chapters. Shah Wali-Allah also touched

upon topics like the classification of human wants, cooperation, opportunity cost, rights to property, the place of economic activities in an Islamic framework, business ethics, balanced growth, etc.

2. *Al-Budūr al-Bāzighah* (The Bright Moons) is the second most important contribution of the author after *Ḥujjat Allāh al-Bālighah* that contains his economic ideas. It deals with different aspects of theology, human nature and social behaviour. It presents a philosophical and rational interpretation of Islam. While discussing new topics, it explicates some of the ideas of *Ḥujjat Allāh al- Bālighah*. Topics mentioned include cooperation, division of labour, nature of tradition as an economic solution, business ethics, evils of interest, justification of taxation and principle of just taxes, the economic wisdom behind various rates of zakah, etc.
3. *Izālat al-Khafā 'an Khilāfat al-Khulafā'* (Removal of doubts from the caliphate of the Caliphs) is another valuable work by Shah Wali-Allah, in which he illustrates Islamic public economy. It also presents guidelines to rulers, noblemen, soldiers and government officials. The provision of grants in the Islamic system, justification of retaining conquered lands in the hands of its previous owners and declaring them as public *waqfs*, classification of wants, and consideration of the poor and their need fulfilment are amongst the important topics discussed in this work.
4. *al-Tafhīmāt al-Ilāhiyyah* (The Divine Explanation) also contains important discussions from the economic point of view. In this work, Shah Wali-Allah interprets subtle issues of rational and spiritual importance in light of personal revelations. He visualizes the economic significance of various prayer times, the wisdom behind the fixation of zakah's *niṣāb*, and the responsibility of the government towards the poor. He insists upon various sections of society to correct their socio-economic behaviour.
5. *al-Khayr al-Kathīr* (A Lot of Goodness) is a book on the philosophy of religion and elucidates the concept of *ma'rifat* and wisdom. Herein, he attempts to explain the fundamentals of faith with an approach combining rational and traditional arguments.

In this work, Shah Wali-Allah Dihlawi remarks that Islamic Law (Shariah) deals with worship (*'ibādat*), great sins (*kabā'ir*), habits (*'adāt*), ethics (*akhlāq*), conduct (*mu'amālat*), household management (*tadbīr al-manzil*), and the management of the city (*siyāsat al-madinah*). Thus, he considered *tadbīr al-manzil* as one of the subjects of Shariah.[1]

6. *Makatib* (His letters) are the numerous letters written in which Shah Wali-Allah addressed different rulers, governors, nobles and friends. He is seen in these letters to hold economic factors as being outstandingly responsible for the weakening and decline of the Mughal Empire in India, a subject which still perplexes many. Shah Wali-Allah's diagnosis of this sad state of affairs is both interesting and insightful, especially in the context of understanding his economic stance.

In this chapter, we will discuss some of Shah Wali-Allah's economic ideas that have been mentioned above. However, the major concepts like household management, money, interest, public finance, and his concepts of socio-economic development will be elaborated upon each in a separate chapter.

4.2 Study of applied economy

4.2.1 Perception of economic causes in decadence of Mughal rule in India

As noted in Chapter 1, Shah Wali-Allah lived in an age of crisis and chaos created by the Marathas, Jats, Sikhs, Ruhillas and other ambitious governors of India's provinces. The rule of Mughal kings was literally confined to the area between the Red Fort[2] and Palam.[3] Peasants and artisans were badly hit; they had to pay taxes more than once a year to frequently changing wielders of power. Salaries of army men and other officials were not paid for months. The Mughal kings, despite having the image of rightful owners of authority, were helpless. Some of the economic reasons for the decline of Mughal rule, according to Shah Wali-Allah, and his suggestions for reform were as follows:

1. *The indigence of the imperial treasury.* The state treasury is the backbone of any government and cannot function without sufficient resources. According to Shah Wali-Allah, revenues of the country were estimated at eight *crore*[4] rupees, but the authority and power needed to realize this had been lost by central government.[5]
2. *The contraction of khāliṣah lands. Khāliṣah* refers to crown lands, and its revenue was collected directly by officials of the king, in contrast to *jāgir* lands (fiefs) where revenues were collected by the *jāgirdār* (feudal lord). *Khāliṣah* was the most important source of income for the government and every wise ruler tried to expand its area. Wali-Allah also suggested that the *khāliṣah* area should be expanded, especially to the region surrounding Delhi, Hissar and Sirhind. All or most of these must be made *khāliṣah*, as the reason for any weakening of the government is the diminution of *khāliṣah* and the consequent indigence of the royal treasury.[6]
3. *The increasing numbers of jāgirs (fiefs).* The natural corollary of decreasing *khāliṣah* lands was an increase in the number of small *jāgirdārs*, who were generally unable to control their areas, and who rented out their lands, a situation prone to oppression and exploitation. Shah Wali-Allah suggested that the *jāgirs* should be granted to chiefs only. Smaller nobles should be paid in cash, as was the practice during the reign of Shah Jahan,[7] because the small *jāgirdārs* rented out their lands and mostly remained in need of money. They did not fully discharge their duties assigned by the royal court.[8]
4. *Irregularities in payments to army and government officials.* Another important reason for the decline of Mughal rule was the defaults in payment to the army and other officials. No doubt, this was due to the reason mentioned earlier, i.e. the indigence of the treasury. Shah Wali-Allah suggested that their salaries should be paid without delay, otherwise they would be forced to borrow

money on interest, which would cause much loss to them and they might not carry out their duties properly.[9]

5. *The heavy burden of taxation and a decline in production.* To meet government expenses, farmers, artisans and producers were heavily taxed, the direct result of which was decreasing interest in their occupations and a decline in production. In his book *Ḥujjat Allāh al- Bālighah*, Shah Wali-Allah says: '... Another reason (for the bad condition of cities in this age) is the heavy taxation on farmers, traders, artisans, etc. and the harsh treatment meted out in collection of those taxes.'[10]
6. *Luxurious living.* Economic factors were the main but not the only reasons for the decadence of Mughal rule. Giving in to luxurious living, moral decay, social disparity and political anarchy were some of the other reasons pointed out by Shah Wali-Allah, and he endeavoured for their reform.[11]

Shah Wali-Allah's presentation of the aforementioned economic reasoning behind the Mughal's decaying rule of India reveals his analytical insight into socio-economic matters. It also provided him with proof that a sound economic condition was a prerequisite for a stable and strong state.

4.2.2 Economic role of artisans and craftsmen

Artisans and craftsmen constitute very important elements of even the agricultural economy. They play a very significant role in the development of the economy. Shah Wali-Allah realized that they were not playing the role expected from them. They had 'lost the sense of responsibility and honest work.' Their religious and socio-cultural condition was very bad. Addressing the community of artisans and craftsmen, he wrote in his book *al-Tafhīmāt al-Ilāhiyyah*: '... If one of you becomes prosperous, he begins living beyond his means, thus depriving his near and dear ones: or he wastes his worldly means in drinking and prostitute and ruins his Hereafter. ... Allah has created innumerable sources to earn livelihood sufficient for you and your dependents if you adopt moderate living and contend with the earning for virtuous living. But you have become ungrateful to the favor of Allah and adopted unfair means to manage things. Do you not fear the torment of the Hell and the worst abode?'[12] He suggested they adopt the golden economic rule: 'Spend less than what you earn and keep the saving for helping the wayfarer and the poor and keep also something as precautionary measures for meeting emerging and unforeseen needs.'[13] It may be noted that the precautionary motive is one of the three motives of liquidity preference or cash holding pointed out by the twentieth-century famous economist, Keynes; the other two being transaction and speculative motives.[14] In Shah Wali-Allah's prescription, one can discern transaction and precautionary motives for meeting everyday requirements and emerging or unforeseen needs. Instead of speculation, he emphasizes spending for the poor and destitute. This is the difference between materialistic and spiritual economics.

4.3 Theoretical economic ideas

In addition to his study of some applied aspects of the economy, Shah Wali-Allah also dealt with the theoretical issues of an Islamic economy. For example, he discussed basic occupations, the need for the division of labour, the nature and functions of money, undesirable economic practices, an economic analysis of *ribā al-faḍl* and *ribā al-nasi'ah*, issues relating to public finance and public expenditure, etc. The following is an account of these ideas.

4.3.1 Classification of human wants

Shah Wali-Allah classified human wants as necessities, comforts and refinements.[15] As far as luxury is concerned, this according to him is a relative term; it differs from people to people. The luxury of one people for example might be subsistence living for others, and the refinement of some people might be luxuries for others.[16] In the same way, miserliness differs from one class of people to another. For example, what may be called miserliness for a king, may be extravagance for the poor. Thus, the desirable course of action is to abandon bad habits, each within one's own level.[17]

It may be noted that the classification of wants existed in Islamic literature for a long time. A very succinct explanation is provided by al-Ghazali in that all economic activities are undertaken to provide for three basic human needs: food, clothing, and shelter. However, this meaning of basic needs is flexible and may be more inclusive depending upon conditions prevalent in a given society and at a given time, but consistent with the Islamic Shariah. Indeed, according to al-Ghazali, the list may include such economic and socio-psychological needs as furnishings, property, status and prestige, and even marital relations, in addition to the aforementioned basic needs. All of these (and others) are recognized as significant human needs.[18] As part of his Islamic social welfare function, al-Ghazali also explores the extent to which the provision and consumption of the various material things lead to human satisfaction and well-being. At another point in his book, *Mizān al-'Amal*, he distinguishes among three levels of consumption: the lowest, the middle, and the highest—and these may apply to each of the three basic needs (food, clothing, shelter), which may be satisfied at any of the three levels: as a necessity, convenience or luxury.[19] For example, the lowest (minimum necessary) standard of shelter may be living in a cave or a trust (public owned) dwelling. The middle (convenient) standard may be one's own house, with privacy and use throughout one's life; such a house may be the 'average' type, and this is the kind al-Ghazali includes as part of his *kifāyah*. The highest level of shelter (luxury) is a large, well-built, aesthetically superior mansion with many amenities—the kind always sought by the worldly people and those of higher ranks. Further, al-Ghazali states that anyone may own such elaborate shelter without any constraints from the state, but certain groups, such as the ascetics or Sufis, may be discouraged from such ostentatious living since, given the nature of their spiritual pursuits, they ought to live a simple life.[20]

4.3.2 Cooperation

Starting from the premise that man is by nature a social being, Shah Wali-Allah established that cooperation with other members of society is a distinguishing characteristic of humankind.[21] On another occasion, he said that man is social by nature and, therefore, his living will be smooth only by cooperation with others.[22] In his work *Al-Budūr al-Bāzighah*, he mentions that it is Allah's great favour that He created man social by nature: his living is impossible without the company, grouping and cooperation of his fellow species.[23] This necessitates the fulfilment of a number of social norms in everyone's daily lives. If one tries to live by means other than cooperating with one another, then this is destructive of social life.[24]

It is worthwhile to note that Muslim scholars have always emphasized cooperation in economic activities. For example, before Shah Wali-Allah, both Ibn Taymiyyah and Ibn Khaldun considered this natural for human beings. Ibn Taymiyyah writes, 'Mankind cannot live in isolation. Now, when two or more persons live together, then there must be cooperation to do something and to refrain from others.'[25] In another place he says, 'Mankind's welfare in this world or hereafter cannot be achieved without getting together and cooperating. Therefore, there should be cooperation and association to achieve good, and alliance to remove injury. Thus, it is said that man is by nature a social being.'[26] Ibn Taymiyyah does not elaborate upon the idea nor on its economic implications. Ibn Khaldun is more explicit on this subject. He starts his *Muqaddimah* with the same statement that 'man is by nature a social being.'[27] According to him, prosperity and business activity depends on the degree of cooperation among people. He says 'As it is known and well established, the individual human being cannot by himself obtain all the necessities of life. All human beings must cooperate to that end in their civilization. But what is obtained through the cooperation of a group of human beings satisfies the need of a number many times greater [than themselves]. For instance, no one, by himself, can obtain the share of the wheat he needs for food. But when six or ten persons—including a smith and a carpenter to make the tools and others who are in charge of the oxen, the plowing of the soil, the harvesting of the ripe grain, and all the agricultural activities—undertake to obtain their food and work toward that purpose either separately or collectively and thus obtain through their labour a certain amount of food, [that amount] will be food for a number of people many times their own. The combined labour produces more than the needs and necessities of the workers.'[28] Apart from this long passage, we find many other passages regarding co-operation and division of labour in his *Muqaddimah*.[29]

In addition to Ibn Taymiyyah and Ibn Khaldun, there are several other Muslim writers who argued cooperation and division of labour as necessary and natural for the human being. Therefore, one will not be wrong to say that on this subject Shah Wali-Allah only followed the established intellectual tradition in the Islamic system. [30]

4.3.3 Division of labour

A very close subject to cooperation is the division of labour. In fact, this is a socio-economic necessity and a manifestation of cooperation. Division of labour arises because of the variety of needs required by a single household and which cannot be met by a single person. For example, the need for food involves many jobs. It leads people to the occupation of farming, which requires the training of animals and the services of carpenters, blacksmiths and others. Similarly, the process involved in the preparation of food and the manufacture of clothes cannot be done by one person or a single household. Instead, they require the involvement of all members of society, with division of labour and specialization as the means.[31]

According to Shah Wali-Allah, specialization in a particular job is generally based on two factors:

1. Physical capability. For example, a brave man is good for war, an intelligent person with good memory is fit for bookkeeping and office work, and a strong, healthy man is suitable for carrying loads and other burdensome work, etc.
2. Incidental advantage. For example, the son or neighbour of a blacksmith can easily take to ironwork and a person living near the sea has the facility to take up fishing which others who live elsewhere do not enjoy.[32]

Shah Wali-Allah's exposition of the basis of specialization and division of labour is unique. However, al-Ghazali is more elaborate

> upon this issue. After describing various aspects of the production of daily food, al-Ghazali says: 'A single loaf of bread takes its final shape with the help of perhaps more than a thousand workers.'[33] He argues further by using the example of a needle: 'Even the small needle becomes useful only after passing through hands of needle-makers about twenty-five times, each time going through a different process.'[34]

Ibn Khaldun also mentions the advantage of the division of labour. He maintains that the division of labour is limited to the functioning of the market. Spengler had best summarized Ibn Khaldun's views on the subject when he said: 'Perhaps the most important of the form of cooperation or organization into which men entered was division of labour (by craft or profession rather than by task) which greatly increased output per worker, elevated a community's capacity to produce above that required to supply elemental wants, and gave rise to exchange and commerce in which producers and merchants engaged, with the kind and quantity of what was produced dependent upon the extent of demand and realizable profit.'[35] The passage is self-evident and does not need any elaboration.

In fact, the division of labour has existed in human history since the earliest civilizations, although exactly when is unknown. It was discussed by the Greek philosophers as well. However, there is a difference between its exposition by the Greek philosophers and the Muslim scholars. For example, Plato's notion of the division of labour is seemingly based on a class system. He does not put emphasis upon the 'increase of efficiency that results from division of labour *per se* ...'[36] while Muslim scholars highlight its economic efficiency. Shah Wali-Allah interprets it under the Shariah provision of *farḍ kifāyah* (socially obligatory duty) to facilitate diversity of occupations and specialization. This is especially so in those jobs whereby a concentration of all people would have led to deterioration in their living standards and hence to socio-economic disadvantages. In such cases, it would not have been possible to assign some people to a particular job and others to another job ... as everyone has advantages in something which the other has not.[37] Diversity of occupation and specialization in a job in which one has facilities is necessary for the healthy development of socio-economic life.

4.3.4 Opportunity cost

While discussing socially desirable and beneficial products, Shah Wali-Allah clearly identifies the concept of opportunity cost without naming it. He says: 'If a large number of people involve themselves in such a job [that is, the production of luxuries], they will correspondingly neglect jobs of trade and agriculture. If the chief of the city spends public funds on such items, he will be equally losing the welfare of the city.'[38] The opportunity cost is defined as 'the cost of foregoing one thing ... to get an acceptable alternative.'[39] The use of this term was not known during Shah Wali-Allah's time. The idea came very late in economics. The first time it was used was in 1894 by David L. Green in an article entitled 'Pain Cost and Opportunity-Cost' published in the Quarterly Journal of Economics. The concept of opportunity cost is very important in economic theory. It is based on the fundamental fact that resources are scarce and have alternative uses, and therefore they should be used in such a way as to maximize public benefits. This is very clear in Shah Wali-Allah's statement. His purpose was to draw the authority's attention to take this into account while selecting a project and allocating the limited available resources to various public purposes.

4.3.5 Rights to property

Stating the Islamic belief that Almighty Allah is the Real Owner and everything belongs to Him, Shah Wali-Allah held that the property right is granted to prevent people from conflicting with each other and from remaining in a constant struggle to grab things from each other. To him, 'the ownership right for a man' means he is more entitled to benefit from an object than others.[40] Thus, he was against the Sufis' condemnation of wealth. He emphasized that wealth should not be an object of hate; it is, in fact, a great favour from Almighty Allah.[41] It is the misuse of wealth and ungratefulness that is condemnable. One may be pious and God-fearing in spite of having wealth if one recognizes and fulfils one's obligations due to wealth.[42]

Shah Wali-Allah was against the private ownership of some natural resources like mines. [43] Furthermore, his stance about the three free goods—water, pasture and fire—was such that it is desirable to share them with others even if they are in someone's possession. Nor is there anything to stop such sharing if free goods happen to be in no one's possession. [44]

It may be noted that Shah Wali-Allah is referring here to a hadith[45] in which it has been said that people are equal partners in three objects: water, grass and fire. These are considered as free gifts from Almighty Allah because man has no trouble in acquiring them or using them. Another reason may be that these are necessities, private individual occupation and ownership of which might create hardship and trouble to the society.[46]

It is clear from the above that Shah Wali-Allah did not intend to discuss the subject of property rights in detail; he confined to its few important fundamental aspects only.

4.3.6 Balanced growth

Shah Wali-Allah advocated for the balanced growth of the economy. In this respect, priority should be given to basic industries and the production of goods and services needed by all people. Harmful products must be prohibited. Paying more attention to luxury goods at the cost of necessary goods would invite destruction. He gave an example of this: if there are ten thousand people in a city, then the city administration must take stock of their ways of earning a livelihood. In such a condition, if the majority of them are engaged in industries and administration of the city and only a few of them are engaged in grazing and cultivation, their worldly condition would deteriorate. On the other hand, if they earn their livelihood through distilling wine or manufacturing idols, this would encourage people to consume them as being commonly known to them and lead them to the destruction of their religious lives. However, if occupations and those engaged in them are fairly divided according to wisdom and the hands of those engaged in sinful earnings are checked, everyone's condition will improve.[47]

Similar is the condition when elites are engaged in luxurious objects and patronize female singers and dancers; some people are engaged in the production of pictures and stylish clothes and objects of fine arts, and others are engaged in the production of precious jewelry, and the planning and construction of tall buildings. All these take place at the cost of necessary economic activities like agriculture and commerce. Naturally, when elites spend their money on such luxuries, they ignore the interests of the city. It inflicts injury on those who are engaged in the production of necessities like cultivators, traders, and manufacturers. This leads to multiplying taxes and as a result the whole city is disturbed. Hence why the Prophet, may Allah bless him and give him peace, prohibited or discouraged objects of luxurious living.[48] Essentially, then, an unbalanced distribution of occupations is injurious to the health of the city. For example, if more people are engaged in commerce and leave the occupation of cultivation, or they prefer military service to other occupations. In Shah Wali-Allah's opinion, the farmers' position in the economy should be like the main food served at mealtimes. As far as manufacturers, traders and guards are concerned, their position is akin to salt for seasoning the food.[49] Shah Wali-Allah's observations came in the background of a pre-industrialized agrarian economy. In the wake of comparative cost advantage, it may be suggested to concentrate on the production of something which can be produced at a lower cost. A city can pay attention to produce more in which it relatively has cost advantage. In this case, it can benefit more through exchange and international trading.

From the above, it is clear that Shah Wali-Allah's concern was the realization of a healthy economic atmosphere where priority is given to the production of the most important and cost effective goods and services. Wasting resources is to be avoided. Socially and mentally harmful products should be banned. The development of cities depends on the proper distribution of resources in all kinds of industries as needed by its citizens. In this regard, the government's duty increases manyfold. The responsibility of suitable planning and the appropriate management of public resources falls on the government. This provides justification for the government to collect resources from people and spend on fulfilling its responsibilities. Shah Wali-Allah considered the main position in the economy to belong to the farmers, and considered others, like manufacturers and traders, as only secondary. This bears some resemblance with the idea of physiocracy that developed in the mid-eighteenth century which considered agriculture as the only source of wealth.[50]

4.4 Economic activities in an Islamic framework

According to Shah Wali-Allah, Almighty Allah put the means of people's living in objects found in free lands, pastoral pursuits, agriculture, industry, commerce, and services performed in the administration of cities and people. Violating these sources has an adverse effect on civilized living. Some people resort to harmful means of earning a living, such as theft, usurpation, etc. all of which are essentially destructive. Thus, Allah delineated such acts as forbidden. This is agreed upon by all human beings.[51] On the other hand there are certain practices that are helpful for the socio-economic development of people. These should be adopted.

4.4.1 Partnership

Islam prefers risk sharing instead of risk shifting. For this purpose, there are various forms of partnership in the Islamic economic system. Shah Wali-Allah mentioned a few of them, such as *muḍārabah* in which capital is given by one person and labour is by another person who carries out the trading on specified shares in the profit.[52] Shah Wali-Allah did not, however, take note of any loss that would be borne by the capital owner. He emphasizes that *muḍārabah* is a provision through which the capital owner, not having the time and skill to engage in business, can cooperate and share with a person who lacks capital but has time, knowledge and skill to carry a business.[53]

Shah Wali-Allah also gives an account of *mufāwaḍah*, another form of partnership, in which two people contribute their capital in all kinds of sales and purchases, and in which they share in the profit. Each is the agent and undertaker of the other. Similarly, he defined *'inān* (partnership together with capital and work), *shirkat al-ṣāni'īn* (partnership of manufacturers), *shirkat al-wujūah* (partnership with credits), *wakālah* (agency), *musāqāh* (fruit-sharing), *muzāra'ah* (crop-sharing), *mukhābarah* (a particular type of crop-sharing) and *ijārah* (hiring or leasing).[54] According to Shah Wali-Allah, all these forms of transactions were in practice during the pre-Islamic period. As such, they were not the object of controversy, nor did the Prophet prohibit them—they were retained in Islam.[55] He avoids writing about their various provisions as they are available in books of Islamic jurisprudence.

4.4.2 Economic reasoning in fixation of prayer times

Shah Wali-Allah discovered economic reasoning in the fixation of prayer times; the Shariah took into account when people would be busy in economic activities and when they would be free. Since farmers, traders, manufacturers and others are generally engaged in their jobs from morning to noon—this being the time for seeking Allah's bounty (the Qur'anic expression for earning a livelihood)—and since most jobs need a long span of time, during which preparation for prayers would be difficult, Almighty Allah did not make any prayer obligatory during these hours.[56] That is, from after the morning prayer (fajr) up to the noon prayer (ẓuhr); nearly six hours. Conversely, people are less busy in the afternoon, so the gap between prayers is reduced to about three hours between the noon and afternoons prayers (ẓuhr and 'aṣr). In the evening, people are less busy, and so the gap is further reduced between the sunset prayer (maghrib) and the evening prayer ('ishā').[57] This shows that Islam attributes great significance to economic activities. However, prayers and remembrance to Allah are not stopped altogether in the course of the day, so that a Muslim should be cautious in behaviour and must not adopt any wrong practice.

4.4.3 Following tradition in economic matters

Mankind has used tradition, command and market as solutions to economic problems—what to produce, how to produce and for whom to produce.[58] Shah Wali-Allaḥ was against the blind imitation of the family tradition in economic matters. Rationality, he argued, required that a person take stock of his needs and choose accordingly a reasonable occupation that would suffice him. He said that empirically he had found many people who had chosen an occupation that could not meet their needs. As a result, they faced humiliation and obstacles. To him, deterioration comes about because people follow their fathers and forefathers in economic matters without proper understanding; hence, they adopt occupations that are unsuitable for them.[59] This does not contradict his argument about incidental advantage mentioned above if a person takes stock of his needs and then chooses a particular occupation. According to him, an earner of livelihood should deeply ponder two points before making a decision: he should adopt an occupation that is sufficient to fulfil his needs and then handle this in the best possible way. Secondly, when a person chooses a particular job, he must adopt the tools and techniques required for it. When he has acquired them, he should seek deep and relevant knowledge about them.[60] Extended to the country level, Shah Wali-Allah's suggestion delivers a great lesson in terms of the selection of modern technology and acquiring the latest information about it. No doubt, late starters have an advantage in obtaining the latest technology, but any error in decision-making will only lead to the waste of already scarce resources.

4.4.4 Business ethics

Shah Wali-Allah was a strong advocate of business ethics. To him, various transactions prescribed by the Shariah aim at promoting economic objectives or moral values. For instance, while sales, purchases, hiring, and renting benefit the two parties economically, gifts and lending promote benevolence, sympathy and fellow feeling.[61] To strengthen these two objectives, it is required that in any exchange transaction, the sold object, its price, and delivery time should be well-defined. Similarly, in cases of hiring, wages and works or benefits should be well-known by all parties. It is for these reasons that such contracts must be based on an offer and its acceptance, to show the consent of the two parties, and the various options prescribed.[62] On the other hand, if certain contracts lead to disputes and enmity, then such contracts are prohibited.[63] Shah Wali-Allah analyzed various forms of forbidden contracts and demonstrated that the reason behind their prohibition is the fact that such transactions may hurt the contracting parties or society. Sometimes they lead to dispute, enmity and jealousy.[64]

Shah Wali-Allah enumerated upon the harmful economic activities that inflict injury upon city life. For example, gambling, interest doubling-quadrupling, bribery, cheating in measure and weight, adulteration of goods, forestalling, hoarding, and predatory pricing.[65] To him, false oaths, incorrect measures and weights, gambling, and usury also fall into the category of harmful acts. Charging an excessive tithe is also like robbery, or even worse than that.[66]

4.5 Measures to avoid disputes in economic transactions

4.5.1 Elimination of *gharar*

Shah Wali-Allah has also dealt with economic evils and has especially analyzed those practices which are prohibited in Islam. In his opinion, since the purpose of buying and selling or exchange of goods and precious metals is to fulfil one's need and to earn money, it is necessary that one should not be ignorant about the thing sold, its price, benefits accruing from it, and its ability to fulfil the particular need. Thus, there should not be any element of *gharar* (uncertainty). It is also necessary that there should be a proposal from one party and an acceptance from the other, or the two parties exchange the object hand to hand, so that both sides feel satisfied over the exchange and that their consent is established. The parties concerned must think over it properly. However, there may be an option of rejection or otherwise if the thing exchanged is proved defective (*khiyār al-'ayb*). If it is a matter of renting or leasing (*ijārah*) an object, a time limit should be fixed. In the case of a *salām* contract (prepaid sale with deferred delivery), full details of the object should be given. It is also necessary that the parties entering into an agreement should be sane so that they are able to distinguish what is right and what is wrong.[67]

4.5.2 Documentation of debts

About lending money and deferred dealings, Shah Wali-Allah strongly advocates adopting the Qur'anic rule (*al-Baqarah* 2: 282) that such debts should be written down in the presence of witnesses or be strengthened through mortgage. This is so because mankind is by nature stingy, and as such, denial or delay in paying debts is possible, leading to great disputes.[68]

4.5.3 Prohibition of gambling and interest

Gambling (*maysir* or *qimār*) is also a prohibited practice. In this game, getting money is the goal only by a contract without any compensation. Ignorance and folly incite men to gambling, and on account of greed, undertaking risks to which they become blinded. Interest or usury, known as *ribā*, is forbidden too. This is the desire to make more money on one side, exploiting the needs of the other. The needy person borrows money with the condition that he should pay extra money as interest which eventually becomes very difficult to pay. As a whole, the only permissible practice is the exchange of goods with money or benefits in exchange for money, or one should donate money generously and willingly. Earning money outside these two ways is not permitted and is considered incorrect.[69]

4.5.4 Proscription of bribery

Bribery (*rishwah*) is forbidden because money is spent to procure what belongs to others. Shah Wali-Allah suggests that it must be considered in every contract what will happen in the future, namely, potential differences, quarrels, and procrastination or delays in the repayment of debts. Measures must therefore be taken that no disputes arise in the transactions, and all those that may lead to quarrels or generate conflict must be avoided.[70]

4.6 Major contributions

In addition to the economic ideas noted in the preceding pages, Shah Wali-Allah discussed some major economic institutions, namely *Tadbīr al-Manzil* or household management, public finance, and *al-irtifāqāt* or the socio-economic development. It seems reasonable to briefly introduce them in the following sections and then deal with each of them in separate chapters.

4.6.1 *Tadbīr al-manzil* or household management

Tadbīr al-manzil or household management is one of the socio-economic concepts discussed by Shah Wali-Allah in much detail. The term is an Arabic rendering of the Greek term *Oikonomia*, which was used by Muslim scholars when they learned the Arabic translations of Greek philosophical ideas after the second and third centuries after Hijra. However, the concept and practice of household management already existed in Islamic traditions, its origins going back to the basic sources of Islam—the Qur'an and the Sunnah. As the term indicates, *tadbīr al-manzil* discusses how to efficiently manage the household and its various components—wife, children and servants—while the man has to look after affairs outside the house. According to Shah Wali-Allah, the basic principles of the technique of *tadbīr al-manzil* are the same in all nations, Arabs and non-Arabs. The difference is only in the forms and figures (*al-ṣuwar wa al-ashbāh*).[71] The next chapter is a detailed study of Shah Wali-Allah's views about *tadbīr al-manzil*.

4.6.2 Public finance

The subject of public finance has always been the focus of Muslim scholars throughout Islamic history as this was the need of the government. Discourses on this topic declined when Muslim governments lost their power. Shah Wali-Allah lived in a period when decadence to the Mughal

Empire had just begun. He was quick to describe the public treasury's indigence and deteriorating condition as the main reasons behind the empire's weakening and decay, and emphasized the need for its enhancements and avoidance of extravagance. He gave various suggestions in this regard while discussing various components of public finance, such as sources of revenue and principles of expenditure. Due to the importance of the topic of public finance, the entirety of Chapter 7 is devoted to its discussion.

4.6.3 *al-Irtifāqāt* or the socio-economic development

Shah Wali-Allah Dihlawi also presented a theory of development under the heading *al-irtifāqāt*. For him, starting from simple primitive village life to an international community, the socio-economic development of human society can be divided into four stages. The first stage is dominated by simple economic struggle, while the last stage is developed to maintain a just political order on an international level to safeguard the socio-economic interests of the different states and establish peace and justice among them. All the economic ideas of Shah Wali-Allah Dihlawi revolve around and are related in some way or another to his concept of *irtifāqāt*. The importance of this concept requires a full chapter and is therefore dealt with in detail in Chapter 8.

Notes and References

1. Dihlawi, *al-Khayr al-Kathīr*, p. 83.
2. Located in the heart of Delhi city, the seventeenth-century famous historical building, the Red Fort (Lal Qil'ah), was built by Emperor Shah Jahan (r. 1627–58), which became the seat of rule for subsequent kings. Independent India's Prime Minister addresses the nation from its pulpit on every Independence Day, i.e. 15 August.
3. Palam is a village on the western border of Delhi where presently Delhi's international airport is located.
4. An amount of one *crore* is equal to ten million (10,000,000).
5. Nizami, *Shāh Wali-Allāh ke Siyāsī Maktūbāt*, p. 53.
6. Ibid., p.52.

7. Mughal Emperor Shah Jahan (r. 1627–58), the builder of the famous Taj Mahal at Agra.
8. Ibid., p. 42.
9. Ibid.
10. Dihlawi, *Ḥujjat,* 1: p. 45.
11. Ibid., p. 106; Nizami, *Shāh Wali-Allāh ke Siyāsī Maktūbāt,* pp. 43, 52, 83, 84.
12. Dihlawi, *al-Tafhīmāt al-Ilāhiyyah,* 1: 17.
13. Ibid.
14. Keynes, *The General Theory of Employment, Interest and Money,* pp. 149-50.
15. Dihlawi, *Hujjat* 1: 38.
16. Ibid., p. 110.
17. Ibid., 2: 190.
18. al-Ghazali, n.d., *Ihyā',* 4: 230.
19. al-Ghazali, *Mizān,* p. 377.
20. Ibid., p. 378.
21. Dihlawi, *Hujjat,* 1: 80; 2: 103.
22. Ibid., 2: 146.
23. Dihlawi, 1970, p. 84.
24. Dihlawi, *Hujjat,* 2: 125.
25. Ibn Taymiyyah, *al-Ḥisbah,* p. 116.
26. Ibid, p. 8.
27. Ibn Khaldun, *Muqaddimah,* p. 33.
28. Rosenthal, *Muqaddimah,* 2: 271–72.
29. For example, see Rosenthal, *Muqaddimah,* 1: 89–91; 2: 235, 238, 273–274, 286, 301–02, 316, 329, 336–41.
30. For example: al-Shaybani, 1986, pp. 75–76, al-Ghazali, *Ihya',* 4: 118–119, al-Asfahani, 1985, pp. 374–75, and al-Dimashqi, 1977, pp. 20–21.
31. Dihlawi, *al-Budūr,* p. 85.
32. Ibid., p. 87; Dihlawi, *Hujjat,* 1: p. 43.
33. al-Ghazali, *Ihya',* 4: 118.
34. Ibid., p. 119. One can see how close this is to the classical pin-factory example of Adam Smith in his work *the Wealth of Nations,* pp. 4–5, seven centuries later in making the same arguments.
35. Spengler (1964, pp. 295–96.
36. Schumpeter, 1997, p. 56.
37. Dihlawi, *Ḥujjat,* 1: 97.
38. Ibid., 2: 106.
39. Woelfel, 1994, p. 870.
40. Dihlawi, *Hujjat,* 2: 103.

41. Ibid., p. 85.
42. Ibid.
43. Ibid., p. 104.
44. Ibid., p. 111.
45. The hadith says: 'Muslims are partners in three things: water, grass, and fire.' (Abu Dawud, *Sunan Abi Dāwūd*, 3: 295, hadith number 3479).
46. Islahi, *Economic Concepts of Ibn Taimiyah*, p. 116.
47. Dihlawi, *Hujjat* 2: 105.
48. Ibid., 2: 105–6.
49. Ibid., 1: 44.
50. For details about physiocracy refer to Whittaker, *Schools and Streams of Economic Thought*, Chapter Four or Schumpeter, *History of Economic Analysis*, Part II, Chapter Four.
51. Dihlawi, *Hujjat*, 1: 82.
52. Ibid., 2: 116.
53. Dihlawi, *al-Budūr*, p. 90.
54. Dihlawi, *Ḥujjat*, 2: p. 117.
55. Ibid.
56. Ibid., 1: 188; Dihlawi, *al-Tafhīmāt* 2: 113.
57. Ibid.
58. Heilbroner and Thuro, *The Economic Problem*, pp. 8–12.
59. Dihlawi, *al-Budūr*, p. 88. Shah Wali-Allah is, thus, against the Greek idea that one must follow his family's jobs. According to Baloglou, 'In the Arabic text of Bryson's treatise, we find a strange theory about the fixity of professions: he maintains that, since there is a need in a polis for all crafts, it is praiseworthy to remain within one's own class (Plessner, 216, 217) without desire to improve oneself by taking a superior craft. Otherwise, in time, everybody would be doing the same job and civilization would vanish (Plessner, 221, 29–31). This idea seems to be original; we are not able to say if this idea was connected with the economic conditions of the Roman Empire, or if it reflected Arab concepts.' (Baloglou, 38). Shah Wali-Allah's statement is enough to correct Baloglou that confining to one's family job or remaining within one's own class is not an Arab-Islamic concept.
60. Dihlawi, *al-Budūr*, p. 88.
61. Ibid.
62. Ibid., p. 89.
63. Ibid., p. 90.
64. Dihlawi, *Hujjat*, 2: 108–111.
65. Ibid., 1: 44, 82.
66. Ibid., 1: 82.

67. Dihlawi, *al-Budūr*, p. 89.
68. Ibid.
69. Dihlawi, *Ḥujjat*, 2: 107-108.
70. Dihlawi, *al-Budūr al-Bāzighah*, p. 90.
71. Dihlawi, *Ḥujjat*, 2: 122.

5

Tadbīr al-Manzil (Household Management)

5.1 Origins of *tadbīr al-manzil*

Shah Wali-Allah Dihlawi has extensively dealt with *tadbīr al-manzil*. As previously mentioned, this term is the translation of the Greek word *oikonomia*, which means management of the household. It is commonly known that the origin of economics go back to Greek *oikonomia*, but its scope was not as wide as the present-day discipline of economics. To quote Baloglou: 'The Greeks did not create an autonomous Economic Science, nor did they aim at doing so.'[1] *Oikonomia*, as we shall see below, was limited to household administration. It dealt with the man—the master of household— the woman or wife, property or money for household management, slaves and servants, and the training of children. It is interesting to note that Shah Wali-Allah also considers them as the subjects of *tadbīr al-manzil*.[2] So we will discuss below his ideas with respect to *tadbīr al-manzil* in the same order. Firstly, let us shed more light on the origins and development of the term. Although the word *tadbīr* and *manzil* occurred separately in the basic sources of Islam,[3] the phrase *tadbīr al-manzil* is found in Arabic literature only after the translation of Greek philosophical ideas into Arabic in the second and the third-century After Hijrah.

Since the origins of the science of Economics are traced back to the Greek *Oikonomia*, hardly any book dealing with the history of economic thought is free from a chapter, a section, or a reference to Greek economic ideas. See, for instance, Baeck's *The Mediterranean Tradition in Economic Thought* (1994), Oser and Blanchfield's *The Evolution of Economic Thought* (1975), Schumpeter's *History of Economic Analysis* (1997), and Spiegel's *The Growth of Economic Thought* (1983). However, there are very few studies fully devoted to Greek economics. In this respect, Dotan Leshem's name can be mentioned as the author of a few articles dealing with the Greek *oikonomia*.[4] But he does not deal with the translation of *oikonomia* as *tadbīr manzil*. In 1934, Heffening wrote an article '*Tadbīr al-Manzil*' in the old edition of the *Encyclopaedia of Islam* in its fourth volume in which he quoted German author Helmut Ritter saying that '*the whole economic literature of Islam* [emphasis added] can be traced to economics of Neo-pythagorean Bryson'. This has been refuted by Islahi.[5] There exists one article only by Sabri Orman entitled 'From Oikonomia to 'Ilm Tadbīr al-Manzil – Intercivilizational Exchange of Knowledge'. Herein, the author shows 'the relationship between the Islamic '*Ilm Tadbīr al-Manzil* and Ancient Greek Oikonomia' to examine 'the attitude of Islamic civilization towards intercivilizational exchange of knowledge' as illustrated by the translation of *oikonomia* to *tadbīr manzil*.[6] However, to the best of our knowledge no work has fully explored the process of the translation and transmission of Greek *oikonomia* to the Islamic tradition, its already existing elements in the basic sources of Islam and their nature, the impact of Greek philosophy on Muslim *ḥukamā* (philosophers), the improvement and additions by ulama and scholars, and its importance in the present-day discipline of Islamic economics.[7]

5.2 *Tadbīr al-manzil* in the Islamic tradition

As noted above, *tadbīr al-manzil* or household management is one of the sciences that Muslim scholars inherited from Greek philosophers and further developed, having made original contributions in this respect. However, the notion of *tadbīr* has been used in the Arab-Muslim literature in various disciplines. It does not necessarily belong to the economy, does not necessarily follow Greek philosophical writings, and is not necessarily confined to the Muslim philosophers.

According to Baloglou 'Oeconomica' had great acceptance in the medieval Arab-Islamic World.[8] There exists a translation of the first book on the topic entitled *Thimār maqālāt Aristātālīs fi tadbīr al-manzil* (Extract from the Treatise of Aristotles on Administration of the Household), written by the philosopher and medical expert Abu' al-Faraj Abdallah Ibn al-Tayyib (d. 435/1043), who lived in Baghdad.[9]

A line of Muslim authors copied and elaborated in more or less detail the Arabic version of *tadbīr al-manzil*. Namely, Farabi (873–950) with his work *Ara' ahl al-madīnat al-fādilah*, Ibn Sina or Avicenna (980–1037) with his *Tadbīr Manzil*, Abu Hamid al-Ghazali or Algazel (1058–1111) with his *Ihyā 'Ulum al-Dīn*, Naṣir al-Din al-Tusi's (1201–74) *Akhlāq-i-Nāṣiri* (Nasirian Ethics), and As'ad Dawwani's *Akhlāq-i Jalālī* (translated by W.T. Thompson as *Practical Philosophy of the Muhammedan People*).

Oikonomia was translated by Muslim philosophers as *'ilm tadbīr al-manzil* (the science of household management). It was one of the three branches of Greek philosophy, the other two being ethics (*'ilm al-akhlāq*) and politics (*'ilm al-siyāsah*). According to Spengler, Muslim scholars extended this branch of knowledge 'far beyond the household, embracing market, price, monetary, supply, demand phenomena, and hinting at some of the macro-economic relations stressed by Lord Keynes'.[10]

The Arabic translation of *Oikonomia* as *tadbīr al-manzil* as published in AL-MACHRIQ (*al-Mashriq*)[11] notes only four components of a house—wealth, servants, wife, and children. All these elements already existed in the basic sources of Islam. Thus, the Tunisian writer Essid is not correct when he says that the Qur'an is 'providing only a body of legal rules concerning marriage and the breaking of the bond of marriage'.[12] Ironically, just after ten pages in this work he admits the existence of 'an interesting parallel to this type of association in Islam' that should preside over family relations.[13] It is true that despite clear teachings found in the basic sources of Islam about all the elements of a household, *tadbīr al-manzil* was not developed as an *'ilm* (science) before the Greek translation. Perhaps none of the past scholars had dealt with the topic of the administration of the household with the Islamic perspective as extensively as did the eighteenth-century Indian scholar Shah Wali-Allah Dihlawi.

5.3 Shah Wali-Allah on *tadbīr al-manzil*

Shah Wali-Allah defines *tadbīr manzil* as 'the science examining the way to preserve the ties existing between the members of the household according to the second degree of the supports of civilization (*al-irtifāq al-thānī*). In it are four departments: marriage, having children, being the master, and associating with one another'.[14]

He mentions the term *tadbīr al-manzil* on various occasions in his works without reference to earlier writers.[15] To him, household management deals with the number of units occupying a house: spouses, children, slaves and servants.[16] These are the same topics that have traditionally been discussed under the subject of *tadbīr al-manzil*. According to Shah Wali-Allah, *tadbīr al-manzil* is to some extent done by animals too. Their males and females cooperate in rearing babies, feeding them together and, in the case of birds, teaching them how to fly. But it is usually perceived as a characteristic of mankind to do it in cooperation with fellow human beings.[17] It is a concern preoccupying all people, in every land, irrespective of their religions and geographic distances.[18] They cannot survive without cooperating with others of their species as they do not feed on wild grass or raw fruits like animals, nor are they kept warm with fur and so on. By nature, mankind is at an advanced level concerning the management of a house.[19]

Shah Wali-Allah stressed that the Lawgiver made us familiar with two types of knowledge each with their distinct rules: the knowledge of beneficial purposes (*maṣāliḥ*) and the knowledge of divine laws and religious rules (*Sharā'i*). The first type of knowledge deals with self-reform (*tahdhib al-nafs*) through moral character (*al-akhlāq*), household management (*tadbīr al-manzil*), economy and manners of living (*adāb al-ma'āsh*), as well as the management of the city (*siyāsat al-madinah*).[20] Essentially, Shah Wali-Allah regarded moral values as the key to economic behaviour leading to a good life. He said that the rules for managing one's home have been known to all nations, whether Arabs or non-Arabs, with only some differences in their forms. Furthermore, as the last Prophet was raised among the Arabs, he followed the rules of managing a home in the Arabic tradition.[21] In this statement, there is a clear refutation of those who claim that everything related to *tadbīr al-manzil* in Islam belongs to the Greeks.[22] In his work *al-Khayr al-Kathīr*, Shah Wali-Allah (1352 AH, p. 83) remarks that Islamic Law (Shariah) deals with worship (*'ibādāt*), great sins (*kabā'ir*), habits (*'ādāt*), ethics (*akhlāq*), conduct (*mu'āmalāt*), household management (*tadbīr al-manzil*), and management of the city (*siyāsat al-madinah*). Thus, he makes it clear that *tadbīr al-manzil* is one of the subjects of Shariah.[23]

To Shah Wali-Allah, marriage is the foundation of a family. It is necessary to live a life of piety and devoutness, especially for youths. He supports his opinion with a hadith in which the Prophet, may Allah bless him and give him peace, exhorts the youngsters to get married if they can afford it as that helps protect the eyes and private parts from abuse. For the one who cannot afford it, he should fast, and that would be a shield for him.[24]

He stressed that there is no contradiction between piety and marriage. He reminds how the Prophet, may Allah bless him and give him peace, admonished his companion Uthman ibn Maẓ'ūn when the latter decided to remain unmarried. The Prophet said, 'Lo by God, I am more God-fearing than you, and more pious but I fast some times and break it some other times, I pray in night, and sleep as well; I am married with women. One, who does not like my way of life, is not among us.'[25]

5.4 The subject matter of *tadbīr al-manzil*

Shah Wali-Allah has discussed the subject matter of *tadbīr al-manzil* in much detail in his work *Ḥujjat Allāh al-Bālighah*: 'The majority of the issues in this field concern recognizing the causes why marriage is required and how it is dissolved, the proper way to marry, the qualities of the husband and wife, the responsibilities of the husband in dealing kindly with his wife and protecting her from humiliation and vices, wife's duties with respect to faithfulness and obedience to the husband, and exerting her capacity in household matters; the way to resolve cases of spousal mistreatment, the method of divorce, the mourning period of the woman who has lost her husband, the bringing up of the children, honouring the parents, the way of managing slaves and treating them kindly, the way for slaves to serve their masters, the way to manumit slaves, how to behave with relatives and neighbors, how to give charity to the poor of the locality and cooperate in alleviating the calamities which assail them, the proper behaviour of the leader of the group and how he should monitor their condition, how to divide the legacy among the heirs, and how to preserve the lineages and the lines of descent.'[26]

5.4.1 Cooperation between men and women

Shah Wali-Allah puts needs in household management in two degrees: 'One degree is not fulfilled until each considers the hurts and benefits of the other as if they were his own, and this will not happen unless each expends all he is capable of in the friendship of the other, and in spending on him and ensuring his inheritance rights. In sum, circumstances require on both sides that each take the profit with the loss. The people who are the most suitable for this degree are relatives, for their mutual love and companionship is a natural matter. The other degree is fulfilled by less than this. Thus it is necessary that consolation and empathy for those struck by calamities be an accepted practice among all, and that the bond of kinship should be firmer and stronger than anything else.'[27]

In the opinion of Shah Wali-Allah, *tadbīr al-manzil* is a natural scheme. He writes: 'Therefore you will not find any nation among humanity which does not have convictions about the principles of these topics and which does not strive to establish them, despite their varying religions and the distance between their countries, and God knows better.'[28]

5.4.2 The art of economic transactions (*mu'āmalāt*)

According to Shah Wali-Allah, to upkeep the family unit and manage the household properly, exchanges, cooperation, and means of earning become necessary. He gave it the name of *fann al-mu'āmalāt* (The Art of Economic Transactions). He says, 'This is the science examining the manner of establishing exchanges, cooperation, and means of earning, at the second stage of the socio-economic development.'[29]

Shah Wali-Allah visualizes how various forms of contracts and institutions of cooperation evolved in the society. He says, 'Exchange is either property for property, which is barter; or property in exchange for usufruct, which is hire and lease. Since the organization of the city could not be accomplished except through good will and love among people, and good will often leads to giving without a return, or delaying payment, therefore gifts and loans evolved. This good will is also only accomplished through sympathy for the poor; and thus charity evolved. Material circumstances required that there be among them fools, competent ones, impoverished ones, and wealthy ones, those who disdained lowstatus work and those who did not, those whose needs were pressing and those who were free from need. Thus, no one's livelihood could be achieved without the cooperation of another, and there could be no cooperation except through contracts, (setting) conditions, and conventions according to a customary practice. In this way the branches of share-cropping, limited partnership (*muḍārabah*), hire and lease, partnership, and power of attorney came into being. Needs arose which led to borrowing and keeping in trust; then some attempted deception, lying and delaying of payments; so they were forced to institute witnessing, writing up documents, mortgaging, guarantee and bills of exchange'. He observes: 'The more their level of comfort increased, the more the types of cooperation diversified, and no community of people exists which does not practice these transactions and recognize justice from injustice, and God knows better.'[30]

In his work *Al-Budūr al-Bāzighah*, Shah Wali-Allah further sheds light on the role of man and woman in fulfilling the affairs of the family together. He observes that man is created upon pride, rulership, display of power over what he holds, and the desire to expand his means of earnings.

A woman is created upon diffidence, obedience, and weakness in what she holds and has control over a limited part of livelihood. However, it has been agreed that man is less free for indoor works such as sweeping, cooking, grinding and looking after children. An agreement has also been arrived at to the effect that women may remain in their houses because of the infirmity of their internal composition and weakness of their hearts.[31]

Shah Wali-Allah suggests what measures should be adopted to improve relations with one's near and dear. In his opinion, those more entitled to good company are family members and kin, the neighbours, and the neighbour who is not of kin such as fellow travellers, class-fellows in learning, and the slaves and servants of the same master. To strengthen relations with them, it is necessary to pay visits to each other, present gifts, do correspondence, cooperate in the affairs of living, display sympathy and leniency in speech, and extend help when needs occur—thus, grow intimacy and show affection. There ought to be an exchange of salutations, asking permission before entering others' houses, lowering the gaze from other women, and displaying concern even in small matters, because sometimes hatred creeps into the hearts as does the ant by acts like taking precedence in walks and speech, quarrelling, disputing and slandering. The rights and obligations are of different degrees towards different members of the society and one should behave accordingly, keeping in view to whom one is dealing with.[32] There is no doubt these suggestions are based on teachings provided in Islamic sources.

5.4.3 Responsibilities of man, the master of the household

To Shah Wali-Allah, the husband should be able to take care of the family properly and possess good qualities and character. He should not be a beggar, nor a great beater; he should not fly in anger, should not be unsteady, impotent nor affected with elephantiasis, nor should he be a leper, mad and a burden incapable of earning anything. It is thus necessary that there should be love between husband and wife to be continued as far as possible. If an unexpected thing were to affect that love adversely, it may be restored through a suitable plan. This could be done by giving the dowry, indicating the existence of the desire to patch up; which may be followed by a marriage feast..[33]

A person must avoid luxuries in excess

According to Shah Wali-Allah, people are of various kinds. Some live in maximum luxuries and are immersed in those luxuries. Some are in the middle class, while others are short of the first and the second, unable to fulfil their needs except as much as the animals do.[34] In his opinion, the middle stage should be made as the balance of the philosophy of living. A person must avoid luxuries in excess, for one will not be free from exertion, weariness, and loss of wealth as one's needs will multiply, making certain one's destitution.[35]

According to him, there are two opinions radically opposed to each other about the use of luxury. One says that it is a fine thing and has good effects on the human personality. The other says that it is a bad thing because it causes disputes, quarrels, anxieties and diverts a person from the unseen and from making provisions for the Hereafter (ibid.). His advice is to follow the middle path and adopt the average standard of living.[36] He writes, 'There are persons who are immersed in the luxuries of life and have made them as their main aim in life. They, therefore, may not be free from the worldly hardships, nor be safe from the punishment of the grave and that of the Day of Gathering.'[37]

Eating manners and etiquettes

Shah Wali-Allah also teaches manners and etiquette on how to take meals in family and groups. He suggests that: 'When man sits to take food, he must be at rest; he must have washed his hands, face, mouth and nose, and should place the food on the table and not on the ground or on a tray. He should not eat his food, before having placed it in front of him, without showing rashness, and hastiness, and without putting in large morsels, as all this is a sign of greed and shame. He must not eat or drink except when he is overtaken by real hunger and thirst. The best kind of food or drink is one which is easy to get and is completely digestible and is wholesome for the stomach as well. He must see that the food and drink are placed in the earthenware or wooden vessels, not on the earth, nor in vessels of gold and silver.'[38] These manners can be supported by various sayings of the Prophet, may Allah bless him and give him peace. Thus, his source is the Sunnah, although he does not mention it explicitly.

Must stop intoxicating drinks

Wali-Allah warns of the bad consequences of taking intoxicating drinks: 'As for the drinks, the intoxicating one is the most hateful, as it causes the loss of reason and corrupts the behaviour, it makes a man an object of mockery for the children. Besides, it means waste of wealth, and the domestic as well as the urban interests are ruined.' 'As far as drinking water is concerned, he should observe certain rules which are necessary for health. He should not breathe in the vessel of water, he should keep it sufficiently away from the mouth when breathing. He must avoid swallowing of water in one gulp and should not bend over a vessel (as do the animals) for drinking. They are the signs of spoiled behaviour and result in disease of the liver. He should sip in with three breaths as that is good for the stomach and is very near to a good manner.'[39] It is needless to say that the rules prescribed by Shah Wali-Allah are derived from the basic sources of Islam and approved by scientific research. Thus, they are additions to the Greek ideas of household management.

Dwelling

Regarding the dwelling, Shah Wali-Allah suggests that it should be such as to protect against heat and cold, as well as against thieves; it should protect its inmates and their goods so that the intended socioeconomic development may take a practical shape. One should not take too much trouble in building a plastered house painted with pictures, nor should it be built very spacious or narrow.[40] Here again, Shah Wali-Allah emphasizes having average types of houses. Perhaps he is observing the famous saying, 'The best of every affair is its average.'

Dress

After describing the place of dwelling, it was but natural to deal with the kind of clothes that are suitable. He says that as for the dress, all the people of the world agree that nakedness is shameful and clothing has an elegance. The display of both private parts, and also some others, is a vice. A fine wear is one by which the whole body is covered. What covers nakedness in the body (such as the private parts and the thigh) should be in addition to the one which covers the rest of the body, leaving the hands to act freely for the fulfilment of needs, and to not be held back. The man should avoid clothes indicating vanity, shamelessness, and dissipation, such as silken, dyed and saffron-applied clothes, or clothes through which the skin of the body can be seen. However, for the woman there is no harm as she is created as a kind of delight for the attraction of her husband. A man who effeminates himself is cursed; he is away from Allah as well as the people. Similarly, a woman who tries to be man-like is cursed and is away from Allah and the people.[41]

Man and woman complete each other

According to Shah Wali-Allah, man and woman complete each other. Things lacked by women are provided for by men and vice versa. However, a man is the head of the family because he reasons more soundly. He is more concerned with defending his honour, more enthusiastic in throwing himself into difficult tasks, and more bent on domination, dispute, and so on. Thus, the livelihood of the latter would not be complete without that of the former, and the former needs the latter.[42]

Handling expenditure correctly

There should be proper managing of expenditure. If a person spends in charity while his family is hungry, in this case, although he is doing a good deed, he is going against the principles of house management.[43] The Prophet, peace and blessings of Allah be upon him, said: 'The people of a house will not go hungry if they have dates.' And he said: 'A house that does not have dates, its people remain hungry.'[44] From this saying, Shah Wali-Allah concludes that one who is responsible for the management of a household must always keep something in the house for eating that can be used at the time of emergency, such as dates, carrots, etc. It is clear from this that the caretaker of the house must ensure the fulfilment of the household's basic needs.

Role of women as the household caretaker

It is an established convention in all peoples as a natural necessity that men should be the maintainers (*qawwām*) of women and should have the power of decision-making as well as bear all expenditures. Women are to be their helpers (*a'wān*). This is also in accordance with the Qur'anic verse *'al-rijāl qawwāmūn ala al-nisā"* (*al-Nisa'* 4: 34).[45]

Woman is best suited to be the caretaker of household

Shah Wali-Allah has discussed the role of woman as the caretaker of the household in much detail. First, he mentions how the household is formed. He says: 'It is the providence of Allah that He suggested to human beings to forge the connection through marriage in the customary and conventional manner. By marriage I mean the marriage with the unforbidden ones by way of proposal and acceptance to be solemnised in the presence of witnesses with the fullest participation of the guardians, by way of giving dowry in advance and through betrothal ceremony, so that, women obey men, serve them and manage for them their domestic affairs while men may earn the livelihood outside the house.'[46] No doubt, their roles are based on the division of labour. According to Wali-Allah, by nature the woman is the one of them who is more guided to bring up the children and the less intellectual of the two, the one less able to bear hardships, and the more modest and attached to the home. She is more meticulous in doing humble tasks and is more completely obedient.[47]

Qualities of a bride

In selecting a bride, Shah Wali-Allah suggests: 'It is preferable that the woman may be beautiful, virgin and capable of bringing forth children, chaste, very kind and affectionate towards the children, should have love for her husband, loyal to his property, know the administration of the house, be neither wrathful nor swift in showing weakness.'[48] On another occasion, he suggested that a woman should have her hands dyed, her head-hair anointed with oil and properly combed, and should be attired in such colourful garments to attract her husband, as well as adorn herself in ornaments of gold, etc.[49]

Shah Wali-Allah is very emphatic that the best management of the household depends on the quality of a woman, specifically, how virtuous and energetic she is. He supports his view by the saying of the Prophet: 'The world is an object to enjoy, and the world's best object is the good woman.'[50] In his interpretation of the Prophet's saying that 'A woman is married for four things, i.e., her wealth, her family status, her beauty and her religion. So you should marry the religious woman (otherwise) you will be a losers.'[51] Shah Wali-Allah says that different people prefer different qualities of a woman. It is advisable to choose a woman who is more religious so that she can cooperate and support in religious matters.[52]

Kafā'ah (compatibility)

Shah Wali-Allah says it is desirable that a potential wife should be from a clan and tribe whose women are known for excellence because the clans and tribes are like mines of gold and silver; their customs and habits dominate their people and become their natural quality. According to him, that is why the Prophet, may Allah bless him and give him peace, said that the women of the Quraysh tribe are the best women who take care of children and protect the husbands' wealth, slaves, and so on.[53] These are among the greatest purposes of marriage and the management of the house which is done by women.[54] It may be noted that the primary objective of marriage is to have a healthy marital life coupled with a good relationship. This is only possible when the natural inclinations and backgrounds of the two are the same. In the absence of such unity, living together successfully despite great effort is indeed difficult, as proven by many marital breakdowns due to incompatibility or the absence of *kafā'ah*.

Religious and moral qualities are very important in the up-keeping of a family. The Prophet, may Allah bless him and give him peace, said: 'If you receive a proposal of marriage from someone and you are satisfied with his religious and ethical condition then you must marry him, if you do not do this, there will be strife in the land and great corruption.'[55] According to Shah Wali-Allah this does not mean that suitability and compatibility (*kafā'ah*) will not be considered. It only means that after being satisfied by the most important qualities, like religiosity and morality, one should not delay the matter in search of trivial things such as money, beauty, prestige and positions.[56]

Solemnization of marriage

The solemnization of marriage should be fully known to people so that no one contests the man or thinks about marrying married women. This is the aim of performing the marriage ritual (*nikāḥ*) in a gathering of people, with a sermon and witnesses.[57] Thus, according to Shah Wali-Allah, the declaration of marriage and a celebration is necessary, within the permitted limits.

The Prophet (may Allah bless him and give him peace) said: 'The difference between *ḥalāl* (valid) and *ḥarām* (invalid) marriage is the announcement of marriage and the playing of *daff* (a simple light musical instrument).'[58] He also said: 'Declare this marriage and make it in the mosques. And play *daff*.'[59]

Dowry and wedding feast

Shah Wali-Allah is against fixing an inflated dowry. It is not desirable to inflate the dowry to the extent that it becomes difficult to pay. The amount should be reasonable as was prevalent during the Prophet's time and among the majority of people after him.[60]

Shah Wali-Allah enumerated several benefits of the wedding feast (*walīmah*). It is according to the popular custom among people to serve a feast before consummating the marriage. It serves as an announcement of the solemnization of the marriage so that none should think it adultery. The wedding feast will help spread the news of the marriage and is an honour to the bride and her family. This will also prevent any doubt about the lineage of the children.[61]

The marital bond is the greatest bond

The marital bond is the greatest bond and the most beneficial among mankind. Likewise, the relationship between spouses is the greatest and most useful of ties of the whole household. It has been an established convention among the people, Arabs and non-Arabs, that the women must cooperate with men in meeting the requirements of life (*al-irtifāqāt*) and ensuring that the food, drink, and clothes are made ready, and that his valuables are properly stored. Needless to say, in his absence, she should take care of managing the household in his place.[62] It has already been mentioned on several occasions that the man's duty is to protect her and make provisions for her and all dependents. Additionally, he has to bear all the expenses of the family and see to their maintenance.

It is prohibited to create conflict between the wife and the husband. This is very clear from the saying of the Prophet who warned that 'a person is not of us who cheats a woman against her husband or a slave against his master.'[63]

In the opinion of Shah Wali-Allah, one of the reasons for the corruption of housekeeping is that a person instigates the woman against her husband or the slave against his master, something which is the opposite of what is required from that person to do.

Justice with women

In the case where there are many wives, the man must do justice with them. He should not prefer one over the other in the distribution of means and meeting days. He should not keep the fate of others hanging. Shah Wali-Allah supports this with a verse of the Qur'an: 'And you will not be able to do justice among women, even if you wish (to do so).' (*al-Nisa'* 4: 129)[64]

In the following passage, Shah Wali-Allah presents the wisdom behind various rules surrounding marriage and divorce in Islam, such as why a woman is to marry one man only, why there should be a dowry and engagement, why very close relatives cannot marry her, and why some very close blood relations are prohibited from marrying each other:

Why close relatives are prohibited to marry each other

According to Shah Wali-Allah, the rivalry among men for women and their sense of jealousy concerning them requires that their relationship is not deemed proper unless the man's exclusive possession of his wife is settled in the presence of witnesses. The man's desire for the woman and her honour's dependency on her guardian defending her, necessitates the dowry, engagement, and her own guardian[65] remaining disinterested (in her as a wife). If the guardian was allowed to desire the relative under his protection, this would cause great harm to her since she would be prevented by him from marrying the one she wanted, and she would not have anyone who would demand marital rights on her behalf despite her great need for this. The offense against ties of kinship through the quarrels of co-wives and the like, in addition to sound temperament require that a man should not be (sexually) attracted to the one who bore him, or towards the one who was born from him, or the one who is like a branch of the same tree with respect to him (i.e. his sister). [66]

In the opinion of Shah Wali-Allah, the binding practice and a matter which all people, Arabs or non-Arabs, agree on and an original nature according to which God, may He be exalted, created mankind is that men support women and have responsibility over them in matters of livelihood, and women are helpful in the home, raise the children, and are obedient. The spouses will not expend efforts to cooperate, in such a way that each of them feels the other partner's harms and benefits as affecting himself or herself, unless they have committed themselves to continuing the marriage. Still, there must inevitably be preserved a way to disengage if they do not accede to one another's wishes and come to terms with one another, and this is the most hateful of permitted things. Therefore in the case of divorce one should pay attention to certain stipulations and to a waiting period. Likewise on the death of the husband, [there is a waiting period] out of respect for marriage in the minds of people, in order to render certain rights of continuity, out to fidelity to the time of companionship, and in order to avoid confusion about the lineage.[67]

Thus, Shah Wali-Allah elaborates upon a woman's role in terms of household management, starting from the first day of marriage to rearing children, looking after domestic works, cooperating with each other and working as a single body, up to the end of her life. Of course, if somehow husband and wife cannot live together, they would have to follow the way prescribed by Islam to get separated as beautifully as they joined hands together.

5.4.4 Slaves and servants

Slaves in the old days and domestic servants in the later period till the present day have been an important component of the house and, therefore, dealing with them formed a subject of household management. According to Shah Wali-Allah, it is from the providence of Allah Almighty that He has made men of different degrees. Some of them are slaves by nature, not independent in their living due to the weakness of their resolution. Their only business is to serve their masters, become their dependents, and obey their orders. Such persons cannot find rest till they find a master, either the one who owns him or someone else, who could deal with him as does a controlling master.[68]

The variations in the capacities of human beings requires that among them are masters by nature, who are the most intelligent, independent in their livelihood, and by nature possess strategy and luxury; and there are servants by nature who are foolish and subordinates who do whatever they are ordered to do.[69]

On the other hand, 'there are men who are chiefs by nature, they are persons of authority and high ambition and have plenty of means of earnings. Their business is to bear the burdens of the family and remain their governing master. Then some events happen and opportunities occur in which some take others as captives and become their masters, subjugate them as the animals are subjugated. Subsequently arise for the masters many needs which cannot be met except with the cooperation of slaves. Similarly, slaves have their needs which cannot be met but through the help of the masters. By this plan (mutual cooperation), the affairs of their living are arranged in the best possible way.'[70]

Rights of the slaves

When discussing the rights of slaves, Shah Wali-Allah emphasizes that the Prophet, may Allah bless him and give him peace, enjoined certain things that people must abide by, whether they wanted to do so or not. For example, the Prophet, may Allah bless him and give him peace, said: 'Whoever has got a slave of blood relation, it is prohibited to enslave him; he would be set free.'[71] As far as the Prophet's injunctions for good treatment towards the slaves are concerned, they are on two levels: one is obligatory, and the other is optional, though encouraged to do without compulsion. An example of obligatory good treatment is his saying that: 'He who is in possession of a slave, he should provide him with his food and clothing, and he should not compel him to do jobs which are beyond his strength.'[72] This is because the slave works for his master thus it is obligatory upon him to look after his necessities.

The example of optional conduct is illustrated in the Prophet's saying that: 'If a servant prepares food for any one of you and he brings it to you, ask him to eat with you as he bore the heat and the smoke. If the quantity is small, give him at least a little.'[73]

Emancipation of slaves

Shah Wali-Allah also highlights Islamic teachings regarding the good treatment of slaves and the encouragement to set them free. He says: 'If a master beats his slave without any fault, then the former would be pardoned only if he sets the latter free.'[74] The Prophet (may Allah blessing him and give him peace) encouraged a Muslim to emancipate a servant as this will set his neck free from the fire.[75] He has also said: 'If a person emancipates a half of a slave, he shall be completely free if he has money.'[76]

Ibn Taymiyyah in his work *al-Ḥisbah* explained how to decide this. He says that in the case of emancipating a jointly-owned slave, the just price (*qīmah 'adl*) of the slave should be determined without any addition or reduction (*lā wakasa wa lā shaṭaṭa*) and each one should be given his share, and the slave should then be set free.[77]

It was previously noted that a blood relation cannot be kept as a slave; they will be free due to the importance of blood relations in Islam. Similarly, if a slave girl is pregnant by her master, she will be free after his death. Shah says that this is to give honour to the child, and his or her mother should not belong to other than his or her father.[78]

It is importat to note that Shah Wali-Allah highlighted the Islamic teaching regarding humane treatment at a time when slaves were still treated worse than animals and legislation had not started yet to ban slavery.

5.4.5 Children

Children are one of the very important components of householed management. Shah Wali-Allah has paid due attention to them. He has dealt with this topic extensively in his two works *Ḥujjat Allāh al-Bālighah*.[79] In his work *Ḥujjat-Allāh al-Bālighah* while discussing various Islamic provisions regarding household management, Shah Wali-Allah, under the section of training of children and slaves (*tarbiyat al-awlād wa'l-mamālīk*), gives more space discussing the former.[80] Perhaps he realized that the latter had not much practical relevance during his time.

As for the question on how to manage children, he says that the newborn is to be given a proper name, his hairs are to be removed and an animal sacrifice is to be offered called the tradition of *'aqīqah* (sacrifice of animals), which is done on behalf of children. This *'aqīqah* was a necessary tradition with the Arabs. It had many social, civil, and psychological advantages. Therefore, the Prophet, may Allah bless him and give him peace, retained it and encouraged people to perform it. It worked like an announcement that a child was born to him and no unpleasant rumor could spread. It was a kind of generosity as opposed to miserliness. It was a substitute to what Christians do as baptism and it is also reminiscent of Prophet Abraham's readiness to sacrifice his son Ishmael, which was replaced by the instruction to instead sacrifice a goat. It also reminds us what sacrifices Muslims do at Mina during the hajj.[81]

There are some noteworthy points in the ceremony regarding the removal of the newborn's hair. Firstly, announcing the child's relation and this acknowledgement that this is his baby. Secondly is to display happiness and offer thanks to Allah the Benevolent. Thirdly is to have love for the child and mother, while the fourth is to offer the animal sacrifice.[82]

How to raise children

According to Shah Wali-Allah, it is necessary to look into a plan for the child's growth. They should be given simple toys to play with. They should avoid things that are likely to inflict injury or break down. When they become sensible and start speaking, they should be helped to speak fluently and become free from any impediments. They should then be instructed in good moral conduct, and abstinence from what is contemptible, including the display of authority. They must learn to avoid extravagance, particularly in eating, drinking and speaking, and should observe rules of etiquette in the presence of their elders. It then becomes necessary to impart education in such sciences as may be useful for them in life on the earth and the Hereafter. When they grow up and attain youth, arrangement should be made for their marriage and to learn the professions which are suitable for them. It is the duty of the son to serve his parents, respect them, commit his affairs to them and refrain from disobedience and grumbling.[83]

According to Shah Wali-Allah, 'the need of children for parents, and the parents' natural sympathy for their children require that the training of the children be such as to preserve and boost their natural instinct. The precedence of the parents over the children is necessary, for even when they grow up their parents' superiority in wisdom and experience continues, along with the requirement of sound morality that kindness should be exchanged for kindness. Honouring parents is a compulsory practice, since they suffered in bringing them up to an extent that needs no elaboration.

In household management, both man and woman/men and women have to perform the role which is by nature appropriate to them. Since rearing the child and breastfeeding is possible for the mother, she has to do it. On the other hand, it is easy for the father to spend money on the child and bear the expenses of the mother who is prevented from earning money and suffers from all kinds of pain and fatigue due to her condition. This is the requirement of justice.'[84]

5.5 Other areas of *tadbīr al-manzil*

5.5.1 Distribution of inheritance

Most of the abovementioned ideas were found within the Greek concept of *Oikonomia* as well, although not exactly; Muslim scholars have adapted them with Islamic faith and values and have made improvements. However, there are certain additions to the topic of household management that Shah Wali-Allah adopted from Islamic teachings. One such provision is the distribution of inheritance based on natural company, mutual help and close relations, not on incidental events, as they cannot be specified and cannot be a basis for distributing inheritance. The governing rule in this respect is 'the blood relations are more entitled of each other in the Book of Allah.'[85] It is, therefore, that inheritance is for the blood relatives, including husband and wife who are treated like blood relation due to certain reasons, especially because they manage the household together.[86]

5.5.2 Cooperation and division of labour

Cooperation and the division of labour are closely related topics that are necessary to smoothly manage the household. At a broader level, they are important for the economy as a whole, hence we have addressed these topics in the previous chapter while discussing Shah Wali-Allah's economic ideas. Here it suffices to say that in his opinion, since man is social by nature, living will be smooth only by cooperating with others.[87] Cooperation with other members of society is a distinguishing characteristic of mankind.[88] Furthermore, the division of labour is necessary because a household faces a variety of needs, which cannot be met without the help of others. Using money facilitates this cooperation and the division of labour. Man, as the leader of the house, is responsible for earning money to buy the things needed by the household. The next chapter will address Shah Wali-Allah's ideas on money in more detail.

In his writings, Shah Wali-Allah shows how the wisdom of household management in search of comforts and an elegant life requires effort by which they may attain all that they need in the best and noblest possible manner. If it is not done this way, they might face difficulty and hardship; needs will then rush in on them, resulting in a situation where it will be tough to fulfil any of them elegantly.[89]

In this connection, Shah Wali-Allah demonstrates the importance and inevitability of cooperation and the division of labour. He writes that the reason why people adopt different professions is the rush of needs on them to such an extent that it is not possible for the members of a single house to procure all that they need without the help of other households. For example, when in need of food, they have to undertake tillage, and for this they would need animals as well as to domesticate them. This they cannot accomplish instantly, particularly when they intend to accomplish the task in the best possible manner, creating beauty as well as excellence. Similarly, there is the need for carpentry and black smithery, and if people intend to do this work in the best possible way, they will need a long time of practice, experimentation and knowledge of the sciences, which is well beyond the scope of a single individual.[90] Likewise, food involves bread and condiment. If a person intends to get the best result from them, it cannot be done alone, nor can it be done by members of a single household; this will require a lifetime in acquiring and finding out better varieties of food. People also need clothing which, in turn, requires the cultivation of cotton, spinning and weaving, which is not possible for one man to do, let alone to make everything excellent. If people need to drink, they unavoidably have to find water and learn the method of digging wells, and at times even carry water to the water-bags. People are also in need of dwellings and would need to work together to build these. In short, what is possible for the members of every house is to work for what suits the first phase of socio-economic development.[91]

From household to surroundings

What suits the second phase, namely the consideration of excellence and beauty in every need, is certainly not possible for members of a single household to attain. At this stage, what is needed is the population's division into different groups, enabling each group to pay attention to one of the works and improve upon it by individual attention and repeated practice. Only then will a man become an expert in that business; he will be able to find out its fine aspects and make it a means for attaining any of the other needs which overtake him. Thus, through the human society (*hai'at ijtimaiyah*), the household's affair will be set in order according to the second phase.[92]

According to Wali-Allah, it is suitable for a brave man to become the helper of his leader. The strong man who is not brave and cannot show gallantry in war like the real fighters is suited for carrying the loads. One who knows the subtleties of dealings is best suited for trade. Some people hasten to adopt a profession under the pressure of necessity, whether it is good or bad. It is well said that 'for every fallen thing, there is one to pick it up'. However, it suits persons endowed with manliness and vigour to adopt professions that are not base, nor contemptible. A man's sense of understanding requires that he may look into his needs and choose a profession that may fulfil his need. A hungry man having chosen a profession which does not fulfil his needs hastens to adopt beggary and degrades himself. Then there is a man who is very lustful but he does not earn save what is sufficient for himself only. Consequently, he hastens to indecency and shamelessness. Had his profession conformed with his need, he would not have been overtaken by shame. Then there is the case of a man with an angry temperament who happens to choose a profession that results in his ignominy. The corruption of people is generally the result of their following and imitating their elders without understanding what they are doing. They rush blindly into the professions of their companions, even though they are/those professions are not suitable for them, except when there happens to be a disgrace for them. In that case, a person tries to get rid of a mean profession. This is a fact fully known to the wise.[93]

Shah Wali-Allah suggests that when a particular profession begins to have doubtful consequences, it should be given up, as 'every man is created for a particular thing'. Every profession has two facts, which should therefore be adopted and followed carefully, after deep thinking. One is the acquisition of workmanship which may suffice a person's needs. The other is to care for what his intention is and thus make the right selection. When a person enters some business, it is his duty to first look into its principles and the instruments to be used; when he has understood them properly, he should then look to its finer points and related requirements.[94]

Exchange and need for money

Division of labour cannot exist without exchange facilities. Wali-Allah, like many other scholars, held that money was invented to facilitate exchange, to play the role of a medium. He said that when every man became distinguishable and distinct on account of his profession, and when it was realised that every profession could not fulfil all needs, people unavoidably went for exchange in order to complete the desired phase (*al-irtifāq*). However, he makes it clear that there are certain cases in which exchange is done without money as a medium. This happens when the exchange is not for commercial purposes, or when it is goods for goods, also known as barter exchange. In the case of gifts, the exchange is for the sake of each other's goodwill; it is closeness which is basically aimed at, and through it needs are fulfilled and support is obtained. In certain conditions, magnanimity, faithfulness and blood relations strongly encourage a person to spend money and give away benefits as an act of benevolence. Shah Wali-Allah gives examples of such transactions. *Bay'* (buying and selling) is the exchange of goods with the medium of money for the sake of money. As far as *ijārah* (renting) is concerned, it is hiring out something for money for the sake of benefit/utility. *Hibah* is gifting something for free without money. There may be an expectation of some returns either in this world or in the Hereafter. *I'ārah* is loaning or offering an object to someone to enable him to enjoy its benefits without any monetary gain. *Dayn* (loan/debt) has a similarity with both *i'ārah* and *bay'*. It is similar to *i'ārah* if dirhams and dinars are given in a loan, and is similar to *bay'* as it happens in *bay' al-salam* in which money is advanced to get goods at a later date.[95] Thus, to Shah Wali-Allah, cooperation, division of labour and exchanges are needed by individuals, the society and the whole economy. Money performs the function of a medium between the different agents.

5.6 The present discipline of economics and the Greek *oikonomia*

The origins of the discipline of economics are traced back to Greek *oikonomia*. But the Greek *oikonomia* did not mean what we understand from Economics today. *Oikonomia*, translated as *tadbīr al-manzil*, meaning household administration was one of the three branches of Greek practical sciences, the other two being ethics (*'ilm al-akhlāq*) and politics (*'ilm al-siyāsah*). *Oikonomia* was confined to the management of a house that comprised the master of the house or man, his wife, monetary resources required for managing the family, children, and servants or slaves. Compared to household administration, politics dealt with the management of cities, which required public revenue, public expenditure, production and distribution, market supervision and control—what we may now refer to as political economy. The Greek philosophers did not discuss much about this aspect of public economics, so much so that one author remarked that 'the term oikonomia referred to "household management" and while this was in some loose way linked to the idea of budgeting, it has little or no relevance to contemporary economics.'[96] Since Islamic primary sources already contained all the elements of *oikonomia*, Muslim scholars adopted the concept and further developed it when it was translated into Arabic as *tadbīr al-manzil*. At the same time, they made many improvements and additions to the Greek *oikonomia*.[97]

Among the authors who have used the term and developed it are: Ibn Abi al-Rabi' (218–272/833–85), Ibn Abi al-Dunya (208–81/823–91), Qudamah ibn Ja'far (250–320/864–932), Ibn al-Jawzi (510–697/1126–1200), Ibn Jama'ah (639–733/1241–1333), Ibn Khaldun (d. 808/1406), Ibn al-Azraq (832–96/1427–89), al-Maqrizi (766–845/1364–1442), etc. The notion of *tadbīr al-manzil* is an application, not a general framework. Ignoring this reality can lead to misinterpretation and erroneous conclusions, hence the need for a multidisciplinary approach to study the subject.

5.7 Market versus 'family'

Writers on 'household management' all extended the term *tadbīr al-manzil* to the whole economy, although basically it meant, as noted above, dealing with family constituents. From the works of Shah Wali-Allah, it appears that he preferred the term *adāb al-ma'āsh* for socio-economic relations other than the family unit.[98] This does indeed seem to be an improvement upon the Greek's *oikonomia*.[99]

The Western scholarship transferring *oikonomia* to economics and making their focus the market rather than the family ignored the significance of household administration. This resulted in family disintegration. Disappointed with the over-emphasis on market and its undesirable effects, many Islamic economists are emphasizing the importance of family. For instance, Chapra writes about Mawlana Mawdudi:

'Since the human-being is the most important input for any economy, and the family is the primary source of this input, he attached a great deal of importance to the role of the family in the realization of human well-being. This role of the family has, however, not received worthwhile attention in both Conventional and Socialist Economics. The state, the society and the economy as well as the individual would all suffer if the family disintegrates. It is the family which creates the right environment for the proper moral upbringing and character uplift of the new generation. It is also the family which provides love and affection to the individual and thereby creates a proper climate for the promotion of not only peace of mind and emotional stability in the individual but also cooperation and harmony in the society. Disintegration of the family promotes bitterness and ill-will and creates an environment in which the new generation does not get the kind of attention that it needs. The quality of the individual deteriorates and with him the quality of all aspects of his society, including the economy.'[100]

Another distinguished Islamic economist, Professor Siddiqi, writes in one of his letters: 'Maybe, one has to go to Ibn-e Sina/Miskwaih and Ghazali, and others to find out what did Muslim thinkers add to Greek legacy. In the Qur'an there is the concept of nurturing with care [*ka mā rabbayānī ṣaghīra*] for the child, and of love and affection [*mawaddatan wa raḥmah*] between husband and wife. I did not find that element in Greek literature as reported by Essid. Where do I find it among Muslim Philosophers? I want to build a bridge between the family and the market.'[101]

Notes and References

1. Baloglou, Christos P., 'The Tradition of Economic Thought in the Mediterranean World from the Ancient Classical Times Through the Hellenistic Times Until the Byzantine Times and Arab-Islamic World' in J.G. Backhaus (ed.), *Handbook of the History of Economic Thought*, p. 72.
2. Dihlawi, Shah Wali-Allah, *Ḥujjat-Allāh al-Bālighah*, I: 41.
3. The Qur'an (32: 5) uses the present tense from *tadbīr* in the verse as *yudabbiru al-amr min al-samā'i ila al-arḍ* (He [Allah] manages the affairs from the heaven to the earth).
4. Dotan Leshem's name can be mentioned as the author of a few articles dealing with the Greek *oikonomia*:
   Leshem, 'Oikonomia Redefined', pp. 43–61.
   Leshem, 'What Did the Ancient Greeks Mean by *Oikonomia?*', pp. 225–231.
5. Islahi, 'The Myth of Bryson and Economic Thought in Islam', pp. 57–64.
6. Orman, 'From Oikonomia to 'IlmTadbīral-Manzil - Intercivilizational Exchange of Knowledge', p. 179.
7. For a brief account of translation activities in the early period of Islam refer to Islahi: *History of Islamic Economic Thought*, pp. 9–15.

8. Baloglou, 'The Tradition of Economic Thought', p. 28.
9. Ibid.
10. Spengler, 'Economic Thought of Islam: Ibn Khaldun', p. 304.
11. AL-MACHRIQ (*al-Mashriq*), vol. 19, no. 3, p. 162.
12. Essid, Yassine. *A Critique of the Origins of Islamic Economic Thought*, p. 181. It is surprising when Essid (p. 181) remarks that: 'The Qur'an does not define the family as such, providing only a body of legal rules concerning marriage and breaking of the bonds of marriage.' The author says this with reference to Gardet, Louis, *La Cite' Musulmane*, p. 251). Being an Arab, Essid could have checked himself. No doubt, one would not find in the Qur'an the definition of 'family' on the pattern of legal or sociological texts. Otherwise, the Qur'an gives a clear concept of a family that consists of mother and father, husband and wife, children, slaves and other relatives. Their rights and obligations—legal and social—have been fully narrated in various chapters of the Qur'an.
13. Ibid., *A Critique of the Origins of Islamic Economic Thought*, p. 191.
14. Hermansen, Marcia K., *The Conclusive Argument from God* (Translation of Shah Wali-Allah's *Ḥujjat-Allāh al-Bālighah*, p. 123.
15. Dihlawi, *Hujjat*, 1: 41–42, 78, 81, 129; 2: 136, 138, 122
16. Ibid., 1: 41–43; 2: 122–148
17. Ibid., 1: 81
18. Ibid., p. 43.
19. Ibid., p. 81.
20. Ibid., p. 129.
21. Ibid., 2: 122
22. Heffening, W., "*Tadbīr*' in *The Encyclopaedia of Islam*, Old Edition, vol. 4, p. 595. Influenced by Haffening, Essid says: 'The contact with Hellenistic ethics on this theme (*tadbīr al-manzil*) was particularly fruitful for Arab-Muslim thought, since Arabic literature had hitherto been relatively silent on the subject' (Essid, *A Critique* p. 181).
23. Dihlawi, Shah Wali-Allah, *al-Khayr al-Kathīr*, p. 83.
24. Dihlawi, *Hujjat*, 2: 1. The hadith has been reported by al-Bukhārī, Muhammad b. Isma'il, *al-Jāmi' al-Ṣaḥīḥ*, vol. 3, p. 334, hadith no. 1905.
25. Dihlawi, *Hujjat* 2: 123. The hadith reported by al-Bukhārī, *al-Jāmi' al-Ṣaḥīḥ*, vol. 7, p. 2, hadith no. 5063
26. Dihlawi, *Hujjat* 1: 42–3; Hermansen, *The Conclusive Argument*, p. 125–26.
27. Hermansen, *The Conclusive Argument*, p. 125.
28. Dihlawi, *Ḥujjat*, 1: p. 43; Hermansen, *The Conclusive Argument*, p. 126.

29. Dihlawi, *Ḥujjat,* 1: 43.
30. Ibid., pp. 43–4, Hermansen, *The Conclusive Argument,* p. 128.
31. Dihlawi, *Ḥujjat,* p. 78.
32. Ibid., pp. 84–5
33. Ibid., p. 80.
34. Ibid., p. 70.
35. Ibid.
36. Ibid.
37. Dihlawi, Shah Wali-Allah, *al-Budūr al-Bāzighah,* p. 74.
38. Ibid.
39. Ibid. p. 72.
40. Ibid. 73.
41. Ibid. 73.
42. Dihlawi, *Ḥujjat,* 1: p. 41. Hermansen, *The Conclusive Argument,* p. 123.
43. Dihlawi, *al-Budūr* p. 78
44. Ibid., 2: 205
45. Ibid., 2: 127
46. Ibid.
47. Dihlawi, *Ḥujjat,* 1: p. 41; Hermansen, *The Conclusive Argument,* p. 123
48. Dihlawi, *al-Budūr,* p. 80.
49. Ibid., p. 73
50. Dihlawi, *Ḥujjat,* 2: 123. The hadith has been reported by Muslim, *al-Jāmi' al-Ṣaḥīḥ,* 4: 178, hadith no. 3716.
51. The hadith has been reported by Muslim, *al-Jāmi' al-Ṣaḥīḥ,* 4: 175, hadith no. 3708. 'your two hands should be dusty' is a way of expressing love and affection, not its literal meaning.
52. Dihlawi, *Ḥujjat,* 2: 123
53. The hadith has been reported by al-Bukhārī, *al-Jāmi' al-Ṣaḥīḥ,* 7: 85, hadith no. 5365.
54. Dihlawi, *Ḥujjat,* 2: 123
55. Ibid., 2: 124
56. Ibid.
57. Ibid.
58. Abu'l-Husayn, Abd al-Baqi, *Mu'jam al-Ṣaḥābah,* 3:16, hadith no. 957.
59. Dihlawi, *Ḥujjat,* 2:128; al-Tirmidh, Muhammad b. Isa, *Sunan al-Tirmidhī,* 3: 398, hadith no. 1089.
60. Dihlawi, *Ḥujjat,* 2: 128–29.
61. Ibid., p. 130
62. Ibid., p. 135.

63. The hadith has been reported by Abu Dawud, *Sunan Abi Dāwūd,* 2: 220, hadith no. 2177.
64. Dihlawi, *Ḥujjat* 2: 137
65. Her father or brother, in most cases.
66. Dihlawi, *Ḥujjat,* 1: p. 41. Hermansen, *A conclusive,* pp. 123–24.
67. Dihlawi, *Ḥujjat,* 1: 42, Hermansen, *A conclusive,* p. 124.
68. Dihlawi, *al-Budūr,* pp. 78–9.
69. Dihlawi, *Ḥujjat,* 1: 42, Hermansen tr. *A conclusive,* p. 124.
70. Dihlawi, *al-Budūr,* p. 79.
71. Abu Dawud, *Sunan.* 4: 45 H.N. 3951.
72. The hadith has been reported by Muslim, *Ṣaḥīḥ.* 5: 93, hadith no. 4406.
73. Dihlawi, *Ḥujjat,* 2: 147.
74. Ibid. The hadith has been reported by Muslim, *Ṣaḥīḥ.* 5: 94, hadith no. 4407.
75. The hadith has been reported by Muslim, *Ṣaḥīḥ.* 5:90, hadith no. 4389.
76. See al-Bukhārī, *al-Jāmiʿ al-Ṣaḥīḥ,* 8:181, H.N. 6715.
77. al-Baghawi, al-Husayn b. Masud, *Sharḥ al-Sunnah,* 9: 358.
78. Ibn Taymiyyah, *al-Ḥisbah wa Mas'ūliyyah al-Ḥukūmah al-Islāmiyah* or *al-Ḥisbah fi'l-Islām,* p. 42.
79. Dihlawi, *Ḥujjat* 2:147.
80. Dihlawi, *Ḥujjat,* 2:142–46, and *Al-Budūr al-Bāzighah,* pp. 82–4.
81. Dihlawi, *Ḥujjat* 2:143.
82. Ibid., 2: 144.
83. Dihlawi, *al-Budūr,* p. 82.
84. Ibid., p. 83.
85. Ibid. *Hujjat,* 2: 146.
86. It is the middle part of the Qur'anic verse *al-Tawba* 8:75.
87. Dihlawi, *Hujjat,* 2: 118.
88. Ibid., 2: 146.
89. Ibid., 1: 80; 2: 103.
90. Dihlawi, *al-Budūr,* p. 85.
91. Ibid. pp. 85–6.
92. Ibid. p. 86.
93. Ibid., p. 86.
94. Ibid. pp. 87–8.
95. Ibid. p. 88.
96. Ibid. p. 89.
97. Leshem, 'What Did the Ancient Greeks Mean by *Oikonomia?*' p. 225.

98. For details, refer to Islahi, Abdul Azim, *History of Islamic Economic Thought*, pp. 61–3.
99. Before Shah Wali-Allah, the fourteenth century Muslim scholar Ibn Khaldun (d. 808/1406) also used the term *adāb al-maʿāsh* to discuss economic matters.
100. Chapra notes this with reference to Mawdudi, *Pardah* pp. 92–3.
101. Prof Siddiqi wrote this to Abbas Mirakhor on 31 August 2012, which the former forwarded to Islahi.

6

Shah Wali-Allah on Money and Interest

Money is the most important instrument of economics. Geoffrey Crowther who authored the famous textbook *An Outline of Money* observes that money is 'one of the most fundamental of all man's inventions'. According to him: 'Every branch of knowledge has its fundamental discovery. In economics, in the whole commercial side of Man's social existence, money is the essential invention on which all the rest is based.'[1] This is clear from the fact that right from the time of Greek philosophers to Muslim scholars, economists have discussed money in all ages. Shah Wali-Allah's reflections on various aspects of money are considerable.

6.1 Money as seen by the Greek philosophers

Money evolved as a convention only. No society could exist without the exchange of goods, no exchange could effectively take place without equivalence, and no equivalence could be determined without a common measure—money. Since, in most cases, Shah Wali-Allah agrees with the thought of Greek philosophers and past Muslim scholars, in addition to offering some new insights, it is worthwhile to briefly discuss the development of money in Greek and Islamic traditions before we study his ideas on the subject.

In his treatise on *tadbīr al-manzil,* '[B]ersis'[2] lists money as the first thing through which man's administration of the household could be completed.[3] Stating the need for money, the Greek philosopher remarks that man needs food grown in the field for his survival. He also needs animal products; these products needing a number of industries to reach their final forms.[4] Man has to manage his food, process it and prepare it. He also needs various industries which are interdependent. Since no single person can master all industries, one has to concentrate on one industry and get the product of other industries through exchange. The difficulties of the barter exchange led humankind to invent money—a measure of value and a medium of exchange.[5] Gold, silver and copper were considered the best substance for coinage due to their particular qualities.[6]

6.2 Money in the early period of Islam

In the early period of Islam during the Prophet's time, different types of Sassanid silver coins and Roman gold coins were used by Muslims. The Prophet, may Allah bless him and give him peace, accepted the existing system and did not issue his own money. His first caliph, Abu Bakr, also followed the same pattern. It is commonly reported that the Umayyad caliph Abd al-Malik ibn Marwan (d. 86/705) was the first to mint dirham. However, al-Maqrizi states that the second caliph Umar and his successors Uthman and Mu`awiyah, respectively, issued dirhams and dinars.[7] And then came the time of Abd-Allah ibn al-Zubayr (d. 73/692) and his brother Mus`ab (d. 72/691) to mint coins. Perhaps credit goes to Abd al-Malik for issuing standardized dirhams and dinars used in the calculation of zakah.[8] However, we do not find much discussion about the nature and functions of money among Muslim scholars in the early period of Islam. In later centuries, the Arabic translation of Greek ideas influenced the Muslim philosophers who generally accepted Greek ideas about money with added comments and explanations.

6.2.1 A survey of Muslim scholars' views on money

It is worthwhile at the outset to present Muslim scholars' views on money by briefly surveying their major ideas. This will help us appreciate Shah Wali-Allah's contribution to the subject, as born in the twelfth/eighteenth century, he must have benefitted from the intellectual heritage of Islam.

Qudamah ibn Ja'far[9], an earlier scholar, states that money has been invented out of the human need to exchange goods with each other and specialization in one's profession. He has visualized various difficulties of the barter exchange, termed by modern economists as the non-proportionality of exchangeable objects, indivisibility of goods, absence of a common measure of value, problem of double coincidence of wants, etc. This led people to use gold as a common denominator for transactions due to its qualities like durability, easy minting and availability in a reasonable quantity.[10] As noted above, these elements existed in Arabic translations of Greek ideas.

According to Miskawayh,[11] another scholar who always tried to synthesize between Aristotle's views and Islamic teachings on ethics, money measures the value of various goods and services, establishing equality between them which is not possible in direct exchange without the medium of money.[12] He considers gold, in its capacity of money, as 'the standard for all and everything'. It is the best store of value because 'he who sells many things and picks up gold in exchange for the articles and as a substitute for all of them, has done the right thing, since he can get thereby whatever he wishes and whenever he wishes.'[13] The suitability of gold and silver to work as money has also been emphasized by many later scholars. For example, in the opinion of Ibn Khaldun gold and silver are created to be used as money and perform the function of the medium of exchange, measure and store of value. 'All other things are subject to market fluctuations from which gold and silver are exempt. They are the basis of profit, property and treasure.'[14]

The following passage of al-Ghazali notes that:

> Various forms and types of goods need a medium which could rule justly and determine their value or worth according to

> their place in exchange. When their place and grades are ascertained, it is then possible to distinguish which one is equal to which other and which is not. Thus, Almighty Allah created dinars and dirhams (gold and silver coins) as two rulers and medium of exchange for all goods, and the value of goods is measured through them, so it is said a camel is, say, equal to 100 dinars and this much quantity of saffron is worth 100 dinars. Since each of them is equal to a given amount, the two quantities are equal to each other. This equality of worth or value becomes conveniently possible through these two types of money only because they are not needed for themselves.[15]

Ibn Rushd introduced Aristotle's definition of *nomisma* (the Greek word for money) and his concept of money as a common measure 'between separate things, so that equality prevails in business between things where it is difficult to measure equality in existence.' Ibn Rushd, like his many predecessors, reiterates that money is needed because of the difficulty of transacting business in a barter economy. In this way he emphasizes the first and most obvious function of money—the medium of exchange.[16] According to Grice-Hutchinson, 'Averroes's original contribution to theory is very small. Yet he is of importance in the history of economic thought owing to the part he played in the transmission of Greek economics to the Christian West.'[17] In a comment on al-Dawwani's views on money,[18] Spengler observes that 'al-Dawani also developed the equality maintaining role of money .... Money in its capacity as unit of account intermediated as a common denominator between producers of unlike goods and thereby facilitated their inter-exchange ... '[19]

By comparing the views of three philosophers—Miskawayh, Ibn Rushd and al-Dawwani, we find that they strictly based their ideas about money on the Greek philosopher Aristotle, touching the same aspects of money that he did. But the other scholars, like al-Ghazali, Ibn Taymiyyah, and Shah Wali-Allah, as we will see below, expanded their thinking on the subject much beyond the philosophical ideas to include most of the functions of money and related issues.

6.3 Difficulties of the barter system

To visualize the vital role of money in our life and how it facilitates our transactions, al-Ghazali discusses the difficulties of the barter system which humankind experienced in the pre-monetary period. He clearly understood and pointed out the three major difficulties of the barter system:

(a) Lack of a measure of value in terms of which goods and services may be expressed.
(b) Indivisibility of most goods required for exchange.
(c) The problem of ensuring double coincidence of wants.

Following is an account of these difficulties:

Since the same people do not produce and possess everything they need, voluntary exchange is a natural phenomenon. However, this requires that the value of goods being exchanged must somehow be clearly known and understood. Although some goods may be directly exchanged for others, many are so peculiar in their use and characteristics that value of one cannot be easily expressed in terms of another. Al-Ghazali mentions several examples, such as exchange of a house with cloth, flour with a donkey or camel with saffron, in each case, the indivisibility problem arises because one item is very large while the other is very small and the large goods could not be divided into small pieces for exchange with the small quantities of the other. 'A camel owner cannot exchange his whole camel for a quantity of saffron.' For completion of barter exchange, it is necessary that the two transacting parties must be in need of the good of each other. But this is also not always possible. 'There can be a problem if the cloth owner needs food, and the food-owner does not want cloth, he wants cattle.'[20]

Shah Wali-Allah agrees with al-Ghazali in that the division of labour and specialization lead to the need for exchange, which can be easily done through an object used as a medium. This ultimately led to the invention of money. He says:

> When needs become numerous and excellence is sought in them, and these (needs) are aesthetic and emotional, it becomes

> impractical for everyone to undertake them. Some found food in excess of their needs but did not find water, and others had extra water but no food. Thus each desired what another had, so exchanging appeared to be the only solution. This exchange arose due to necessity, so that they were forced to agree among themselves that each one would accept to take care of one need, and achieve mastery in it and make efforts to attain proficiency in the use of its tools, and to make it a means for achieving further needs through the medium of exchange (money), and this became a practice on which they agreed.[21]

Thus, the division of labour and the need for exchange led humankind to the invention of money. Due to certain qualities of gold and silver, these precious metals were chosen as money. Shah Wali-Allah observes:

> Since many people would desire a certain thing or dislike a certain thing, and could not find anyone to trade in it in that case, they were forced to provide a way to commission things and have them prepared in advance and they were forced to agree to set the convention of mineral substances which would last a long time as a means of exchange among them. The most suitable among these were gold and silver due to their small size, their homogeneity, their greatly beneficial effect on the human body, and since they could be used for adornment, so these two became the natural currency while other things were given conventional monetary values.[22]

6.4 Functions of money

Elsewhere we have discussed that money performs different functions like measuring value, functioning as a medium of exchange, store of value, and a standard of deferred payments. In the opinion of many economists, its function as a medium of exchange is the most important of all.[23] To quote Crowther, 'Money must serve as a measure of value, as a medium of exchange, and as a store of wealth. Of these three functions, the second is the most essential ... Money must be something that performs all three functions, and pre-eminently the function of being a medium of exchange.'[24] A.C.L. Day has also emphasized the same point as he says, 'The most important use of money is in settling by far the larger part of transactions between different individuals or organisations in modern economies.'[25]

Al-Ghazali fully emphasized the functions of money as a medium of exchange and as a measure of value. Money is used in the payment of all goods and debts. As far as its function as a store of value is concerned, he says, 'When one owns money, one owns about everything, not like the one who owns cloth, as he owns cloth and nothing else.'[26]

There is no doubt, Al-Ghazali's exposition is as lucid as we find in a typical contemporary textbook. On another occasion we have analyzed this in detail.[27] The problems of barter exchange and the function of money as a medium of exchange, unit of account and store of value, have also been discussed by al-Dimashqi.[28]

As far as Shah Wali-Allah is concerned, he emphasizes the function of money as 'the medium of exchange' only.[29] However, in his work *Al-Budūr al-Bāzighah* he says that 'the purpose of exchange is to acquire a particular thing or to get the two substances of money (*naqdayn*) which represent the acquisition of all other things taken together'.[30] This seems to be a reference to the function of money as a store of value. He further observes: 'The purpose of exchange is to acquire a particular thing or to get the two substances of money (*ḥajarayn*) which represent the acquisition of all other things taken together.'[31] This is similar to al-Ghazali's statement noted above: 'When one owns money, one owns about everything.'

6.5 The use of gold and silver as money?

According to Schumpeter, the origin of the idea that precious metals are created to serve as money goes back to Greek philosophers.[32] Most of the Muslim scholars, as seen above, also held the same opinion. However, Ibn Taymiyyah has a different view. As against al-Ghazali, Ibn Khaldun and many other Muslim scholars, including Shah Wali-Allah, Ibn Taymiyyah regards it as a matter of convention. He says, 'Gold and silver coins have no natural or Sharīʿah specification. They depend on people, their custom and social consensus'[33] so that any commodity could serve as money. He writes that: 'Even the coins (token money) in circulation will rule as precious metals in measuring the value of goods.'[34]

As we noted elsewhere:[35] 'Muslim leaders and scholars had the perception of token money as early as the 1st/7th Century. Caliph Umar (d. 23/644) once intended to issue money of camel skin but he refrained because some of his close people expressed apprehension that this might adversely affect the growth of camel stocks.[36] Perhaps based on this report, Imam Malik (d. 179/795) says that 'if people accept skins as money, he would not like their exchange for gold and silver with deferred delivery' as it may lead to usurious practices.[37] It may be noted that the exchange of gold for gold and silver for silver with inequality in terms of quantity and time of delivery differences has been prohibited because it is considered as *ribā* as discussed below. Another great scholar Ahmad ibn Hanbal (d. 241/855) is reported to have said that if people decide something as money (other than gold and silver), it would be quite acceptable.[38]

Shah Wali-Allah seems to have an opinion in between the two. In his book *Al-Budūr al-Bāzighah*, he says that money should not necessarily have its own utility. The only condition is that it should be accepted in exchange.[39] It may be noted that 'common acceptance' is the essential element of the definition of money. This means it is not necessary for an object used as money to be a valuable thing, to have an intrinsic value of its own. However, in *Ḥujjat Allāh al-Bālighah*, Shah Wali-Allah mentions that 'gold and silver are the most suitable metals used for money because they are easily divisible into small pieces. Furthermore, their different units enjoy similarity, and they are of *great benefit to the human physique and may be used for adornment*. Thus, they are money by nature while other materials may be treated as money by convention.'[40] In this way he went against al-Ghazali and many others who said that money should not have its own use. While regarding it as 'money by convention', he seems to have an opinion similar to Ibn Taymiyyah.

6.6 Interest—an ill-use of money

A topic very closely related to money is interest. It is generally accepted that money was invented to serve as a measure, medium of exchange of goods and services, and to ensure a just measure of values. It was never desired for itself. However, the practice of lending money on interest made the money something desired for itself and a source of injustice and exploitation. Therefore, interest has been very strictly prohibited in Islam, so much so that the question of why interest arises and how its rates are determined became irrelevant to Muslim scholars. Therefore, they never discussed it.[41] They only tried to visualize its negative effects and exploitative nature.[42] They never made a distinction between interest on consumption loan and interest on production loan. The imaginary time value of money, in lending and borrowing, is not acceptable to them. 'The possibility of the lender investing his money and earning profit is a matter of conjecture; it may or may not materialize. So to demand a higher amount over and above the sum lent, on that conjectural basis is a kind of injustice and exploitation.'[43]

The provision of profit sharing (*muḍārabah*) has been considered by Muslim scholars as the alternative to interest for running the business. It has been emphasized by Shah Wali-Allah as well.[44] Muslim scholars agree that under *muḍārabah* partnership no one can get a guaranteed profit irrespective of the outcome of the business. Profit is to be shared with a predetermined ratio, not on a percentage to be earned on the capital supplied. In the case of loss, the capital owner bears the capital loss while the working partner bears the loss of his labour, that is, the labour goes 'unrewarded'. Of course, he is held responsible if the loss occurred due to negligence of the working partner (*muḍārib*). It may be noted that Muslim scholars prescribed the *muḍārabah* provision as the way to run interest-free banking. Siddiqi, in his treatise *Rationales of Islamic Banking* argues that 'profit-sharing banking system will not only save the society from the evil consequences of interest based banking, it will serve the good of society by securing justice, effecting a better distribution of income, and contributing towards greater stability and peace.'[45]

Before we discuss Shah Wali-Allah's views on interest proper or interest on lending money (*ribā al-Qur'an*), which is prohibited by clear text of the Qur'an, we would like to first deal with a particular type of interest—*ribā al-faḍl* and *ribā al-nasī'ah*. This may be referred to as *ribā al-ḥadīth* as its prohibition is known from the traditions of the Prophet, may Allah bless him and give him peace.

6.6.1 *Ribā al-faḍl* and *ribā al-nasī'ah*

A unique contribution of Islam to economic thought is that it envisaged the occurrence of interest in certain cases of barter that involve exchanges unequal by way of quantity or time of delivery termed as *ribā al-faḍl* and *ribā al-nasī'ah*, respectively.[46] The prohibition is based on a group of traditions that report the Prophet saying that 'Gold for gold, silver for silver, wheat for wheat, barley for barley, dates for dates and salt for salt be exchanged, like for like, equal for equal and hand to hand; one who demanded extra or paid extra, indulged in *ribā*.[47] The tradition further reports: '...When these commodities differ, then sell them as you like [with the difference of quantity] provided that the exchange is hand to hand [i.e. the transfer of ownership takes place at once].'

Scholars have different opinions regarding the nature and purpose of this prohibition. Al-Ghazali relates this prohibition with the violation of the nature and functions of money.[48] Since Shah Wali-Allah is much influenced by al-Ghazali on this issue, it seems worthwhile to give an account of the latter's view on *ribā al-faḍl* and *ribā al-nasī'ah* in his own words. He says:

'One who practices interest on dirhams and dinars is denying the bounty of Allah and is a transgressor, for these coins are created for other purposes and are not needed for themselves. When someone is trading in dirhams and dinars themselves, he is making them as his goal, which is contrary to their objectives. Money is not created to earn money, and doing so is a transgression... The two kinds of money are means to acquire other things; they are not meant for themselves. If a person is permitted to sell (or exchange) money with money, then such transactions will become his goal, and as a result money will be imprisoned and hoarded like anything. Imprisonment of the ruler or a postman is a transgression, for they are then prevented from performing their functions; same is the case with money. It is a transgression. If it is asked why one of the two kinds of money is permitted to be exchanged for the other and why exchanging dirham is permitted with the same amount of it? Then, you should know that the two kinds of money are different from each other in being means of obtaining something else. Sometimes one of them is more useful in being because it is in larger quantity, like dirham which is disbursed on different needs in smaller units. If this exchange is forbidden, then their special purpose, i.e. their use as means of getting other things is destroyed. As for selling dirhams with the same amount of dirhams is concerned, it is allowed, but no rational person or trader will do so, for, they are both the same. It is just like doing something in vain—putting a dirham on the ground and then picking it up again. There is no need to prohibit such exchange... This exchange may be done if one dirham is better quality than another. But, this is also not likely because one who has better quality will not (knowingly) accept equal but inferior quality of the other. So the transaction could not happen. The intention from this exchange may be to obtain a greater amount of the inferior one. Of course, this is what we oppose and affirm that good and bad quality dirhams are both equal, for good and bad should be seen only about those things which are needed for themselves. And it is not quite proper to examine the minute differences in quality of things—such as dirhams and dinars—which are not needed for themselves. And, it is a transgressor who mints coins with differences in quality (i.e. counterfeits) and thus makes them desirable for their own sake; that must not happen.'[49]

He applies the same reasoning in the case of exchanging foodstuffs. Foodstuffs are meant for nutrition. A barter exchange of the same commodity will hinder its use for nutrition and result in hoarding. This requires that such an exchange should be prohibited so that a person must sell food with money, and it may reach one who actually needs it. This exchange is allowed with the condition of simultaneous payment if the commodities are different, as the two commodities will have different purposes. In all these exchanges, no consideration of qualities is made to curb the luxury-seeking mentality of man. He says:

Similar is the position of foodstuffs. They are created to be used as nutrition so they should not be misused. If exchange within them is freely allowed it will result into their longer stay in hands and delay their use as nutrition for which they are created. Foodstuffs are created by Allah to be eaten which is a dire need. This requires that they should go from the hands of that who does not need them to one who needs them. Only that person will do a transaction on food who does not need it. Because if a person has food why does he not eat it if he is in need of that; why is he using it as a trade commodity? If he wants to make it a trade commodity, he should sell it to that who needs it with something other than the same foods. If someone is buying with exactly same food, he is also not in need of it, this is the reason that *Shari'ah* cursed the hoarder. Of course, a seller of barley with dates is having excuse because one of them cannot work for the other. A seller of one *ṣā'* (a measure = 2.176 kg) of wheat with the same does not have an excuse but he is doing something in vain, so he does not need prohibition. Such a thing will be done only if one of the amounts is a better quality but in this case, the owner of better quality will not be ready to do it. One unit of a good can be exchanged with the two inferior of that, but since the foodstuffs are necessities and good and inferior both fulfil the necessity while they differ only in being luxuries, the *Shari'ah* has rejected the consideration of luxury in that which is basic and necessary thing.[50]

As we will see below, Shah Wali-Allah also prescribes the reason behind the prohibition of this type of exchange as to keep in check people's inclination towards an excessive pursuit of luxurious living and materialistic attitudes.

6.6.2 Shah Wali-Allah on *ribā al-faḍl* and *ribā al-nasī'ah*

Shah Wali-Allah considered interest in lending as the actual form of *ribā* (*al-ḥaqīqī*). He also took note of barter exchange with inequality in terms of quantity or time of delivery, termed as *ribā al-faḍl* and *ribā al-nasī'ah* in the Shariah. He regarded them as interest in similitude (*maḥmūl 'alayh*). Here the word *ribā* is used because of the similarity between the two and also to express the perversity of such a transaction. Additionally, due to the frequent use of the word for this kind of transaction, it became established in this sense as well.[51] Shah Wali-Allah's division of interest in lending as the actual form of *ribā* (*al-ḥaqīqī*) and interest in barter exchange as interest in similitude (*maḥmūl 'alayh*) is similar to Ibn al-Qayyim's division of interest into two categories—open (*jalī*) and disguised (*khafī*). The disguised interest or *ribā al-khafī* is *ribā al-faḍl* which is prohibited to stop it from becoming an aid to interest. The open interest is the same as an increment on debts which people used to offer in the pre-Islamic period.[52]

As noted above, like al-Ghazali, Shah Wali-Allah holds that the reason for the prohibition of *ribā al-faḍl* is to restrain people's inclination towards an excessive pursuit of luxurious living and materialistic attitudes, because the exchange of a similar quality of the same good may not satisfy one's thirst for obtaining a better quality of the same good.[53] This argument, however, does not seem very convincing—no one would be ready to part with, for example, a higher quality of wheat for an inferior one. Here Ibn al-Qayyim's argument is more convincing. According to him, the prohibition of *ribā al-faḍl* is to prevent the practice from being instrumental to interest. Had the simultaneous payment not been provided along with equality in quantity, the difference in the period of payment might lead to differences in quantity according to the time.[54]

Jurists have differed over the question as to whether the restriction is confined to the six aforementioned commodities or whether there are fundamental principles involved in the prohibition in which case it would apply wherever those principles do. Shah Wali-Allah was of the opinion that the prohibition is based on a certain cause (*'illah*) and any commodities exchanged in an analogous situation are to be included in the prohibition. In his opinion, the most appropriate reason for prohibition in the case of the two precious metals is *thamaniyyah* (their capacity for use as a standard of value or medium of exchange), while with the four remaining commodities is their capacity of being preservable food items (*muqtāt muddakhar*). The reason for the ascertainment of these two causes is the fact that they have been given high importance in the Shariah in many cases.[55]

Shah Wali-Allah elucidated the reason for making it obligatory to take possession of items and payment in the same meeting: the need for food and money is the most pressing and urgent need and one can benefit from them only after consuming and spending on them respectively. It would be a matter of great dispute if one of them were to remain in credit while the other suffered a loss. Thus, to prevent such an occurrence, it has been made compulsory that the two parties must not leave without taking possession and nothing is left in credit. The same reason is considered in the prohibition of the sale of foodstuffs before taking full possession and forbidding the two parties from departing while anything remaining is in credit if gold is collected in place of silver. He further said: 'If money (gold and silver) is on the one side and food is on the other side, in this situation money should be spent first as it is the means to acquire something. In another situation, when both sides are money or foodstuff (that is, exchange of money for money or grain for grain), in this situation it would be arbitrary to ask only one of them to pay on the spot. If none is paying on the spot, it would become a sale of deferred for deferred, which is prohibited. It is also possible that the other party may deny the payment. Thus, it is a requirement of justice and for the prevention of dispute that both are enjoined to take possession before separation.'[56] Thus, to Shah Wali-Allah the prohibition of such an exchange is a preventive measure, not something prohibited for its own sake. It may be noted that Ibn Taymiyyah and Ibn al-Qayyim, the two great scholars of Islam, also regarded *ribā al-faḍl* and *ribā al-nasi'ah* as precautionary measures.[57]

6.7 *Ribā* (interest)

As for interest (*ribā*), Shah Wali-Allah considered it as one of those undesirable practices that led to enmity and exploitation in the pre-Islamic period, hence its prohibition in Islam. He stated that in those days one used to lend money to someone on the condition of its return with an extra amount. Failing that, the person lending would make the total the original amount and the addition the principal and stipulate further increase over the original and so on. In this way, the sum used to grow larger and larger. Therefore, this was abolished in Islam, and only the demand for original capital was sanctioned.[58] Thus, Shah Wali-Allah removed the doubts raised by some contemporary writers whereby in the pre-Islamic period there was initially no interest on loans, interest was only imposed when the borrower failed to return the amount. Based on this, such writers try to legalize interest initially, stipulated by 'mutual consent'.

To Shah Wali-Allah, the needy borrower's consent to pay interest is a pseudo-consent. Helplessly, he agrees to a condition which he can hardly fulfil.[59] On another occasion, he observed that the extra income from a loan with a condition to return more or better than what is lent is a wrongful, invalid earning as the majority of such borrowers are poor and helpless people who are unable to repay on the due date. Thus, the amount becomes doubled and quadrupled and they never get rid of it. This leads to widespread problems and conflict. If this kind of earning is allowed, people will depend upon it rather than invest in agriculture and industries, which are basic sources of living.[60] This is an argument reminiscent of al-Razi,[61] who wrote in his famous commentary on the Qur'an that interest draws capital-owners away from enterprise. This is so because when the money-lender has the possibility to earn more money in cash or deferred payments, he will shun other economic activities and will never be ready to enter trade, commerce or industries involving risk and hard labour.

6.8 Is prohibition of interest exclusive to the poor?

> In his work *Al-Budūr al-Bāzighah* ,[62] Shah Wali-Allah said 'the *ribā* is prohibited which is an extra earning from a person that enters into contract while he is helpless and needy (*'ind iḍṭirār al-'āqid wa iḥtiyājihi*). Because of his need, he agrees to pay an excess amount to a person on his loan, which he finds very difficult to repay later'. In the same work, he remarked: 'It is their (money-lenders') habit to lend money to a needy person and stipulate an extra amount if he is unable to repay on a particular date. Since he is poor, mostly he is unable to return the amount. They (lenders) press their demand and force him so he accepts an obligation to an increase over it to a similar amount. This continues indefinitely. They quarrel and fight and the borrower never gets rid of this ordeal. Therefore, this *ribā* is forbidden.

> If the borrower has money, he is to return the principal. If he has nothing, he will be given time till it is easy for him to repay or it may be remitted by way of charity.'[63]

On the basis of the preceding two quotations, one may think that Shah Wali-Allah considered forbidden *ribā* only that which is charged from a poor and helpless borrower. The fact is that he presented an existing situation and tried to visualize a painful and exploitative practice in a *ribā*-based society. This is similar to the Qur'anic qualifications of *ribā* as *aḍ'āf-muḍā'afah* (doubling and quadrupling),[64] which occurred in most cases. This does not mean that simple interest or one charged from the prosperous borrower is permissible. Had it been so, it would have been made explicit. In fact, to Shah Wali-Allah all kinds of interest are completely prohibited, as is clear from the following section.

6.8.1 A misrepresentation of Shah Wali-Allah's view on *ribā*

Athar Abbas Rizvi in his work *Shah Wali-Allah and His Time* writes: 'Besides religious grounds, Shah Wali-Allah condemned usury on economic grounds. He pleaded that the lust to become rich through usury undermined interest in agriculture, crafts and other productive professions. People were tempted to enrich themselves by realizing high rates of compound interest. To Shah Wali-Allah this was an extremely unhealthy means of earning money. In pre-Islamic Arabia, he wrote, unending enmity and wars between different tribes and clans due to usury prompted the Qur'an to make it illegal. However, the Shah did not totally forbid the taking or giving of loans on interest, but asserted that it was the duty of the authority enforcing the *shari'a* to set a limit to the interest rate.'[65] Rizvi misunderstood Shah Wali-Allah's statement and attributed to him something incorrect and baseless. This blunder came about due to his misunderstanding of the term *Shāri'* (i.e. the Lawgiver, Almighty Allah), which he translated as 'authority enforcing the Shariah'. After describing the evils of gambling and *ribā*, Shah Wali-Allah observed that 'it is upon the *Shāri'* (Lawgiver) to fix a limit below which it may be permitted and above it to be prohibited, or stop it altogether. Gambling and interest were common among the Arabian people, which resulted in great disputes and wars. Since *a little of them leads to a lot of them* [emphasis added], it would have been the most correct and right step to observe their bad and corrupt aspects and forbid the two completely (*fa yunhā 'an-humā bi'l-kulliyyah*)'.[66] This quotation is clear proof that Shah Wali-Allah believed in the total prohibition of interest. He never said that 'it was the duty of the authority enforcing the Shariah to set a limit to the interest rate', which is something that Rizvi wants his readers to believe.

Notes and References

1. Crowther, *An Outline of Money*, p. 4.
2. It is said that [B]ersis (Bryson) was a Greek philosopher whose personality was 'unidentified' and 'whose work was unknown to the West' (Spengler, 'Economic Thought of Islam: Ibn Khaldun', p. 276 footnote). It may be noted that there is no mention of Bryson in Schumpeter's encyclopedic work *History of Economics Analysis*, which presents minute details of the history of the intellectual efforts 'from the earliest discernible beginning' (Schumpeter, *History of Economic Analysis*, p. 3). Bryson's name came from an Arabic translation of an unknown manuscript entitled *Kitāb Tadbīr al-Manzil* (The Book of Household Management). Its author and the translator both are obscure. There is no consensus on the correct form of his name. It is guessed to be a Latin or Greek name such as 'Barses', 'Brasius', 'Beresius', 'Bersius', 'Thrasius', 'Tarasius', 'Teresius', 'Neresius', 'Nerses', 'Narcissus', etc. The reason for these differences is the fact that in the manuscript, his name is written as سيسرب in which the first Arabic letter is blank, without the dor or *nuqṭah* (Shaykhu, *Kitāb Tadbīr al-Manzil*, in *al-Mashriq* 19/3, p. 161). Furthermore, at the end of the manuscript, his name is written as سلورب, again without any dot. We do not know how they changed it to 'Bryson'.
3. Shaykhu, *Kitāb Tadbīr al-Manzil*, 19/3 (*al-Mashriq*): 162.
4. Ibid., p. 163.
5. Ibid., p. 164.
6. Ibid., p. 165.
7. al-Maqrizi, *Shudhur al-'Uqud*, pp. 7–8.
8. Ibid., pp. 10–13.

9. Qudamah bin Ja'far (250–320/864–932) converted from Christianity to Islam during the period of caliph al-Muktafi Bi'llah (r. 289–295/902–908), and held the position of finance secretary in the caliphal administration in Baghdad. The title of his work is *Kitāb al-Kharāj wa Ṣinā'at al-Kitābah*. Shemesh translated part of the book in his *Taxation in Islam*, vol. II Leiden, E.J. Brill, 1965. The book is a compendium of positive law, marked by the applied aspect.
10. Ibn Ja'far, Qudamah, *al-Kharaj wa Sina`at al-Kitabah*, p. 434.
11. Ahmad b. Muhammad Miskawayh (320–421/932–1030) was a philosopher and historian who practiced the two disciplines with great competence. Translation of his work on history *Tajārib al-Umam* (Experiences of Nations) is in seven volumes published from London in 1920–21. As a philosopher Miskawayh is distinguished by the central importance he attached to ethics. His work *Tahdhīb al-Akhlāq* presents Greek, Persian and Arab and Muslim traditions. He had a profound impact on al-Ghazali, Nasir al-Dīn al-Tusi and Jalal al-Dīn al-Dawwani (also written as Dawani, and in Persian, Davani).
12. Miskawayh, *Tahdhib al-Akhlaq*, p. 110.
13. Miskawayh, *Risalah fi Mahiyat al-`Adl*, edited and translated by M. S. Khan, p. 29.
14. Rosenthal, *Muqaddimah of Ibn Khaldun*, 2: 274, 285, 313.
15. al-Ghazali, Abu Hamid, *Ihyā' 'Ulūm al-Dīn*, 4: 91.
16. Grice-Hutchinson, *Early Economic Thought in Spain, 1177-1740*, p. 70. She quotes Rosenthal's *Averroes' Commentary on Plato's Republic.*
17. Ibid. pp. 70–74. Since Ibn Rushd's original commentary, in Arabic, on the Greek philosopher is lost, our information of his views is based on secondary sources.
18. Muhammad b. As'ad Jalal al-Dīn al-Dawwani (830–-907/1427–1501) was born at Dawwan (or *Davan* in Persian), a village near Kazirun in the southwest of the Iranian plateau. He died in Shiraz shortly after the founding of the Safavid dynasty, but before Shah Isma'il I captured the province of Fars. He was a leading philosopher, theologian, jurist and poet of fifteenth-century Iran. He wrote numerous commentaries on well-known works of philosophical and mystical literature in both Arabic and Persian. Of his Persian works, the best-known is his edition of Nasir al-Dīn al-Tusi's *Akhlāq-i-Nāṣirī* which was itself a translation of *Kitāb al-Ṭahārah* of Miskawayh, entitled *Lawāmi' al-Ishrāq fī Makārim al-Akhlāq* or more briefly *Akhlāq-i-Jalālī*, translated , translated in London, 1839,

by W.T. Thompson under the title 'Practical Philosophy of the Muhammedan People'.

19. Spengler, Economic Thought of Islam: Ibn Khaldun', *Comparative Studies in Society and History*, (1964) 6: 281.
20. al-Ghazali, *Ihya'*, 4: 91.
21. Dihlawi, *Ḥujjat*,1: 43.
22. Ibid.
23. Islahi, *Economic Concepts of Ibn Taimiyah*, p. 139.
24. Crowther, *An Outline of Money*, p. 20.
25. Day, *Outline of Monetary Economics*, p. 1.
26. al-Ghazali, *Ihya'*, 4: 91.
27. Islahi, 'An Analytical Analysis of Al-Ghazali's Thought on Money and Interest', pp. 2-4.
28. al-Dimashqi, *al-Ishārah ilā Maḥāsin al-Tijārah*, p. 21. Abu'l-Faḍl Ja'far b. Ali al-Dimashqi lived in Syria during the sixth/twelfth century, according to another estimate during the fifth/eleventh century. His life details are not known. From his work it appears that he was a practicing businessman. The title of his work is *al-Ishārah ila Maḥāsin al-Tijārah* (The Guide to the Virtues of Trade).
29. Dihlawi, *Ḥujjat*, 1: 43.
30. Dihlawi, *al-Budūr al-Bāzighah*, p. 89.
31. Ibid. p. 86.
32. Schumpeter, *History of Economic Analysis*, p. 62.
33. Ibn Taymiyyah, MFS, 19: 250, 251, 248–249.
34. Ibid., 29: 469.
35. Islahi, *Muslim Economic Thinking and Institutions in the 10th AH/ 16th AD Century*, p. 99.
36. al-Baladhuri, *Futūḥ al-Buldān*, p. 456.
37. Malik b. Anas, *al-Mudawwant al-Kubrā*, 3: 90–91.
38. Ibn Qudamah, *al-Mughnī*, 4: 176.
39. Dihlawi, *al-Budur*, p. 86.
40. Dihlawi, *Ḥujjat*, 1: p. 43.
41. Islahi, *History of Islamic Economic Thought*, p. 40.
42. cf. Ibn Taymiyyah, MFS, 29: 419, 455; al-Razi, *al-Tafsīr al-Kabīr*, 5: 92; Dihlawi, *Hujjat*, 1: 106.
43. al-Razi, *al-Tafsīr*, 5: 92.
44. Dihlawi, *Ḥujjat*, 2:115.
45. Siddiqi, *Rationales of Islamic Banking*, p. 5.
46. Islahi, *Economic Concepts of Ibn Taimiyah*, p, 131.
47. Muslim, *al-Jāmi' al-Ṣaḥīḥ*, 5: 44, Ḥadith number 4148.
48. al-Ghazali, *Ihya'*, 4: 192–93.
49. Ibid., 4: 192.

50. Ibid., 4: 192–93.
51. Dihlawi, *Hujjat,* 2:107.
52. Ibn al-Qayyim, *I'lām al-Muwaqqi'in,* 2: 135.
53. Dihlawi, *Hujjat,* 2:107.
54. cf. Ibn al-Qayyim, *I'lām,* 2: 130.
55. Dihlawi, *Hujjat,* 2: p. 107.
56. Ibid. pp. 107–108.
57. Islahi, *Economic Concepts of Ibn Taimiyah,* pp. 131–32.
58. Dihlawi, *Hujjat* 1: 106.
59. Ibid., 2: 103.
60. Ibid., 2: 106.
61. al-Razi, *al-Tafsīr,* 5: p. 92.
62. Dihlawi, *al-Budūr,* p. 89.
63. Ibid. p. 297.
64. *Al 'Imran,* 3:130.
65. Rizvi in his work *Shah Wali-Allah and His Time,* p. 315.
66. Dihlawi, *Hujjat* 2: 106.

7

Public Finance

7.1 Muslim thinkers on public finance

One of the distinguishing features of Islamic economics is that the subject of public finance was first to attract the attention of Muslim thinkers, making an appearance in several works in the early period of Islam.[1] This was but natural in the wake of the expanding territory of the Islamic state, the availability of new sources of income, confronting new heads of expenditure, and facing other socio-economic challenges. Works on taxation in Islam (*Kitāb al-Kharāj*) and public finance (*Kitāb al-Amwāl*) first appeared in the second/eighth century, and within the next few centuries more than two dozen treatises were written. Shemesh provides, from various sources, a list of twenty-one works on taxation written during the early centuries of Islam.[2] However, most of these works were lost. The books that could have survived include those of Abu Yusuf, al-Qurashi,[3] Abu Ubayd,[4] Ibn Zanjawayh,[5] al-Dawudi,[6] Ibn Rajab,[7] and portions of Qudamah ibn Ja'far and al-Makhzumi.[8] In addition to exclusive works on the subject, issues of public revenue and expenditure constituted parts of juristic and political writings. For example, al-Ghazali wrote a special treatise on the role of the state and the functions of the rulers entitled *Naṣīḥat al-Mulūk* (Book of Counsel for Kings). In this volume and elsewhere, he provides considerable discussion on the subject of public finance as well—namely, sources of revenue, including public borrowing, and areas of public functions and expenditures. Ibn Taymiyyah wrote *al-Siyāsah al-Shar`iyyah* at the request of the Mamluk Sultan Nasir ibn Qalawun (d. 742/1341) to use it as a guide. The work gives an account of the heads of revenue and expenditure of an Islamic government. Ibn Taymiyyah's contribution to the theory of public finance is enormous, which we have discussed elsewhere in detail.[9]

It may be noted that al-Ghazali's discourse is most elaborate on public finances. He distinguishes between Shariah as well as 'extra-Shariah' sources of revenues, and he is bold enough to condemn the prevalent 'anti-Shariah' levies. Furthermore, while he would want to implement Shariah-mandated levies, he allows additional taxes under certain conditions, chief among them being the need for *maṣlaḥah* or social welfare of the community. Moreover, al-Ghazali recognizes and advocates the well-known 'ability-to-pay' principle of taxation; he is also aware of the 'benefits-received' principle when there is mention of levies-upon non-Muslims. Indeed, al-Ghazali is also concerned about tax administration and compliance when he criticizes the malpractices of tax-collectors.[10] Coming in the eighteenth century, Shah Wali-Allah was aware of the writings of these great scholars of Islam. Thus, there is no surprise that we find similar ideas with Shah Wali-Allah as well, as will be pointed out in the following pages.

Public finance is the backbone of any government. Decay starts with the deteriorating condition of the treasury. During Shah Wali-Allah's time, when the binding thread of Mughal rule was falling apart, he rightly paid much attention to this important aspect of the economy. He regarded the indigence of the public treasury or *bayt al-māl* and its deteriorating condition as the main reason for the weakening and decay of Mughal rule in India, as discussed in Chapter 4. He stressed that this was also true about the empires of Persia and Byzantium in the days of the Prophet.[11] Shah Wali-Allah accused the rulers of his country of still living in luxury. To afford the same lifestyle, they resorted to heavy taxation on cultivators, merchants, artisans, etc. and harsh treatment in the collection of those taxes.[12] Thus, Shah Wali-Allah emphasized the need and importance of having a treasury that is always full as this ensures the ability of the government to equip itself with the necessary provisions, both in times of war and peace, and to fulfil its obligations to its subjects. At the same time, tax rates should be reasonably low so that people can easily pay and their incentive to work is not disturbed.

7.2 Public revenue

After enumerating upon traditional Shariah sources of income for an Islamic state, such as *ghanīmah* (spoils of war), *fay'* (booty), *kharāj* (land tax), *'ushūr* (custom duty), *jizyah* (poll tax),[13] unclaimed property, heirless property, and *ṣadaqāt* (charities) including zakah,[14] Shah Wali-Allah observed that in an unmixed Muslim country the scope of taxes other than zakah is minimal. That is, 'in pure Muslim countries except for zakah there would not be much revenue'.[15] It was, therefore, in the expenditure of zakah revenue that he recommended wide-ranging use.

7.2.1 Justification of taxation without overburdening

Shah Wali-Allah justified taxation on the basis of services provided by the government. In this respect, funds must be collected to support the army and officials; given that they present their services for the sake of the people, it is therefore obligatory upon the people to support them.[16] According to him, in a pure Muslim state voluntarism and altruism are natural characteristics, and so most people's financial needs are not very pressing for the government. The administration of a mixed Muslim country, however, requires greater finance. In governmental budgeting, collection of funds should be according to expenditure (*al-jibāyah bi ḥasb al-maṣārif*.[17] With this, Shah Wali-Allah tacitly permits extra taxes if the situation demands so. It may be pointed out that this position on the part of al-Ghazali, as well as some other prominent Islamic scholars, has been the subject of considerable controversy. Thus, while al-Ghazali allows the imposition of new taxes, there are two guiding principles evident from his discussion: for the defense of the Islamic state i.e. when resources are deficient in the state treasury and the security and survival of the state may be at stake.[18] Thus, taxes may be imposed to avoid and minimize the threat to the state. These two reasons were very much existing during Shah Wali-Allah's time as discussed in Chapters 1 and 4.

7.2.2 Imposition of extra-Shariah taxes

It may be noted that the question of imposing extra-Shariah taxes has been a controversial issue among Muslim scholars. Those who oppose additional taxes permit it only in exceptional circumstances such as war emergencies. Shah Wali-Allah does not draw a line when it is justified to ask for more. He emphasized preserving justice in the imposition of taxes and avoiding unfairness, oppression and the confiscation of property. The authorities should chalk out rules that sufficiently help officials but which at the same time do not inflict injury upon any subject. Any surplus revenue must be kept in the public treasury (*bayt al-māl*) for unseen situations.[19]

7.2.3 Low tax and large revenue

Muslim scholars always argued for a low tax rate so that the incentive to work is not killed and the payment of taxes is made happily.[20] The most prominent advocate of low tax rates was Ibn Khaldun. According to him, when the government is honest and the people friendly, as it happens to be at the beginning of a dynasty, then 'taxation yields a large revenue from small assessment. At the end of a dynasty, taxation yields a small revenue from large assessment'.[21] In his opinion, 'the strongest incentive for cultural activity is to lower as much as possible the amount of individual imposts levied upon persons capable of undertaking cultural enterprise. In this manner such persons will be psychologically disposed to undertake them, because they can be confident of making a profit from them'.[22] Ibn Khaldun has rightly been considered as the forerunner of 'Laffer's curve 600 years before Laffer'.[23] In this regard, his ideas are 'comparable with those of supply side economics'.[24]

According to Shah Wali-Allah, a reasonable tax rate contributes more to the treasury and adds to the prosperity of a state's subjects. A state can only prosper if light tributes are collected and the necessary number of civil servants are employed.[25] This is an idea that came to be known in the twentieth century as Laffer's curve. Describing Shah Wali-Allah's views on taxation, Rizvi observes: 'Additional taxes should be realized from affluent sections of society, such as those with considerable assets of gold and silver or livestock, or those involved in prosperous forms of trade. Should these sections fail to fulfill the financial needs of the government, then additional taxes had to be levied on artisans.'[26] El-Ashker and Wilson also examine Shah Wali-Allah's ideas on taxation: 'The Treasury, through government, may resort to various kinds of taxes that should be levied without overburdening the tax payers beyond what their income can bear. Taxes can be imposed on those of high wealth and income, such as property owners whose passions are continuously increasing, traders and owners of industries. However, Shah Wali-Allah seems to have advocated a tax threshold, as he emphasized that taxes should be imposed on only the extra income beyond that is needed to cover necessities.'[27]

7.2.4 *Jizyah* is not predetermined by Shariah

Regarding the *jizyah,* Shah Wali-Allah noted that different amounts were charged by the Prophet, may Allah bless him and give him peace, and his successor Umar. By this, he inferred that there is no fixed rule about it. It is left to the ruler to decide about it in the best interests (*maṣlaḥah*) of the people. In his opinion, the same option or discretion should be granted wherever differences in the practices of the Prophet and his successors are reported.[28] Before Shah Wali-Allah, Imam Abu Yusuf has made it clear that 'rates of poll tax and land tax are not predetermined by Shariah.' They are variables subject to 'ability of the tax payer' and 'condition of the land.'[29] This is also the opinion of Shaykh al-Islam Ibn Taymiyyah.[30] Al-Ghazali also advocates observing the principle of certainty, benefit and ability to pay as he says '... they (rulers) must demand them only at the proper seasons and times; they must know the usages and fix (burdens) in accordance with capacity and ability (to pay).'[31]

7.2.5 Emphasis on a just tax system

As for the rule of taxation, Shah Wali-Allah suggested that there should be a just system of levying and collecting taxes so that people are not hurt and the revenue is adequate to meet the expenses of the state. Taxes should not be imposed on every person and all goods. Instead, it should be on people having farms, wealth, and growing assets, such as breeding cattle, agriculture, and trade. If more money is needed, the physically earning population may be included.[32] It is also recommended that the imam (leader) should have some personal means of support, such as uncultivated lands to be appropriated and herds of cattle. This would make him independent and thus relieve people of the burden of supporting him.[33]

According to Shah Wali-Allah, tax collection is justified on the ground that there are certain public goods that cannot be provided for by individuals, so the government undertakes their supply through meeting their cost through public finance. As a whole, the government has to establish a court of justice, defend the country, construct fortresses and city walls, promote markets, construct canals and bridges, excavate canals, arrange the marriages of orphans and protect their properties, distribute charities among the poor, distribute inheritance among survivors, and administrate revenue collection and expenditure.[34] Specifically for the purpose of the collection and expenditure of taxes, the head of the state should appoint a governor who has sufficient knowledge of such matters.[35]

7.3 Economics of zakah

Zakah is one of the five pillars of Islam. It is a religious duty as well as a financial obligation. Shah Wali-Allah analyzed the institution of zakah on these two grounds. In his opinion, one objective of zakah is the moral development of oneself (*tahdhīb al-nafs*) and so the personal, individual inner purification. It prepares a person to adopt high human values and abandon bad habits like miserliness, selfishness and jealousy. It is a source of winning Allah's pleasure and improving one's angelic qualities; this is why zakah is bracketed with prayer in the Qur'an in so many places.[36]

Another objective of zakah is to help society in general, given it is comprised of weak and needy elements, which are frequently exposed to calamities. If there is no such provision, these people may die and perish. In a city, there may be many people engaged in the management of public affairs and the fulfilment of citizens' needs, and so are unable to earn their livelihood. This also requires that there should be financial arrangements in place to take care of them, and this is borne by well-to-do citizens.[37] Zakah is also a permanent source to meet such needs.

It may be noted that in his exposition of the significance of zakah, Shah Wali-Allah seems to be influenced by the eighth/fourteenth-century scholar Ibn al-Qayyim (d. 751/1350), as we will see below.

7.3.1 Reasonable rates of zakah

After the imposition of zakah, the need was felt to fix it to reasonable rates that one who seeks to reduce the contribution may not diminish it, and the one who wants to violate the system is unable to do so.[38] According to Shah Wali-Allah, fixing the amount of zakah is one of the innovations of this lastly chosen Shariah, as in earlier Shariah, it was an undetermined right of the poor and orphans to the wealth of the rich.[39] This amount is not so trivial that the rich may not take it seriously or that it cannot cure their miserliness. Nor is it too heavy that they feel it difficult to pay.[40] In other words, the amount fixed in zakah is average and is highly practical. Ibn al-Qayyim has elaborated this point before Shah Wali-Allah: 'According to the former, the purpose of *zakāh* is the development of the quality of kindness, brotherly love and goodwill. For this reason, a specific rate of *zakāh* has been fixed; it can serve this purpose easily, without causing any disconcertment. The amount paid in *zakāh* is not too much for the payers to feel aggrieved, while it is enough for the have-nots to fulfill their basic needs. If it were a very high rate it might have led the rich to evade *zakāh* and resort to different tricks to escape the payment of *zakāh*. On the other hand, the poor would have become accustomed to receive the *zakāh* money without deserving it. The two extreme positions would have defeated the very purpose of *zakāh*.'[41]

7.3.2 Reasonable times of zakah collections

Similarly, in fixing the time for its collection, the period is not so short as to be unable to sustain it, nor is it so long that it becomes ineffective with the needy and poor receiving money after a long time only. A yearly collection period is something that is an accepted norm in all nations.[42] In other words, zakah is payable only after one full year had passed with the ownership of goods, with the exception of a treasure-trove where collection is due immediately upon finding such treasure, and crops where zakah is collected when harvested. Here again Shah Wali-Allah seems to be influenced by Ibn al-Qayyim. According to him, a one-year period is the most suitable and adequate period for the collection of zakah. If zakah had been collected every month or every week, it would have harmed the interests of zakah payers, and if it had been collected once in a lifetime, it would have destroyed the poor. Thus, its imposition on an annual basis is most justifiable.[43]

There are some other arguments in favour of the annual collection of zakah. For example, if zakah is on productive property; this requires that a suitable period should be given before zakah is imposed so that a man can utilize his productive property and get its benefits. The one-year period seems to be enough to invest money and see its result. If zakah had been required every month or every week, it would have created a lot of problems for payers in assessing their income, keeping the accounts, and withdrawing money from investments to pay zakah. On the part of the state, the administration and collection of zakah would have become more expensive and difficult.[44] In the opinion of Shah Wali-Allah, since various economic activities like trade trips from far away places, harvesting crops, and picking fruits generally require one year's duration, an annual collection of zakah is the best.[45]

7.3.3 Productive zakah bases

As far as zakah bases are concerned, the points considered are exactly those that are characteristic of a good tax that is accepted by all sound thinkers and has pious rules affixed to it, such as collection from productive property, levying on those who have the ability to pay, for example, the rich and prosperous; it is also collected from a treasure trove which is obtained without much effort, and it is also imposed on those who are engaged in earning and productive activities (*ru'us al-kasibin*),[46] with the condition of fulfilling *niṣāb* (zakatable assets above the maximum exemption limit). Before Shah Wali-Allah, Ibn al-Qayyim also pointed out that zakah is not imposed on every kind of property. It is imposed on those goods only which have the ability to increase, grow and give a return. Goods meant for consumption like clothes, houses, equipment, riding animals, etc. are free from the zakah levy. Only four kinds of property are subject to zakah, namely, cattle, crops and fruits, gold and silver, and merchandise. These are commonly used and needed commodities. In fact, these are the things that can be shared.[47]

There is a consensus that zakah is levied on those assets that grow or that have the ability to grow if put to work, such as crops, cash, merchandise and precious metals. The ability to pay is also a consideration, and the criterion is for full ownership of *niṣāb* (above the maximum exemption limit of an asset). A treasure trove has the highest rate of zakah, equating to one-fifth, but there is no zakah on the basis of only being earning men. But a sturdy, earning person is not entitled to receive zakah. In the imposition of *jizyah*, however, it will be considered whether a person is earning.

7.3.4 Labour consideration in fixing the zakah rates

Normally, there are four types of rates of zakah: one-fortieth or 2.5 per cent, one-twentieth or 5 per cent, one-tenth or 10 per cent and one-fifth or 20 per cent. According to Shah Wali-Allah, the sources of earning in most countries are in four sectors, namely, merchandise, agriculture with artificial means of irrigation, crops grown through rainfall, and treasure troves or mines. Accordingly, four types of rates have been fixed. The variation is based on high yield and low cost or labour involvement.[48] That is, where yield is highest or cost is lowest, the highest rate is fixed and vice versa. There is thus an important economic causation behind the fixing of the various zakah rates, which has many implications. In his work *Al-Budūr al-Bāzighah*, Shah Wali-Allah wrote that the lowest rate is in cases of money, gold and silver assets, because they are the support for people's living and their means to acquire all necessary objects, so people feel the highest injury in departing with it.[49] It means the rule of equal sacrifice is also observed in fixing the various rates. The principle of equal sacrifice requires that 'the burden of taxation should be so distributed that the direct real burden on all tax payers is equal'.[50]

Before Shah Wali-Allah, Ibn al-Qayyim has also discussed in two places of his writings the significance and economic reasoning behind these different rates of zakah. According to him, the involvement of labour has been taken into consideration for the fixation of these rates. The greater the amount of labour involved in the production or procurement of a property, the lesser the rate of zakah and vice versa. A very small amount of labour service is employed when a person discovers a treasure-trove. The highest rate of zakah is imposed, therefore, in this case; that is, the rate is 20 per cent of the treasure-trove. The rate is 10 per cent in the case of crops watered by rainfall where human work is only to prepare the land, plough it and sow the seeds. The rate has been reduced to 5 per cent if more labour is involved, for example, if a man not only ploughs the land and sows the seeds but also irrigates the land by artificial means. The rate has been decreased to 2.5 per cent in cases where throughout the year, continuous labour service is required, for example, the accumulation of gold and silver and merchandise.[51] However, both Shah Wali-Allah and Ibn al-Qayyim are silent on its application in changing situations. That is, if in a different time and place the situation is reversed and in various sources of income the involvement of labour or high yields and low costs are altered, then what will be the effect on zakah rates? Can they be appropriately modified?

7.3.5 Wisdom behind the minimum exemption limit

As far as the exemption limit or *niṣāb* is concerned, Shah Wali-Allah tried to show that it is the minimum amount needed to upkeep an average family. For example, zakah is levied on agricultural produce when it reaches five *wusaq*.[52] In his opinion, the minimum number of family members comprises husband, wife, and a child or a servant. The daily consumption of people is a maximum quantity of a *mudd*.[53] With this rate, if they consume for a year, the amount would suffice for the whole family and something would be left for other needs.[54] Similar is the exemption limit of five *uqiyyah*[55] of silver, as this amount is sufficient for the expenditure of a family for the whole year if prices are suitably stable.[56] This is a unique interpretation of Shah Wali-Allah. To the best of my knowledge, I could not find it with others.[57]

In fixing *zakāt al-fiṭr* as one *ṣā ʿ*[58] of dates or barley, the same objective is observed, that is, a family's one-day diet.[59] It may be noted that four *mudd* equals one *ṣā ʿ*. Earlier, Shah Wali-Allah said that the daily consumption of people was a maximum quantity of a *mudd*. Perhaps this is for a single person. By one *ṣā ʿ* or four *mudd* foodstuffs, he means this as necessary for a family nucleus. However, one can object to this on the basis that Shah Wali-Allah's analysis presumed the minimum number of family members while normally this is not the case. However, in Shah Wali-Allah's support, one can say that a family's assets are not confined to a particular kind of income or wealth. Taken together, various forms of assets and their *niṣāb* is enough to support even a larger number of family members.

7.4 Public expenditure

In mainstream economics, exclusive writing on public finance started very late, and the aspect of public expenditure in particular remained neglected even for a much longer time.[60] Contrary to this, in the Islamic tradition, writing on public finance constituted the earliest works related to economic problems in which public expenditure occupied a considerable portion. Rules governing the disbursement of *ghanīmah* and zakah and their heads of expenditure have been mentioned in the Qur'an itself.[61] There is hardly any difference of opinion on that. A major concern of Muslim scholars had been the welfare revenue or *amwāl al-maṣāliḥ*, a term used by al-Ghazali[62] because the revenue was primarily meant for public welfare (*maṣlaḥah*).[63] The welfare revenues or *amwāl al-maṣāliḥ* comprise *amwāl al-fay'*, one-fifth (*khumus*) of the spoils of war (*ghanīmah*), land tax (*kharāj*), and other miscellaneous incomes. We do not find this terminology with Shah Wali-Allah. He simply uses the term '*al-amwāl*' (finance)[64] Perhaps he thinks that the welfare revenues or *amwāl al-maṣāliḥ* are to be spent for the welfare of people, so it is considered the people's money.

For the balanced growth of a city, there is a need to provide infrastructure, such as defense walls for security, inns and fortresses, a market and bridges, sources of water, means of transportation, and arrangements for the accommodation and hospitality of strangers, as this encourages foreign trade. Farmers should be urged to not leave lands uncultivated. Manufacturers should produce standardized products. Educational institutions should be fully developed and information systems should be well-organized.[65]

7.4.1 Revenue and expenditure in a purely Muslim country

While discussing expenditure, Shah Wali-Allah divided countries into two categories—those that are of a purely Muslim population and others that include other religious entities as well. In his opinion, in the first category, government expenditure would be smaller as it would not require much expenditure on defence and the maintenance of internal security. A lot of work would be done voluntarily by the Muslim population, so the required number of government officials would be smaller. In such a country, sources of public income would also be limited. The major source would be zakah, which would be spent as prescribed in the Qur'an.[66] Shah Wali-Allah divided the recipients of zakah into three major groups: those who are entitled to zakah because of their needs, mentioned in the Qur'an as needy, poor, wayfarer and indebted; those who receive zakah because of their protective or administrative services, mentioned in the Qur'an as fighters or collectors, and thirdly, zakah revenue would be spent to ward off evil that may fall upon the Muslim community, that is, through paying those who are weak of the new Muslims who may change camp or by paying money to infidels to protect Muslims from their wickedness.[67] A similar analysis has been provided by Ibn al-Qayyim.[68] However, he divides this into two categories. First, those who receive zakah because they are needy; they will receive according to their need. This category includes the poor (*fuqarā'*), the needy (*masakīn*), the captives (*fi'l-riqab*) and the wayfarer (*ibn al-sabil*). Secondly, some will receive because of their utility. They are collectors (*'amilun alayha*), those whose hearts are to be reconciled (*mu'allafah al-qulub*), indebted for a good purpose (*al-gharimun*) and fighters in the way of Allah (*fī sabīli llāh*). If the recipient is not needy, nor has any benefit for Muslims, they have no share in zakah.[69]

Revenue other than zakah would be spent on excavating canals, constructing bridges, building mosques, digging wells and springs, etc.[70] Shah Wali-Allah did not perceive that for the provision of such infrastructure, huge financing was required. The sources mentioned by him are not very large, sure or certain, such as unowned property, heirless inheritances, unclaimed lost found objects, etc. Perhaps he left many other requirements of development to the voluntary provision by the rich as he mentioned that this aspect should be very significant in a pure Muslim country.

7.4.2 Revenue and expenditure in mixed Muslim country

As far as a mixed Muslim country is concerned, its heads of expenditure would be larger in number, and so would the sources of income. He noted that the spoils of war (*ghanīmah*) would be spent as prescribed in the Qur'an.[71] From the one-fifth of it, the share of the Prophet would be spent after him on the general welfare of Muslims, following the most important and the next most important object (*al-ahamm fa'l-ahamm*).[72] The shares of his relatives would be spent on members of the family of Banu Hashim and Banu Muṭṭalib, irrespective of gender and financial condition. The authority was to have the discretion to fix the amount. Similarly, the shares of orphans, the poor and wayfarers would be determined by the authority, following the criterion of the most important and the second most important.[73] The imam (the leader) would announce some incentives to various participants of war if he found it in the interests of the people. The same principle of expenditure (*al-ahamm fa'l-ahamm*) would be followed in spending booty (*fay'* revenue).[74] Accepting the wider scope of ijtihad (original thinking) and discretion in matters of distribution, Shah Wali-Allah noted the pattern of the Prophet and the practices of his successors. The Prophet, may Allah bless him and give him peace, used to distribute booty as soon as it was obtained, allotting two shares to a married man and one share to a bachelor. Abu Bakr, the first caliph, followed the criterion of satisfying the need while Umar, the second caliph, considered the need as well as other preferences such as the person's seniority, sacrifices, dependents, and needs. According to Shah Wali-Allah, all of them did this in the larger interests of the people during their time and based on ijtihad. From this, he inferred that expenditure matters are left to the leader in the best interest of the people in a particular situation.[75] However, he enumerated the objectives of public expenditure as to provide maintenance to those suffering from old age, to protect the town from the wickedness of infidels by garrisoning it and strengthening the fighters through spending on arms and ammunition, to administer the city and manage it by providing guards and a judiciary meting out Shariah punishments, by appointing market and moral supervisors (*al-Ḥisbah*), and protecting the nation from general degeneration by appointing sermon givers, leaders, admonishers and teachers. Public goods also form an important head of public expenditure, like digging canals and constructing bridges and similar public goods and services.[76]

The abovementioned are in no way, however, the only heads of expenditure. They are just guidelines and, as Shah Wali-Allah reiterated, it is left to the ruler and his advisory council to decide specific issues according to the prevailing situation and existing conditions. Such flexibility may help in undertaking all development schemes and promoting the well-being of both the people and the economy. At the same time, Shah Wali-Allah warned of the consequences of misusing the public treasury and misappropriating resources. He condemned those who try to be burdensome on *bayt al-māl* on various pretexts.[77]

On another occasion, Shah Wali-Allah stated that the different principles adopted by the first two caliphs regarding grants were not on the basis of a difference in Shariah injunctions. Rather, they were in consideration of the public interest. During the time of the first caliph, the spoils of war were not considerable and so were unable to take into account anything except the need. But, during the time of the second caliph, the amount of the spoils of war increased considerably due to various conquests, providing much more than what was necessary to meet people's needs. So, the caliph took into consideration some other criteria for deciding the amount of grants.[78]

According to Shah Wali-Allah, any decision to distribute lands captured from infidels after a war or to retain them in the hands of their former owners would be left to the ruler.[79] In his book, he gives a unique interpretation to the stance of the second caliph, Umar, for retaining the lands in the hands of its previous owners.[80] He says that the Persian people who fought Muslim soldiers were not the owners of the land conquered; the actual owners were peasants and farmers who surrendered without an actual fight. Thus, the caliph treated it as *fay'*[81] and made it *waqf* for all Muslims and those who would come later. Shah Wali-Allah was not against fief (*iqṭā'*), but he opposed grants of any land to individuals whose benefit was required by society.[82] He was also against private enclosure (*ḥimā*). However, the enclosure of pasture lands for cattle belonging to the public treasury and to the weak and poor was permissible.[83]

7.5 Public borrowing

There are instances of borrowing by the Prophet, may Allah bless him and give him peace, for emergency needs and public purposes. However, the early writers on public finance,like Abu Yusuf, Abu Ubayd, etc. are silent on this aspect. The reason for this may be the prosperity and surplus of funds in the public treasury of their time period.

Abu Yala al-Farra[84] and his contemporary al-Mawardi[85] are perhaps the first to talk about borrowing by the state. They allowed public borrowing only as a last resort and in exceptional cases. The reason, perhaps, was that they were apprehensive of the government's inability to repay the loan or the inclination of the ruler to indulge in extravagance. Perhaps due to the same reason the later writers also allowed borrowing by the ruler only when the income is delayed; in that situation, the government can borrow to bridge the gap.[86]

Al-Ghazali allows for the possibility of public borrowing under rare circumstances (such as security and survival of the Islamic society), although he would want to ensure the appropriate means of future repayment.[87] In this respect, he is ascribing to the views of an earlier Islamic scholar, Qadi Abu Ya ʿla al-Farra,[88] which were also endorsed subsequently by Ibn Taymiyyah.[89] Looking into the financial conditions of the declining Mughal rule, the rulers were in need and must have borrowed money from various sources. However, strangely enough, Shah Wali-Allah did not discuss the Mughal rulers' borrowings and their terms and conditions, nor did he give his own views about their public borrowing.

7.6 Concern for the poor

Shah Wali-Allah had great concern for the poor. While opposing exorbitant rates of taxation upon cultivators, merchants, and the like, he pointed out that they suffer from great hardship: 'If they refuse to pay taxes, the ruler takes issue with them and chastises them, and if they pay, they are reduced to the level of asses and bullocks ... and they are not even allowed an hour to rest from their labours so that they find no time to pay any heed to the life to come.'[90] He reminded government officers of their duty to poor subjects. In a fierce denunciation, Shah Wali-Allah addressed them: 'O *amirs* (officers) do you not fear Allah when you indulge in short-lived and trivial pleasures and neglect to take notice of your subjects who devour one another? Is it not the fact that wine is consumed publicly and you never denounce it? Are brothels, taverns and gambling-dens not set up but you do not try to change them? Is it not a fact that Sharīʿah punishments (*hudūd*) have not been enforced for more than six centuries? You eat up someone who is weak and leave the mighty untouched ...?'[91]

So did Shah Wali-Allah strive to save the common man from economic hardship? In one of his letters to a minister, he stressed the need for bringing prices down.[92] It may be noted that under normal conditions he was against fixing prices, due to it being unjust to interfere in prices when both parties—sellers and buyers—are equally affected. He suggested price fixation as a policy, if injustice and unfairness are noticed in dealings from sellers, as this is a kind of corruption.[93] Needless to say that by injustice and unfairness, he meant the creation of imperfections in the market and artificially raising prices. It was also in consideration of the poor's interests that he allowed the enclosure of pasture for their cattle.[94] One of the reasons behind the prohibition of *ribā*, stressed by Shah Wali-Allah was that it is clearly an exploitation of the needy and the poor.[95]

Shah Wali-Allah called for economic reform of all sections of society. He warned the elite of the bad consequences of luxurious living and the exploitation of the downtrodden. He advised the military to adopt moderate living. He suggested to them that they keep their expenditure less than their income, such that they could save something to help the poor and wayfarers and also have some amount to cover unexpected needs as a precaution. He criticized those so-called religious people who exploited their devotees. He specially exhorted the common man to earn as much as is sufficient to meet his needs; he should not be a burden on others, and he must have some source of earning for his livelihood.[96]

Notes and References

1. It is interesting to note that in Schumpeter's opinion 'public finance especially modern taxation first developed in the course of the fifteenth century in the Italian city republics, Florence in particular, and in German free-towns *(Reichsstadte)*'. See Schumpeter, *History of Economic Analysis*, p. 200.
2. Shemesh, *Taxation in Islam*, vol. I, pp. 3–6.
3. Abu Zakariya Yahya b. Adam al-Qurashi (140–203/757–818) flourished in Kufa and died in Fam al-Silh, a town situated on Tigris near Wasit. He was a reliable transmitter of traditions. His *Kitāb al-Kharāj* was first published by Juynboll in 1896. Shemesh published its English translation in 1958, Leiden. E.J. Brill, 1969, 2nd ed.
4. Abu Ubayd al-Qasim bin Sallam (157–224/774–838) authored *Kitāb al-Amwāl*, one of the most comprehensive earliest records of the financial system of Islam, widely quoted by contemporary writers on the subject. Recently it has been a subject of a PhD research

by Ugi Suharto at the International Institute of Islamic Thought and Civilization, Kuala Lumpur.

5. Humayd ibn Zanjawayh (d. 251/893) was a disciple of Abu Ubayd. His *Kitāb al-Amwāl* is almost a glossary on the book of Abu Ubayd. It has been edited by Dr Shakir Deib in three volumes, published by Faisal Centre, Riyadh, in 1986.
6. Abu Ja'far Ahmad b. Nasr al-Dawudi (d. 401/1012) authored *Kitāb al-Amwāl* which was studied and critically edited by Najib Abdul Wahhab al-Fili (1989), and translated into English in two volumes as a PhD work from the Exeter University, U.K, in 1989. Al-Dawudi's work is important as it is the only work on the subject from al-Maghrib. It makes use of earlier, now lost, Maliki and non-Maliki studies on the topic.
7. Abd al-Rahman b. Ahmad Ibn Rajab (736–795/1335–1392) was a Hanbali traditionalist, jurisconsult, and author of several voluminous books. Originally from Baghdad, most of his time was spent in Cairo and Damascus. *Aḥkām al-Kharāj* is his work on the subject.
8. Abu' al-Hasan Ali b. Uthman Al-Makhzumi (d. 685/1384). A little is known about him. The title of his work is *Kitāb al-Minhāj fī 'Ilm Kharāj Miṣr*. Part of the book was published under the title *al-Muntaqā min Kitāb al-Minhāj fī Kharāj Miṣr*, Cairo: *Supplement aux Annales, Islamologiques*, in 1986.
9. Islahi, Abdul Azim, *Economic Concepts of Ibn Taimiyah*, pp. 204–20.
10. Ghazanfar and Islahi, *Economic Thought of al-Ghazali*, pp. 60–61.
11. Dihlawi, *Hujjat*, 1: 105.
12. Ibid.
13. Ibid., 2: 176–77.
14. Ibid., 2: 45.
15. Ibid.
16. Dihlawi, *al-Budūr*, p. 95.
17. Dihlawi, *Hujjat* 2: 45; Dihlawi, *al-Budūr*, p. 85.
18. al-Ghazali, *al-Mustasfā*, pp. 303–4.
19. Dihlawi, *al-Budūr*, p. 85.
20. Abu Yusuf, *Kitab al-Kharaj*, p. 121.
21. Rosenthal, *Muqaddimah of Ibn Khaldun*, 2: 89.
22. Ibid., p. 91.
23. Lipsey and Steiner, *Economics*, p. 449. According to Laffer: 'The higher tax rates are, the greater will be the economic (supply-side) impact of a given percentage reduction in tax rates. Likewise, under a progressive tax structure, an equal across-the-board

percentage reduction in tax rates should have its greatest impact in the highest tax bracket and its least impact in the lowest tax bracket' (Laffer, 'The Laffer Curve: Past, Present, and Future').

24. Baeck, *The Mediterranean Tradition*, p. 117.
25. Dihlawi, *Hujjat*, 1: 45.
26. Rizvi, *Shah Wali-Allah and his Times*, pp. 292–93.
27. El-Ashker and Wilson, *Islamic Economics: A Short History*, p. 313.
28. Dihlawi, *Hujjat* 2: 177.
29. Abu Yusuf, *Kitab al-kharaj*, pp. 44, 92.
30. Ibn Taymiyyah, MFS, 19: 253–54.
31. al-Ghazali, *Counsel*, p. 112.
32. Dihlawi, *Hujjat*, 1: 46.
33. Dihlawi, *al-Budūr*, p. 113.
34. Ibid. pp. 93–94.
35. Dihlawi, *Hujjat*, 1: 47.
36. Ibid. 2: p. 39.
37. Ibid.
38. Ibid., 2: 39.
39. Dihlawi, *al-Tafhīmāt* 2: 136.
40. Dihlawi, *Hujjat*, 2: 39.
41. Ibn al-Qayyim, *Madārij*, vol. 1, p. 148; cf. Ibn al-Qayyim, *I'lām al-Muwaqqi'īn*, 2: 92.
42. Dihlawi, *Hujjat*, 2: 39.
43. Ibn al-Qayyim, *Zād al-Ma'ād*, 1: 147–48; Ibn al-Qayyim, *I'lām al-Muwaqqi'īn*, 2: 92.
44. Islahi, *Economic thought of Ibn al-Qayyim*, p. 10.
45. Dihlawi, *Ḥujjat*, 2: 40.
46. Ibid.
47. Ibn al-Qayyim, *Zād al-Ma'ād*, 1: 147; Ibn al-Qayyim, *I'lām al-Muwaqqi'īn*, 2: 20–91.
48. Dihlawi, *Hujjat*, 1: 102; 2:44; Dihlawi, *al-Budūr*, p. 287.
49. Dihlawi, *al-Budūr*, p. 287.
50. Dalton, *Principles of Public Finance*, p. 63.
51. Ibn al-Qayyim, *Zād al-Ma'ād*, 1: 148; cf. Ibn al-Qayyim, *I'lām al-Muwaqq'īn*, 2: 91–92.
52. One *wasq* (pl. *wusaq*) equals 130.56 kilograms. 5 *wusaq* is equal to 825 kilograms in present weight.
53. One *mudd* equals 544 grams of food.
54. Dihlawi, *al-Budūr*, p. 287; Dihlawi, *Hujjat*, 1: 102; 2: 43.
55. One *uqiyah* equals 40 dirhams; 5 *uqiyah* (200 dirhams) equals 595 grams, the *niṣāb* of silver.
56. Dihlawi, *Hujjat*, 2: 43.

57. Our contemporary scholar Prof Monzer Kahf has appreciated this wisdom of Shah Wali-Allah. See the following link: https://www.iiibf.org/papers/english/socioeconomic_justice. Retrieved on 8 April, 2020
58. One *ṣā'* was equal to 2.176 kilograms.
59. Dihlawi, *Hujjat*, 2: 44.
60. As Dalton puts it: 'English economists as a body have had surprisingly little to say concerning the principle of public expenditure'. (See Dalton, *Principles of Public Finance* p. 139). Earlier, Hunter and Allen (*Principles of Public Finance*, p. 19) have said: 'When the entire amount of literature on public finance is taken into consideration, only a small part of it will be found to deal with public expenditure.'
61. *al-Anfal* 8: 41, *al-Tawba* 9: 60.
62. al-Ghazali, *Ihya'*, 2: 166.
63. Abu Yusuf, *Kitab al-kharaj*, p. 127, al-Qurashi, *Kitab al-kharaj*, pp. 60–61, Abu Ubayd, *Kitab al-Amwal*, p. 3.
64. Dihlawi, *Ḥujjat*, 1: 39, 47, 48; 2: 39, 103, 106, 176, or *'amwāl al-nās'* (public finance or the people's money. Ibid, 2: 151, 156, 184.
65. Ibid., 1: 45.
66. Ibid., 2: 45, 177.
67. Ibid., 2: 45.
68. See Islahi, *Economic thought of Ibn al-Qayyim*, p. 11.
69. Ibn al-Qayyim, *Zād al-Ma'ād*, 1: 148.
70. Dihlawi, *Ḥujjat*, 2: 45.
71. *al-Anfal* 8: 41.
72. Perhaps this has been the general rule of expenditure in Islamic public finance. Before Shah Wali-Allah Dihlawi, Shaykh al-Islam Ibn Taymiyyah also noted that in spending public money, priority should be given to the most important items and the next most important and so on, in the context of the general welfare of Muslims (Ibn Taymiyyah, *al-Siyasah al-Shar'iah*, p. 44.
73. Dihlawi, *Hujjat*, 2: 176.
74. Ibid., 2: 174.
75. Ibid., 2: 177.
76. Ibid., p. 177.
77. Ibid., 1: 45.
78. Dihlawi, *Izālat al-Khafā*, p. 69.
79. Dihlawi, *Hujjat* 2: 177.
80. Dihlawi, *Izālat al-Khafā*, 2: 264.
81. The rule concerning *fay'* (booty obtained from the enemy without a fight) is that it should not be distributed among the fighters. In the Qur'an (*al-Hashr* 59: 6–7) it says: 'And that which Allah gave as spoil unto His messenger from them, ye urged not any horse or

riding-camel for the sake thereof, but Allah giveth His messenger lordship over whom He will. Allah is Able to do all things. That which Allah giveth as spoil unto His messenger from the people of the townships, it is for Allah and His messenger and for the near of kin and the orphans and the needy and the wayfarer, that it become not a commodity between the rich among you.'

82. Ibid., 2: 104.
83. Dihlawi, *Izālat al-Khafā*, 2: 234.
84. Abu Ya`la al-Farra, *al-Aḥkām al-Sulṭaniyyah*, p. 253. Abu Yala Muhammad bin al-Husain al-Farra (380–458/990–1066) whose work *al-Aḥkām al-Sultaniyyah* (The Rules of Government), like the one by al-Mawardi (introduced below), has some economic contents. The two scholars had the same titles for their work and contents are also the same except where their respective schools of thought differ (Abu Yala was Hanbali while al-Mawardi was Shafi`i). It is not known who wrote first and who followed suit.
85. al-Mawardi, *Adab al-Dunyā wa'l-Dīn*, p. 214. Ali b. Muhammad al-Mawardi (364–450/974–1058), the son of a rose water merchant in Baghdad, his work *al-Aḥkām al-Sulṭānīyah* (The Ordinances of Government) was commissioned by the caliph. It contains a wide range of subjects including market supervision, taxation and the economic role of the government. The work is translated by Wahba, H. Wafa and published by Garnet Publishing Ltd. Reading, U.K, in 1996.
86. al-Juwayni, *al-Ghayāthī,*, p. 276; Ibn Jama'ah, *Taḥrīr al-Aḥkām fi Tadbīr Ahl al-Islām*, p. 151; al-Shatibi, *al-I'tiṣām* vol. 2, 122.
87. al-Ghazali, *Shifā al-Ghalīl*, p. 241.
88. Abu Ya`la al-Farra, *al-Aḥkām al-Sulṭaniyyah*, p. 253.
89. Ibn Taymiyyhah, *MFS*, 30: 347–48.
90. Dihlawi, *Hujjat*, 1: 105–106.
91. Dihlawi, *al-Tafhīmāt*, 1: 285.
92. Nizami, *Siyāsi Maktūbāt*, p. 147.
93. Dihlawi, *Hujjat* 2: 113.
94. Dihlawi, *Izālat*, 2: p. 234.
95. Dihlawi, *al-Budūr*, pp. 89, 297.
96. Nizami, *Siyāsi Maktūbāt*, pp. 6–8.

8

Shah Wali-Allah on the Stages of Socio-Economic Development

8.1 Early Muslim scholars' holistic approach to development

Humankind is the vicegerent of Almighty Allah. According to al-Raghib al-Asfahani,[1] one of the assignments of God to man is to develop the Earth for the better living of human beings and other creatures.[2] Thus, the development has been a prime concern of Muslim scholars from the early period of Islam. However, only a few of them have presented a systematic theory of economic development, Shah Wali-Allah being one of them. Before we deal with his ideas, it is better to present a brief survey of the other scholars' views on this topic to understand the difference between his ideas and those of others.[3] Those who discussed the issue of development have adopted a holistic approach in which faith and action, spirit and matter, health and education, peace and security, political power and economic elements are inter-connected. For instance, Abu Yusuf remarks: 'God-consciousness (*taqwā*) and personal character of a ruler leads a people to the right direction and absence of these virtues demolishes the foundation of the state.'[4] 'Justice causes development of a country and increases the income. Divine favour is linked with justice and disappears with injustice', he explains further.[5]

Abu Yusuf holds the ruler responsible for carrying out development activities. He says: 'The ruler is accountable for welfare of the people and must do everything that is good for them.'[6] He quotes a companion of the Prophet, Abu Musa al-Ash'ari: 'The best of men in authority are those under whom people prosper and worst are those under whom people encounter hardship.'[7] Economic development requires the availability of infrastructure. Given the importance of agriculture and trade in his time, Abu Yusuf emphasizes the provision of irrigation and transportation facilities.[8] Every effort for development is doomed if the country lacks peace and security. That is why he deals with this issue extensively.[9]

Al-Mawardi also considers it a duty of the ruler to strive for the comprehensive development of the citizens. He includes among his functions to guard faith, execute and preserve justice, protect life and property, establish peace and security, defend the country, manage financial affairs and to give personal supervision to public affairs.[10] In addition to the role of religion and justice,[11] he emphasizes proper education as a prerequisite for comprehensive development.[12] To him the overall progress depends on six factors: religion, self-rule, peace, security, property and optimization.[13] He writes that: 'People will improve their condition only if they are obedient, loving and have sufficient resources from four sectors of the economy: agriculture, animal husbandry, trade and industry.'[14]

On another occasion, al-Mawardi presented an outline of the sustainable development of the state and economy. Establishment of a state requires the foundations of religion, military power and economic resources. State policy should be based on the development of the country, protection of citizens, management of army and administration of revenues. Development of a country requires due attention to both rural and urban areas. He also mentions certain criteria such as a crime-free society, necessary industries, means of employment, enough drinking water, pollution-free environment, wide road, planned cities and districts, education and training facilities, and so forth.[15] It is obvious that most of these factors are considered as necessary for human development even in the present age.

8.2 The role of the state in development

Describing the economic and development role of the state, Nizam al-Mulk al-Tusi[16] observed: 'He (the ruler) shall build underground conduits for irrigation of land, shall have canals dug, bridges built over wide rivers, and see the land is cultivated; he shall build fortifications, found new cities, build noble monuments and splendid residences, and shall have caravanserais established on highways.'[17]

Al-Ghazali also considers the state as a necessary institution, not only for the proper functioning of economic affairs but also for fulfilling divine social obligations: 'The state and religion are inseparable pillars of an orderly society. The religion is foundation and the ruler, representing the state, is its promulgator and protector; if either of the pillars is weak, the society will crumble.'[18] After citing the example of old Persian rulers, al-Ghazali says: 'The efforts of these kings to develop the world were undertaken because they knew that the greater the prosperity, the longer would be their rule and the more numerous would be their subjects.' They also knew 'that the religion depends on authority, the authority on army and the army on supplies and supplies on prosperity and prosperity on justice.'[19] Thus to him, various segments of life are interdependent. Sustainable growth is possible when all sectors are developed simultaneously.

Al-Ghazali assigned so much importance to education and training in socio-economic and human development that he discussed its various aspects in about one hundred pages of his famous work *'Iḥyā' 'Ulūm al-Dīn*— even the title of this four-volume work indicates the same.[20] He considers the development of the economy as part of socially obligatory duties; if they were not performed, life would collapse and human beings would perish.[21] He is not in favour of the population as a whole to confine itself to a mere subsistence level of living. 'If people stay confined to subsistence level and become weak, death rate will increase; work and industry would come to a halt and the society will perish. The religion will also be destroyed, as life is preparation for the Hereafter.'[22]

The Muslim scholars had almost identical views on the question of development. This is due to their common social and political context. They included in the state's responsibility: the elimination of poverty, supply of necessities, provision of justice and fair distribution, the establishment of peace and security, promotion of human values, and building infrastructure for the development of the economy. Elsewhere we have discussed these functions with reference to Ibn Taymiyyah.[23]

8.3 Ibn Khaldun's cyclical model of development

8.3.1 A political-economic theory of development

Ibn Khaldun has studied issues of development in detail, but different from others.[24] His is a political-economic theory of development which is in fact a cyclical model of development. To facilitate a comparison with Shah Wali-Allah's theory of the stages of socio-economic development, let us first elaborate upon Ibn Khaldun's theory. He deals with the processes that recur cyclically during relatively normal phases. He divides them into five stages: (a) conquest and success; (b) stability and self-exalting; (c) economic expansion and enjoying the fruit of development; (d) contentment and compromise; and (e) extravagance, wastage and decadence. A summarized account of these stages is given below.[25]

The stage of conquest and success

Supported and strengthened by group feeling and social cohesion, a new ruling dynasty takes over by suppressing all opposition. Ibn Khaldun writes that: 'In this stage the ruler serves as a model to his people by the manner in which he acquires glory, collects taxes, defends property and provides military protection.'[26]

The stage of stability and self-exalting

In the second stage, 'the ruler gains complete control over his people, claims royal authority all for himself excluding them and prevents them from trying to have a share in it'.[27] Thus it is a stage of stabilization and consolidating forces, further strengthening the group feeling and by rewarding his supporters.

The stage of economic expansion and enjoying the fruit of development

The third stage is characterized by economic prosperity and the enjoyment of the 'fruit of royal authority'. Attention is given to the development of cities, construction of large buildings, and increased allowances of officials and the general public. According to Ibn Khaldun: 'This stage is last during which the ruler is in complete authority. Throughout this and the previous stages, the rulers are independent in their opinion. They build up their strength and show the way for those after them.'[28]

The stage of contentment and compromise

In the fourth stage, 'the ruler is content with what his predecessors have built: He limits his activities, "follows closely in their footsteps"'.[29] He takes no initiative by himself. The expansion in politico-economic power stops and some sort of stagnation starts.

The stage of extravagance, wastage and decadence

In the fifth stage, the ruler indulges in extravagance, lives an extra-luxurious life, and wastes resources accumulated by the previous rulers. Incompetent and unqualified followers are entrusted with the most important matters of the state. Idle court men are rewarded, and sincere critics are humiliated and punished. The ruler loses all kinds of sympathy and group feeling. At this stage, rates of taxes increase while revenues collected decline. The economy is shattered and the social system is disturbed. The government suffers from incurable problems, which leads to its downfall and takeover by a new ruling dynasty, supported by a strong group-feeling and social cohesion.[30] Thus, the cycle of development sets in again.

8.3.2 *'Aṣabiyyah*

The core concept of Ibn Khaldun's theory of development is *'aṣabīyah* (group feeling, social cohesion)[31] which keeps people united behind their leader and solid against enemies. It provides stability and strength to the political setup of the country, a pre-condition for development efforts.[32] The difference in the degree of *'aṣabiyyah* determines the difference in size and quality of socio-economic development. Like anything else, *'aṣabiyyah* grows weaker after reaching its highest degree. As a result, degradation and corruption begins in which excessive taxation and the ruler's luxurious living play an important role.

Social cohesion, group feeling and solidarity are the basis for cooperation which are necessary for building an efficient social organization. These become important as the state develops. To quote Ibn Khaldun, 'Through cooperation the needs of a number of persons, many times greater than their own number, can be satisfied.'[33]

8.3.3 The role of population and finance

Population

In Ibn Khaldun's scheme of development, population size also plays a vital role. A large population is able to engage in all sorts of economic activities, causing an increase in goods and services, prosperity and welfare, and government revenues.[34] Ibn Khaldun's views about population bear the colour of modern demographic theory. Population tends to grow where food is abundant and life is comfortable, though rich diets were less favourable than frugal diets to bodily and natural health.[35] Similarly, 'luxury' and 'prosperity' are initially favourable to population growth, stimulating both natural increase and migration,[36] though in time a luxurious mode of life tends to be unfavourable.[37] At the last stage of civilization, an increase in population accompanies famine and death. At this stage, people generally withdraw from essential economic activities because of the government's oppressive policies and political disturbances resulting in famine and starvation. The increased death rate is because of increased pollution and diseases.[38]

The role of public finance

In the opinion of Ibn Khaldun, the development cycle is also linked to public finance. In the initial stage, levies are kept low, conforming to Shariah taxes. This causes an increase in entrepreneurial activities allowing the tax base and revenue to grow. With the passage of time, the ruler and officials indulge in luxuries. Moreover, government expenditure also tends to increase. It then becomes necessary for the government to increase assessment and tax rates. This creates a disincentive for the businessmen and entrepreneurs, leading to a decrease in productivity and tax evasion. Again the authority increases taxes and again productivity declines further, and thus revenue decreases and a vicious circle starts.[39]

8.3.4 The lifespan of a ruling dynasty

According to Ibn Khaldun, a ruling dynasty has a lifespan like individuals, which is about one hundred and twenty years (three times a generation's age, forty years).[40] Once decline sets in a state, it cannot be reversed.[41] In the final stage of a dynasty, sickness and weakness strangles the state and the whole nation in such a way that there remains no point of escape. The city's culture turns senile by a self-effecting process of urban luxuries, breeding laxity of morals and corrupt customs, immorality, wrongdoing, insincerity and trickery for the purpose of making a living in any manner, proper or improper. The people develop habits of lying, gambling, cheating, fraud, theft, perjury and usury.[42] The socio-economic and moral decay leads to the decline of the old system and allows for the rise of a competing new one.

This cyclical interpretation of development does not mean that the new government is going to start from the same level of economic progress from where the outgoing had started. Some of the infrastructure developed by the past government would remain available to start economic development from a higher point and cover the distance in a shorter period.

It is interesting to note that despite being generally influenced by Ibn Khaldun's work and style, Shah Wali-Allah did not pay attention to Ibn Khaldun's theory of cyclical development. Instead, he presented a different theory of the socio-economic development of human society, starting from simple primitive village life to an international community. He divides this into four stages. The first stage is a simple economic life at the village level and the last stage is a just political order on an international level. In between the two is the stage of town building and the city-state, and the stage of development at the country level. Let us study these in detail.

8.4 Shah Wali-Allah's theory of socio-economic development

8.4.1 His use of the term *al-Irtifāqāt*

Shah Wali-Allah has presented a systematic theory of socio-economic development. For this purpose, he coined the term *al-irtifāqāt* (sing. *irtifāq*). Linguistically, the root of *irtifāq* is r-f-q- which means to become gentle, tender, gracious, courteous or to behave and act gently and softly. The past tense *Irtafaqa bihi* means: He profited or gained advantage or benefitted by him or it.[43] The word *irtifāq* refers to adopting convenient ways, helping devices, beneficial methods, useful techniques, and good manners in one's life. According to Rizvi, *irtifāq* refers to the principles of devising useful schemes to promote social, political and cultural life. [44] In the opinion of Marcia Hermansen, 'Shah Wali-Allah's concept of *Irtifāqāt* has provided much interest among contemporary scholars of his thought. The term in his usage is idiosyncratic and its precise meaning varies contextually.'[45] After giving various interpretations of the term *al-irtifāqāt*, she opines: 'It appears, therefore, that this term may encompass all of these connotations depending on context and does not have a simple English equivalent. The core of Wali-Allah's explanation of the *irtifāqāt* presents the development of human societies through four *irtifāqāt* or stages of increasingly refined order and elaboration of arts of civilized life'[46] In the opinion of Jalbani: 'The ways and means by which, with little trouble and in [a] short time, one can tide over his [sic] social and economic difficulties, are called *irtifāqāt*.'[47] Baljon takes *irtifāqāt* in the sense of 'socio-economic development'.[48] Looking into the context in which the word *irtifāq* has been used by Shah Wali-Allah, this seems to us the most appropriate meaning of the term. As we shall see below, starting from a simple primitive village life existence to an international community, the socio-economic development of human society can be divided into four stages. All of Shah Wali-Allah's economic ideas are related, in some way or another, to his concept of *irtifāqāt*. Let us, then, study these stages separately and in detail.

8.4.2 The First Stage: Rudimentary Life

There are certain basic needs, such as food, drink, shelter, sex etc. which are common, not only among humankind but also among animals. Satisfying these basic needs has been instinctively revealed to every living creature. Shah Wali-Allah presents examples of bees and sparrows, who systematically work together for food, drink, shelter and breeding. Likewise, every species has a course of conduct (shariah) infused into the heart of each individual member of that species. He calls this *irtifāq al-bahā'im* (an animal-like living stage).[49] In the same manner, Almighty Allah inspired human beings how to fulfil their basic needs. However, He added for them three characteristics whereby they become distinguished from other animals:

1. *al-rā'i al-kullī* (an all-inclusive way of thinking).[50] Unlike animals, which are always motivated by natural wants—hunger,

thirst and lust—humans are in many cases motivated by intellectual wants such as the establishment of a just order, perfection of their character and refinement of their soul, with the aim of achieving honour and glory in this life and the Hereafter.[51]

2. *al-ẓarāfah* (an aesthetic urge).[52] Animals only desire something to meet their natural requirements and fulfil their instinctive needs, while man wants to be aesthetically and emotionally satisfied in the fulfillment of these basic needs. For example, humans would like an attractive spouse, a variety of delicious food, stylish dress, and a good-looking spacious house.
   The existence of these qualities makes man distinct from animals and resolves 'the issue arising out of [the] seemingly overlapping instinctive pursuits of man and beast, which led [the] human mind to different confusions concerning the correlation between various species of [the] animal world'.[53]
3. *istinbāṭ al-irtifāq wa iqtidā'uh* (the capability to discover good manners and to follow them). Some individuals possess intelligence and awareness and discover appropriate socio-economic support, while others are not intellectually advanced enough to be able to do so. Such people learn from their intelligent leaders what they have discovered for the common good and adopt their methods, firmly adhering to them because they fit into their own general understanding.[54]

Since these three qualities are not found equally in all people, they have been grouped under different socio-economic levels (*irtifāqāt*).[55] The first *irtifāq* is based on an animal-like living (*irtifāq al-bahā'im*)[56] distinguished in clarity, communication, refinement and intelligence. It exists in people like the Bedouin and tribal groups, dwellers of remote and far-flung areas such as mountain peaks and deserts. Under this stage, man acquires a language to express thought in a natural way.[57] In this stage, he becomes acquainted with foodstuffs suited to his physical constitution, and learns how they are to be eaten and digested. He should also know the methods of their cultivation, irrigation, harvest and preservation, and the ways of preparing and cooking them as well as how to benefit from animals by obtaining meat, milk and butter. Similarly, he should know the uses of vegetables and the ways of getting water and storing it. He should be familiar with taming animals to use them for riding, to benefit from their milk, meat and wool, and for works otherwise hard to perform such as ploughing the land. He should have a shelter to protect himself and his family from rain, heat and cold. Using garments is also an aspect of this stage. A man is led to acquire for himself an uncontested wife to satisfy his sexual urges and to reproduce offspring.[58] In this stage, humankind develops simple crafts for agriculture and the domestication of animals, and seeks the assistance of others through primitive exchange and limited cooperation. Social organization is led by the person who possesses, relatively, a higher quality of sound judgement and power to subjugate others. There should be a set pattern to resolve people's disputes and punish transgressors and offenders. On an intellectual level, there should be at least one person with relatively higher intellectual calibre who discovers ways of *al-irtifāq* according to the peoples' condition, and so that others might follow him.[59]

From Shah Wali-Allah's description of this first stage of *al-irtifāq*, it appears that he keeps in mind the standard of civilization and socio-economic conditions of village folk. It is, therefore, a stage of fulfilling the basic needs of food, shelter, clothing, justice, etc. which man desires by nature. Economic problems of 'what', 'how' and 'for whom' are solved by traditions. This stage has the least division of labour and no development of the market. It is a stage that distinguishes human society from animal life and encompasses all groups. Its existence is a prerequisite for the second stage of socio-economic development.

8.4.3 The Second Stage: Town Building and the City-State

When mankind gets over the problems of the natural needs for food, drink, clothing, etc. and tries to satisfy them in a refined and sophisticated manner, they enter the second stage of socio-economic development. In this stage, the expansion and improvement of the first stage takes place with behavioural knowledge and good morals.[60] Humans have, by nature, a tendency, to seek and pursue improvements in their pattern of living, which is dictated by their aesthetic urge (*ẓarāfah*). The complexity of life increases in this stage and the need arises for suitable institutions and prudent measures conducive to progress. According to Shah Wali-Allah, in this stage the following five kinds of sciences (*ḥikmah*) are needed and discovered by humankind:[61]

1. *al-Ḥikmat al-Maʿāshiyyah* or the science pertaining to good manners of living, with reference to consistency in conduct and practical knowledge about eating, drinking, dressing, dwelling, etiquette, manners of conversation, modes of travelling, etc.
2. *al-Ḥikmat al-Manziliyyah* or the science of good family life, which pertains to married life, rearing children, obligations towards relatives and servants, and manners of companionship, etc.
3. *al-Ḥikmat al-Iktisābiyyah* or the science of earning a livelihood, which involves various occupations people pursue and which fit their personal capacities, and the means that help them in their crafts such as carpentry, smithying, and so on. Division of labour, specialization, diversity of occupation and the use of money are some aspects of Shah Wali-Allah's *al-ḥikmat al-iktisābiyyah*.
4. *al-Ḥikmat al-Taʿāmuliyyah* or the science of mutual dealings, which concerns purchase and sale, giving presents, tenancy, lending, debt, mortgages, *waqfs*, etc. These dealings are inevitable for an economy based on the division of labour and specialization, otherwise, people cannot maintain the second stage of socio-economic development. The motives behind these activities are to benefit from the products of others by exchange or to secure the prosperity of all people necessary for the fulfilment of needs, and cooperation for that purpose. Additionally, one seeks to adopt values such as generosity, honesty, faithfulness, etc. In these mutual dealings, goods or services are extended to others for the pleasure of Allah. Shah Wali-Allah also discussed the wisdom of Islam's different teachings regarding these contracts of mutual dealing in some detail in the second part of his book *Ḥujjat Allāh al-Bālighah*.[62] On another occasion, he mentioned

some more institutions of mutual dealings based on virtue and benevolence, such as *ṣadaqah* (charity), *waṣiyyah* (wills) and *waqf* (religious endowments and trusts).

Shah Wali-Allah maintained that the idea of *waqf* was unknown to people before Islam. This institution was established by Prophet Muhammad, may Allah bless him and give him peace, for different welfare considerations. The merit of *waqf* is that the needy benefit from this source of income generation while its ownership remains with the endowment maker.[63] This view is held by Shah Wali-Allah, although some others do not agree that the donor's right of ownership rests with him. A similar opinion is also reported from Imam Abu Hanifah.[64]

Shah Wali-Allah defined these contracts along the pattern of Muslim jurists and elaborated upon the important instructions of the Shariah to fulfil the requirement of validity and equity.[65] To avoid disputes and exploitation, all deals that involve such negativity have been prohibited by the Shariah, because they have a bad effect on the concerned parties. An example of this is contracts involving uncertainty, deception and double-dealing. Shah Wali-Allah especially took note of bribery, gambling and *ribā*.[66]

5. *al-Ḥikmat al-Ta'āwuniyyah* or the wisdom of cooperation, which relates to standing surety, silent partnership, commercial enterprise, power of attorney and tenure etc.[67]

This last science in the second stage of socio-economic development relates to cooperation among members of society on economic issues. Shah Wali-Allah stated: 'This cooperation necessitates itself as people in society are not equally good for all things. Some of them have good intelligence while others are imbeciles. Some of them have capital, while others are empty handed but can work hard. Some people hate to do petty works, while others do not, and so on. Thus their mundane lives would have become very difficult had they not sought the cooperation of each other. Take the example of *muzāra'ah* (crop-sharing), a person might have land but not bullocks and seeds and may not be able to work himself. Others t have two of these or even three. Or take the example of *muḍārabah* (profit-sharing), a person might have capital but he cannot persuade himself for trade and travelling or any other such kind of job. Thus, they need the cooperation and help of each other. Some people cannot do this directly, so they resort to power of attorney, sponsorship or middlemanship.'[68]

In *Ḥujjat Allāh al-Bālighah*, he defined the different forms of partnership that have been discussed in more detail in most books on Islamic jurisprudence. He said that these forms of contracts were in practice before the Prophet, may Allah bless him and give him peace. Hence, they are acceptable for use unless their validity is disputed in general or are specifically prohibited by the Prophet, may Allah bless him and give him peace.[69]

Out of the five abovementioned types of sciences, the first two, *al-ḥikmat al-ma'āshiyyah* and *al-ḥikmat al-manziliyyah*, are related to sociological studies while the last three, *al-ḥikmat al-iktisabiyyah*, *al-ḥikmat al-ta'āmuliyyah*, and *al-ḥikmat al-ta'āwuniyah*, come under the subject of economics. As mentioned earlier, the second stage of *irtifāqāt* follows the first stage, but there can be no watertight division between the two.[70] Thus, the activities of the first two categories of the second stage are also found in the first stage, the difference being in refinement and improvement. For example, man should fulfil his need for food, drink, cleanliness, decoration, clothing, accommodation, talking, walking, travelling, selling, intercourse, treating diseases, and living with his wife and children according to the noble and elevated ethical requirements of piety as enjoined by the religion.[71] In his book *al-Budūr al-Bāzighah*, Shah Wali-Allah described, in this regard, the details of the standard desirable for an average person.[72]

8.4.4 The Third Stage: Formation of Government and a Country-state

With the completion of the second stage, human society completes its city-stage. Shah Wali-Allah clarified that the city (*madīnah*) does not mean walls, buildings and markets. Instead, the city is a kind of relation between different groups of people based on mutual dealings and cooperation.[73] The need for preserving this relationship and preventing different economic evils leads society to the third stage of socio-economic development. According to him, the city, which is a unit and like a single body, may be exposed to different internal and external diseases. Thus, there is the inevitable need for a physician for the healthy upkeep of the body of the city. The imam or the leader with all his associates represents this third stage. [74] The imam is an institution through which the integrity, interest and independence of the city is maintained. [75] In this third stage, the following five institutions are necessary so that the progress of the state continues and measures are imposed against corruption, abuse, disorder and decay: [76]

1. *al-Qaḍā* or the judiciary. When stinginess, envy and disregard of others' rights enter into social life, disputes and disagreements are bound to arise among the people. Hence, there must be an acknowledged institution available to which one may have recourse for an equitable settlement of disputes.
2. *al-Shahryāriyyah* or the executive. When perverted disposition and pernicious activities prevail over people and they act accordingly, the city-state becomes depraved and disordered. Therefore, there should be a strong body to take deterrent and punitive measures against such people.
3. *al-Jihād* or a police and military force. People with a corrupt nature often take to violent activities such as murder, robbery or rebellion, and deliberately try to disturb the peace and order in a city-state. In order to control such violent situations and preserve the city-state from the misfortune they cause, a defence force constituting brave fighters is essential.
4. *al-Tawallī wa'l-Naqābah* or welfare and public works. The city-state has institutional and corporate bodies that make it a perfect state, whereas the lack of these renders guarding the city-state difficult. For example, things to be taken care of includes defending frontiers, constructing wells, markets, bridges and canals, marrying orphans and protecting their properties, distributing alms among the needy, distributing inheritance among heirs, having information about the condition of the people, and keeping an account of income and expenditure.

5. *al-Maw'izah wa'l-Tazkiyah* or religious and moral business. Since faith and true religion cannot dispense without a person to impart knowledge about them—though both of them are based on such clear proofs that sane people find the way to them by themselves—the numerous men of corrupt nature who follow their lusts and passions and who oppose the truth are in need of a man of wisdom, a teacher of religion to manage the house properly and show them how to conduct themselves correctly towards each other.[77]

Shah Wali-Allah Dihlawi advised the imam to treat the people and his army justly and to pay due attention to the collection of revenue, which is necessary for strengthening the army and official machinery.[78] In this stage, it is the government's duty to see that the proper allocation of employment is done in different industries and services. Additionally, traders and farmers are encouraged in their professions and arrangements are made for their proper education. Shah Wali-Allah pointed out the worsening condition of his time, however, in which the requirements of this third stage of socio-economic development were not properly fulfilled. He stated, 'There were two main reasons for the decay of the cities in his time. One, people overburdened the *bayt al-māl* (public treasury). They became accustomed to getting their livelihood from it on the pretext of being warriors, educationists, saints, poets, etc. Two, the heavy taxation on farmers, traders and industrialists and the harshness meted out to them caused frustration among the obedient, but evasion and uprising among strangers. A city develops with the easy taxation and employment of only the necessary number of officials.'[79] He also enumerated upon the qualities of a successful imam.[80]

8.4.5 The Fourth Stage: Internationalism

In this stage, human society and the institutions of the government adopt an international character. Thus the need arises for a super-government (*Khalifat al- Khulafā*). When the third stage of *irtifāq* is complete and different imams (rulers) control their states, having sources of income and the support and protection of the brave warriors, then enmity, hostility, bitterness and greed lead them to fight each other. This causes heavy losses in terms of lives, the destruction of the means of livelihood and the annihilation of facilities. Therefore, this necessitates the existence of *Khalifat al-Khulafā* (the ruler of all rulers).[81] According to Shah Wali-Allah, such a ruler should be all-powerful in terms of men and material so that none can hope to defeat him.[82] Only by establishing such a super-government can countries and people live peacefully together. Such a caliph may also be forced to wage war against those who want to loot and plunder the property and lives of others.[83] Shah Wali-Allah did not assign any economic role to this government of international character, except that it would need a lot of men and material to perform its duty of keeping peace, providing justice, and curbing exploitation and hostility. Thus, such an institution should know how to manage the levy of different taxes to meet expenses. The chief of this government could deliver financial punishments to rebellious and unruly sections. However, the purpose of such punishment should be reform and to bring them to order, not the collection of funds.[84] In his work, Shah Wali-Allah describes the qualities of a good, successful and imposing caliph, suggesting different measures for making his role firm and effective in discharging his duties.[85]

8.5 *Irtifāqāt:* a natural process in human development

Like his predecessing Muslim scholars, Shah Wali-Allah in his theory of development emphasizes the promotion of religious life, justice, education and overall improvement of economic conditions. He presents this under a comprehensive term *irtifāqāt* and holds that humankind passes through different stages in its struggle for development, which is a natural process.[86] Whatever differences we notice are only ways in how to achieve those *irtifāqāt*, or we see them as resulting from some people's bad habits, ill-nature, indulgence and lust. The institution of prophethood also aimed at assisting the people towards completing *irtifāqāt*, rectifying the means and methods necessary for them and removing hurdles in the way. According to Shah Wali-Allah, housekeeping and the management of cities are two important subjects of Qur'anic Shariah.[87] The task assigned to Prophet Muhammad, may Allah bless him and give him peace, was to correct the second *irtifāq*, set up the third one, make the religion of Allah spread all over the world, and establish it on the pattern of the fourth *irtifāq*.[88] In this way, Shah Wali-Allah combined socio-economic development with the concept of securing Allah's pleasure, termed by him as *iqtirābāt*— that is, the ways and stages of purifying and spiritually developing humankind.[89]

Among the stages of development prescribed by Shah Wali-Allah Dihlawi, the first stage is purely traditional in nature, when people concentrate on the production of necessary and easily exchangeable goods and use simple agrarian methods. In the second stage, the market grows. Specialization and division of labour develops. This necessitates the use of money and relatively improved technologies and production processes. Expansion in socio-economic activities leads to increased mutual contact and cooperation. This is a very important stage of development as most of the basic socio-economic institutions are developed at this stage, their function being to check people from exploiting the economically weaker members of society, to prevent socio-economic evils by wrong-doers, and to provide a healthy environment and infrastructure for overall progress. The need for the state and the use of some sort of command arises as the economy completes this second stage. With this, human society enters the third stage, and the city-state takes the form of a national economy. The state then has to ensure the balanced growth of the economy

To prevent conflict between different states, a more powerful government of international character is required, which is the final stage in socio-economic development. Shah Wali-Allah did not assign any important economic role to this government. The reason perhaps is that internationalism in his time had not assumed the importance it now carries. Thus, talking about international economic organizations and institutions would have been beyond the purview of people's minds. We can safely say that in the present age, world organizations and institutions established for cooperation and helping poor nations come within the line of Shah Wali-Allah's thinking, as do his suggestions for an overlord or *khalifat al-khulafā* to keep conflict among states in check and prevent the exploitation of the economically or militarily weak and socially backward states. This, of course, does not include the powerful and developed nations as they are capable and self-sufficient.

Notes and References

1. Al-Husayn b. Muhammad al-Raghib al-Asfahani (d. 502/1108). A contemporary of al-Ghazali, famous for his Qur'anic studies, especially an excellent dictionary of the Qur'an, *Mufradāt Alfāẓ al-Qur'ān*, and his work on ethics *al-Dharī'ah ilā Makārim al-Sharī'ah*, which are both published. Al-Ghazali is said to have always had a copy of *al-Dharī'ah* by him. They exchanged ideas, which is clear from the similar discussions and examples used in their works.
2. al-Asfahani, *al-Dharī'ah ilā Makārim al-Sharī'ah*, p. 90.
3. In our work *History of Islamic Economic Thought* we presented a survey of Muslim scholars' views on development. Due to its significance, portions of that survey are reproduced in this chapter. See Islahi, *History of Islamic Economic Thought*, pp. 53–56.
4. Abu Yusuf, *Kitab al-kharaj*, pp. 3–4.
5. Ibid., p.120.
6. Ibid., p. 129.
7. Ibid., p. 16.
8. Ibid., p. 119.
9. Ibid., pp. 161–194.
10. al-Mawardi, *al-Aḥkām al-Sultāniyyah*, pp. 15–16.
11. al-Mawardi, *Adāb al-Wazīr*, pp. 3–4, 20.
12. al-Mawardi, *Adab al-Dunyā wa'l-Dīn*, pp. 15–46.
13. Ibid., p. 80.
14. Ibid., pp. 135–38.
15. al-Mawardi, *Tas'hīl al-Naẓar wa Ta'jīl al-Ẓafar*, p. 152.
16. Nizam al-Mulk al-Hasan b. Ali al-Tusi (408–85/1018–92) was born at Radkan, near Tus. The celebrated minister of the Seljuk Sultan Alp Arsalan and Malik-Shah was in all but name a monarch and ruled his empire with great success. Worked for the economic and educational development of the country, established the famous Madrasa Niẓāmīyyah of Baghdad and brought a number of reforms to win the hearts of ulama, elites and commoners. *Siyāsat Namah* written by al-Tusi is a monarch's primer.
17. al-Tusi, *Siyāsat-nāmah*, p.11.

18. al-Ghazali, *Ihya'*, 1: 17; al-Ghazali, *Counsel*, p. 59.
19. al-Ghazali, *Counsel*, p. 56.
20. The title *'Iḥyā' 'Ulūm al-Dīn* (Revival of Religious Sciences) is a comprehensive work. Since in the Islamic tradition 'religion' covers every aspect of life, knowledge that guides in those aspects are part of the religious sciences.
21. al-Ghazali, *'Iḥyā'*, 2: 32.
22. Ibid., p. 108.
23. Islahi, *Economic concepts of Ibn Taimiyah*, pp. 178–86.
24. For Ibn Khaldun's theory of development viewed with a focus on its economic rather than political aspects, see Ahmad, *Taṭawwur al-Fikr al-Iqtiṣādī*, pp. 109–117.
25. For details, see Rosenthal, *Muqaddimah of Ibn Khaldun*, pp. 353–58. It may be noted that sections on *'aṣabiyyah* (Ibid., 1: 313–30), taxation (2: 89–91), population (2: 135), trade (2: 93), etc. are only explanations of various stages of Ibn Khaldun's theory of cyclical development.
26. Rosenthal, *Muqaddimah of Ibn Khaldun*, 1: 353.
27. Ibid.
28. Ibid., 1: 354–55.
29. Ibid.
30. Ibid.
31. Commenting on Ibn Khaldun's theory of *'aṣabīyah*, Timur Kuran says: 'Variants of this idea appear much later in the works of a number of extremely influential thinkers, including Marx and Schumpeter. The idea also forms the basis of Mancur Olson's celebrated *Rise and Decline of Nations* [New Haven, Yale University Press, 1982] although, I might add, Olson fails to cite Ibn Khaldun among the originators of his thesis.' See Kuran, 'Continuity and Change in Islamic Economic Thought', p. 109.
32. Rosenthal, *Muqaddimah of Ibn Khaldun*, 1: 284.
33. Ibid., 2: 271–72.
34. Ibid., p. 273.
35. Ibid., 1: 351–52; 2: 274–76.
36. Ibid., 2: 280–81, 351–53.
37. For more information about Ibn Khaldun's theory of population, see Spengler, 'Economic Thought of Islam: Ibn Khaldun', p. 297.
38. Ibid., pp. 136–37.
39. Ibid., 2: 89–90.
40. Ibid., 1: 343.
41. Ibid., p. 117.
42. Ibid., p. 293.

43. Lane, *An Arabic-English lexicon*, 3: 1125–1126.
44. Rizvi, *Shah Wali-Allah and his Times*, p. 288.
45. Hermansen, *The Conclusive Argument from God* (Translation of Shah Wali-Allah's *Ḥujjat-Allāh al-Bālighah*), p. xviii. Abdel-'Aal in his thesis *God, the Universe, and Man in Islamic Thought: The Contribution of Shah Waliullah of Delhi (1702–1762)* reviews some of the translations or explications offered for the term '*al-tadbīrat al-nafi'ah*' or 'the useful management of human affairs', which was offered by the editors of the Arabic text of *Ḥujjat Allāh al-Bālighah*. Abdul Hamid Halepota's definition of *irtifāqāt* is 'every trait; characteristic, and institution that comes under the subject of sociology' (See *Practical Theology and Ethics of Shah Wali-Allah* cited by Abdel-'Aal, pp. 392–397). Aziz Ahmad, in his work *Studies in Islamic Culture in the Indian Environment*, regards *irtifāqāt* as the stages of history of the growth of human societies and Sabih Ahmad Kamali, in his work *Type of Islamic Thought*, sees *irtifāqāt* as 'civilization and its devices' and a theory of natural law. Jacques Berque concludes that it seems possible that 'the plural of the verbal noun, *irtifāqāt*, may be translated by "uses, commodities, services"' (See Berque, 'Un contemporarian islamo-indien de Jean- Jacques Rousseau.', pp. 113–146). Berque further reads a socio-economic slant into *irtifāqāt* by equating them with 'the services constituting the institutional section of the "collective good" (*al-maṣlaḥah al-'ammah*)' (See Hermansen, *The Conclusive Argument from God*, pp. xviii-xix). In the opinion of Hermansen, 'this term may encompass all of these connotations depending on context and does not have a simple English equivalent' and she, therefore, renders the term *Irtifāqāt* as 'supports of civilization' though prefers to use the same Arabic term at various places in her translation of *Ḥujjat Allāh al-Bālighah* (See Hermansen, *The Conclusive Argument from God*, p. 113).
46. See Hermansen, *The Conclusive Argument from God*, p. xix.
47. Jalbani, *Teaching of Shah Waliullah of Delhi*, p. 165.
48. Baljon *Religion and Thought of Shah Wali-Allah Dihlawi*, p. 193.
49. Dihlawi, *al-Budūr*, p. 64.
50. Other translations of the term *al-rā'i al-kulli* include comprehensive outlook, social purpose, universality of purpose, social welfare, consideration of the general interest, etc.
51. Dihlawi, *Hujjat*, p. 38; Dihlawi, *al-Budūr*, p. 28.
52. Other translations of *al-zarāfah* include aesthetic sensibility and cultural accomplishment.
53. al-Ghazali, *The Socio-Political Thought of Shah Wali-Allah*, p. 45.
54. Dihlawi, *Hujjat*, p. 38.

55. With reference to Simpson, al-Ghazali remarks that 'contemporary sociologists also recognize the significance of language as 'the real incomparably important, and absolute distinction between human and other living organisms' (al-Ghazali, *The Socio-Political Thought of Shah Wali-Allah*, p. 52).
56. Dihlawi, *al-Budūr, al-Budūr* p. 64.
57. It may be noted that in *Ḥujjat Allāh al-Bālighah*, Shah Wali-Allah elaborated upon the wisdom of this stage of *irtifāq* under three chapters: *Bāb fann ādāb al-ma'āsh* (Arts of Living), *Bāb tadbīr al-manzil* (Arts of Household Management) and *Bāb fann al-mu'āmalāt* (Arts of Transactions). An analysis of the 'Arts of Transactions' shows that this chapter includes all the three wisdoms which he mentioned in his work *Al-Budūr al-Bāzighah* under the classification of *al-Ḥikmat al-Iktisābiyyah* (wisdom pertaining to earning a livelihood), *al-Ḥikmat al-Ta'āmuliyyah* (wisdom pertaining to mutual dealings) and *al-Ḥikmat al-Ta'āwuniyyah* (wisdom pertaining to cooperation).
58. Ibid., p. 69; Dihlawi, *Ḥujjat*. 1: 39–40.
59. Dihlawi, *Ḥujjat*. 1: 40.
60. Dihlawi, *al-Budūr*, pp. 62–65.
61. Ibid., p. 62.

    Shah Wali-Allah's statement has great relevance today. From an unpublished paper entitled *Maqāṣid and Finance in Islam* by Prof M.N. Siddiqi (undated): 'In the fast globalizing world of the twenty-first century we Muslims are increasingly becoming part of a plural world society. We must live with the other, interact with the other and seek solutions to the emerging problems in ecology, demography, weaponry, entertainment, and what not together and jointly. This challenge requires coming nearer not moving apart farther. We need to look at what is common between "us" and "them" rather than remain focused on what is not. All men and women, irrespective of their ethnicity and creed seek peace and justice.'
62. Dihlawi, *Ḥujjat*, 2: 112–13.
63. Ibid., 2: 114–16.
64. Ibn Abidin, *Radd al-Muhtar ala al-Durr al-Mukhtar*, 2: 319; 6: 533.
65. Dihlawi, *al-Budūr*, pp.88–9.
66. Ibid., p. 90, 102; Dihlawi, *Ḥujjat*, 2: 106.
67. Dihlawi, *al-Budūr*, p. 63.
68. Dihlawi, *Ḥujjat*, 2: 117.
69. Dihlawi, *al-Budūr*, pp. 50–51.
70. Ibid., p. 65.
71. Ibid., p. 89.

72. Ibid., p. 90.
73. Ibid., p. 63.
74. Ibid., p. 64.
75. Ibid., p. 61.
76. Ibid., pp. 92-93.
77. Ibid., p. 94.
78. Ibid., pp. 94–95.
79. Dihlawi, *Ḥujjat*. 1: 44–45.
80. Ibid., p. 45.
81. Ibid., p. 47; Dihlawi, *al-Budūr*. p. 64.
82. Dihlawi, *al-Budūr*. p. 113.
83. Dihlawi, *Hujjat*, 1 47.
84. Ibid., p. 48.
85. Ibid.
86. Ibid., 2: 48; Dihlawi, *al-Budūr*. p. 125.
87. Dihlawi, *al-Khayr al-Kathīr*, p. 83.
88. Dihlawi, *al-Budūr*. p. 266.
89. Ibid., pp. 241–2.

9

Conclusion: Comparison and Evaluation

Shah Wali-Allah Dihlawi did not discuss economic ideas as one finds presented in textbooks. Rather, he was motivated by the economic issues faced by the society he lived in and within his country as a whole. Strictly Islamic in scope, Shah Wali-Allah's economic concerns revolved around a classification of wants, business ethics, prohibited and promoted contracts, prices, cooperation and division of labour, opportunity cost, property rights, and a balanced variety of occupations. He also discussed issues relating to the management of the house, money and interest, public finance, and mankind's socio-economic development.

Shah Wali-Allah lived in Delhi, India's capital, then ruled by the Mughals. The Mughals were next to the Ottomans in power and prestige, at least until the beginning of the twelfth/eighteenth century when Emperor Aurangzeb passed away. Soon after him, decadence and anarchism engulfed the whole Empire. Regional forces from all over India were on the path of revolt, seeking to annex Delhi and establish their own control. The frequent changes of kings weakened the regime and Mughal rulers lost their wisdom, courage and political insight. Luxurious living, extravagance, an empty treasury and heavy taxation added to the unrest and anxiety of their subjects. In this way, disunity and disintegration were the biggest challenges faced by Muslim-rule in India.

Shah Wali-Allah kept himself away from the court of the king and active politics, but he could not keep himself aloof from the political arena. When he saw that regional forces were about to put an end to centuries-old Muslim rule in India and establish their own hegemony, he wrote to the ruler of Afghanistan for direct assistance. Although the latter acceded to his request, the Mughal ruler of the time did not avail himself of this opportunity to correct both his own behaviour and reinforce his rule. Thereafter, Shah Wali-Allah chose an academic career to carry out reform and renovation. Since the unity of the Muslim umma was the most pressing need of the time, he called upon the removal of rigidity among the followers of Islam by inviting them to rely in their matters on the Qur'an and Sunnah. He stressed *tawḥīd* as the basis of this unity. He criticized heretic Sufism, but approved that form of Sufism which did not conflict with the authentic teachings of Islam. In this regard, he is nearer to Uthman dan Fodio than Ibn Abd al-Wahhab. Shah Wali-Allah's contribution is much wider in scope and deeper in analysis than his two aforementioned contemporary scholars. On economic issues too, he was far ahead of his contemporaries. For a comparative study of the three aforementioned scholars - Uthman dan Fodio, Ibn Abd al-Wahhab, including Shah Wali-Allah, one may refer to Islahi's *Islamic Economic Thinking in the 12th AH and 18th CE Century*.[1] In fact, after Ibn Khaldun, the Islamic world has not seen such a great writer on socio-economic problems. In this respect, Shah Wali-Allah not only revived the economic ideas of past Muslim scholars, but also made his own original contributions. A comparison with his predecessors is therefore in order.

Shah Wali-Allah seems to be more influenced by the works of Abu Yusuf (d. 182/798), al-Farabi (873–950), al-Khattabi (d. 388/998), al-Ghazali (d. 505/1111), al-Razi (d. 606/1209), al-Izz ibn Abd al-Salam (d. 660/1262), Ibn Taymiyyah (d. 728/1328), Ibn al-Qayyim (d. 751/1350), and Ibn Khaldun (d. 808/1406). In his famous work *Izālat al-Khafā*, he generally relied on Abu Yusuf's *Kitāb al-Kharāj*, especially on the economic practices of the Second Caliph. While giving an account of Umar's refusal to distribute the conquered land of Iraq among the fighters, Shah Wali-Allah presented a unique interpretation whereby the lands actually belonged to the farmers who surrendered them without fighting (an essential condition for holding them as *fay'*). On the pattern of al-Ghazali, Shah Wali-Allah classified wants as necessities, comforts, and refinement. To him, luxury is a relative term. Things that are a luxury for the common man may be a necessity for a king. In his description of the economic evils of interest (*ribā*), he seems to have been affected by one of the reasonings given by al-Razi, namely, the practice of interest may detract people from undertaking necessary productive enterprises.

Cooperation and division of labour have been some of the most discussed topics of economic thought. It was inherited from Greek philosophy and discussed by al-Ghazali, Ibn Taymiyyah and Ibn Khaldun, etc. Shah Wali-Allah considered it the foundation for the healthy and balanced development of the economy. He highlighted its basic elements. To him, the implications of the Islamic provision of *farḍ kifāyah* are also a kind of division of labour and non-concentration of all into one job.

To Shah Wali-Allah, like many other Islamic scholars of the past, gold and silver form natural money and other substances are money by convention. Money was invented to fulfil the need for exchange and to facilitate trading. Unlike other scholars, he thought that gold and silver are best to form the function of money because they are useful and valuable in and of themselves. Although other substances also can be used as money, they will be considered money by convention.

In the case of *ribā al-faḍl* and *ribā al-nasi'ah* accruing due to an exchange of gold for gold and silver for silver, he considered *thamaniyyah* (moneyness) as the *'illah* (causation), and in the case of foodstuffs he considered only those which are storable and preservable. This was also advocated by al-Ghazali, Ibn Taymiyyah, and Ibn al-Qayyim. Similarly, he also thought that this prohibition served as a preventive measure only.

While discussing the economic significance of various provisions of zakah, such as its reasonable rate, time of collection, productive zakah bases, consideration of growth and labour involvement, etc. he seemed to be borrowing ideas from Ibn Taymiyyah and his student, Ibn al-Qayyim. However, he did not confine himself to these points only and instead made certain valuable additions. For example, he indicated the rule of equal sacrifice in fixing the *niṣāb* of various types of assets. Another contribution was showing that the fixation of *niṣābs* (exemption limits), in the case of various assets, are the minimum amount needed for the upkeep of an average family.

In his discussion of public finance, Shah Wali-Allah classified countries as purely Muslim or pluralistic. Accordingly, there will be less or more requirement of public expenditure and sources of income. This was also a notion not found with others.

Like Ibn Khaldun, Shah Wali-Allah opined that a low tax rate would be more rewarding to the treasury, an idea which came to be known as Laffer's curve in the twentieth century. It is not known whether he borrowed this from Ibn Khaldun or whether it was his own thinking. The occurrence of similar ideas to different people simultaneously or in different periods is quite possible in economics as in other areas. Several examples of this are given by Islahi in his work *Contributions of Muslim Scholars to Economic Thought and Analysis*.[2]

Among the Muslim scholars of the past, Ibn Khaldun and Shah Wali-Allah are most famous for their theories of development. However, the two followed entirely different approaches. Ibn Khaldun presented a cyclical politico-economic theory based on *'aṣabiyyah* (group-feeling). Shah Wali-Allah presented a theory of socio-economic development (*al-irtifāqāt*) based on human nature. Ibn Khaldun's theory works in a cyclical way in the political sphere, but Shah Wali-Allah's theory works in a straightforward fashion. He also expanded it to the other-worldly sphere, viewing seeking nearness to Allah (*al-iqtirābāt*) and spiritual progression as the ultimate goal of human beings.

Shah Wali-Allah is not only unique in his theory of socio-economic development among Muslim scholars, but is a pioneer of the theory known in the West as the 'stages of history' approach to development. Here is an account of the same: over the last two and half centuries, a number of Western economists have adopted this 'stages of history' approach to development.[3] For example, Adam Smith (1723–1790), known by the West as the Father of Economics, chose the sequence of hunting, pastoral, agricultural, commercial and manufacturing. The German economist Friederich List (1789–1846) lists the stages as savagery, pastoral life, agriculture, agriculture and manufacturing; and finally agriculture, manufacturing and commerce. Another German economist Gustave Schmollar (1838–1917) divided the stages of development as the village economy, the town economy, the territorial economy, the national economy and the world economy. Karl Marx (1818–1883) perceived the stages of development as being from primitive communism to slavery, feudalism, capitalism, socialism, and communism. The twentieth-century economist W.W. Rostow (1916–2003) distinguished five stages of growth for each economy: the traditional society, the preconditions for take-off, the take-off, the drive to maturity and the age of high mass consumption.

Without going into a detailed comparison of all these, one can immediately see that Shah Wali-Allah takes precedence over these Western writers in pointing out the different stages of humankind's development as presented in his theory of the stages of development—and this when such a discussion was not common among scholars. The fact that scholars belonging to different regions of the globe perceived similar stages in mankind's socio-economic development verifies Shah Wali-Allah's statement that these stages are natural to every human society. Gustave Schmollar's 'stages of history' approach is very close to Shah Wali-Allah's stages of socio-economic development. His discussion of these stages may not be that elaborate and technically detailed as we find with later writers but is nonetheless very comprehensive as it is not confined to economic or material aspects only. In this respect, it also takes into account moral and spiritual aspects. The advancement of the human institution is not only the work of worldly philosophers, politicians, social theorists, and reformers but is instead the mission of a true religious institution as well. The development of humankind in the third and fourth stages without the necessary and just institutions, and void of human values, will only lead to the exploitation of the weaker nation and oppression of the masses. Ultimately, this will lead to the breakdown of the whole system, just as Shah Wali-Allah complained during his own time, and has been experienced in every time period. Shah Wali-Allah's theory is also distinguishable from others insofar as he does not consider the development of humankind into a fourth stage and the establishment of an international socio-economic institution as the climax of humanity. Instead, this should lead to nearness to the Creator of this world (*al-iqtirābāt*) through good deeds and following the life patterns of the Final Prophet, may Allah bless him and give him peace. Improvement in this relation will serve to improve the condition of *al-irtifāqāt* and vice-versa. Thus, there is no end of history in Shah Wali-Allah's theory of development. The relevance of Shah Wali-Allah's theory of development today, as he himself pointed, is that where we miss the control of the fourth stage, we should adorn and improve the third stage, and where we lose the third stage, we should concentrate on the betterment of the second stage and so on till we regain the higher stage.[4] National and international socio-economic and political institutions can serve their correct purpose only if their diseases are cured and crime, corruption, exploitation and oppression are eliminated. The increasing concern about improving the human development index and the emphasis on adopting a value-based system on the part of many contemporary writers only shows the relevance of Shah Wali-Allah's ideas in the modern age. His theory of *al-irtifāqāt* is a lasting contribution to the social science, one that is very much relevant today.

Notes and References

1. Islahi, *Islamic Economic Thinking in the 12th AH and 18th CE Century*, (Jeddah: Scientific Publishing Center, King Abdulaziz University, 2011b).
2. Islahi, Abdul Azim, *Contributions of Muslim Scholars to Economic Thought and Analysis* (Jeddah: Scientific Publishing Centre, KAU, 2005).
3. Oser, *The Evolution of Economic Thought*, p. 431.
4. Dihlawi, *al-Budūr*, pp. 119–20.

Bibliography

Arabic References

al-Ālūsī, Nu'mān b. Maḥmūd, *Jalā' al-'Aynayn fi Muḥākamat Aḥmadayn* (Cairo: Matb'at al-Madani, 1981).

Abu Dawud, *Sunan Abi Dāwūd* (Beirut: Dar al-Kitab al-Arabi, n.d.).

Abu Ubayd, *Kitāb al-Amwāl* (Beirut: Dar al-Kutub al-Ilmiyah, 1986).

Abu Ya`la al-Farra, *al-Aḥkām al-Sulṭaniyyah,* (Egypt: Mustafa Babi al-Halabi, 1966).

Abu'l-Husayn, Abd al-Baqi, *Mu'jam al-Ṣaḥābah,* (al-Madinah al-Munawwarah: Maktabah al-Ghuraba' al-Athariyyah, 1418 AH).

Abu-Yusuf Yaqub b. Ibrahim, *Kitāb al-Kharāj* (The Book of Taxation), (Cairo: Dar al-Matba'ah al-Salafiyah, 1392 AH).

Ahmad, Abd al-Rahman Yousri, *Taṭawwur al-Fikr al-Iqtiṣādī* (Development of Economic Thought) (Alexandria: al-Dar al-Jami'yyah, 2001).

al-Asfahani, al-Husayn al-Raghib, *al-Dharī'ah ilā Makārim al-Sharī'ah* (Cairo: Dar al-Sahwah; al-Mansurah: Dar al-Wafa, 1985).

al-Asqalani, Ibn Hajar, *Fatḥ al-Bārī Sharḥ Ṣaḥīḥ al-Bukhārī,* (n.p. Dar al-Fikr, n.d.), vo. 5, *Kitāb al-Buyu'*.

al-Baghawi, al-Husayn b. Masud, *Sharḥ al-Sunnah* (Damascus: al-Maktab al-Islami, 1983).

al-Baladhuri, Ahmad, *Futūḥ al-Buldān,* (edited by Ridwan, Ridwan Muhammad), (Beirut: Dar al-Kutub al-Ilmiyyah, 1983).

al-Bukhārī, Muhammad b. Isma'il, *al-Jāmi' al-Ṣaḥīḥ,* (Cairo: Dar al-Sha'b, 1987).

al-Dawudi, Abu Ja'far Ahmad *Kitāb al-Amwāl.* (See al-Fili, Najib Abdul Wahab (ed.), 1989).

Dihlawi, Shah Wali-Allah, *Izālat al-Khafā 'an Khilāfat al-Khulafā* (Removal of Doubts from the caliphate of the Caliphs), (Bareily, India: publisher unknown, 1286 AH).

Dihlawi, Shah Wali-Allah, *'Iqd al-Jīd fi Bayān Aḥkām al-Ijtihād wa'l-Taqlīd* (Rules of imitation and original thinking) (Bareily: Maktabah Siddiqi, 1305 AH).

Dihlawi, Shah Wali-Allah, *Fuyūḍ al-Ḥaramayn* (Favours of the Two Holy Mosques) (Delhi: Matba' Ahmadi, 1308 AH).

Dihlawi, Shah Wali-Allah, *al-Khayr al-Kathīr* (Manifolds of Goodness) (Dabhel: al-Majlis al-Ilmi, 1352 AH).

Dihlawi, Shah Wali-Allah, *al-lnṣāf fi Bayān Asbāb al-lkhtilāf* (The just stand in dealing controversies), (Beirut, Dar al-Nafa'is, 1398 AH).

Dihlawi, Shah Wali-Allah, *Waṣiyyat-nāmah,* (Lucknow: Matba' Nami Munshi Nawal Kishor, 1873).

Dihlawi, Shah Wali-Allah (1898), *al-Fawz al-Kabīr* (The Great Success, a treatise on principles of interpretation) (Delhi, Matba' Mujtaba'i, 1898).

Dihlawi, Shah Wali-Allah, *Anfās al-'Ārifin,* (Delhi: 1917).

Dihlawi, Shah Wali-Allah, *al-Tafhīmāt al-Ilāhiyyah* (The Divine Explanation), (Dabhel, Surat, al-Majlis al-Ilmi, 1936), vols. 1&2.

Dihlawi, Shah Wali-Allah, *al-Budūr al-Bāzighah* (The Bright Moons), (Hyderabad: Sind (Pakistan), Academy of Shah Wali-Allah Dihlawi, 1970).

Dihlawi, Shah Wali-Allah, *Ḥujjat-Allāh al-Bālighah* (The Convincing Proofs of Allah), (Beirut, Dar al-Ma'rifah, n.d.a), two parts. The first part's translation entitled The Conclusive Argument from God by Marcia K. Hermansen (tr), (Leiden, E.J. Brill, 1996).

Dihlawi, Shah Wali-Allah, *al-Muṣaffā*, (Delhi: Matba Faruqi, n.d.b).

al-Dimashqi, Abu'l-Faḍl Ja'far, *al-Ishārah ilā Maḥāsin al-Tijārah*, al-Shorabji (ed.), (Cairo, Maktabah al-Kulliyyat al-Azhariyyah, 1977).

al-Farabi, Muhammad, *al-Madīnat al-Fāḍilah wa Maḍāddātuhā* (Cairo: Hindawi Foundation for Education and Culture, 2016).

al-Fili, Najib Abdul Wahab, *A Critical Edition of Kitāb al Amwāl by Abū Ja'far Aḥmad al-Dāwūdi (d. 401 H)*, vol. 1 & II, (University of Exeter, U.K, 1989), p. 693.

al-Fullani, Salih b. Muhammad al-Umari, *Īqādh Himām Uli'l-Abṣār li'l-Iqtiḍā' bi Sayyid al-Muhājirīn wa'l-Anṣār wa Taḥdhīrihim 'an al-Ibtidā' al-Sha'i fi'l-Qurā wa'l-Amṣār min Taqlīd al-Madhāhib ma' al-Ḥamiyyah wa'l-'Aṣabiyyah bayn Fuqahā' al-A'ṣār* (Awakening the fervor of those who have insight to follow the Leader (i.e. the Prophet, peace be upon him) of Migrants and Helpers and warning them from common bad innovations existing in towns and cities regarding blindly following their respective jurisprudential schools with biased support and the defense of past jurists). Abridged and edited by Salim al-Hilali (Amman: al-Makatabah al-Islamiyah, n.d.).

al-Ghazali, Abu Hamid, *Ihyā 'Ulūm al-Dīn* (Beirut: Dar al Nadwah, n.d.), 4 volumes.

al-Ghazali, Abu Hamid, *al-Mustasfā min 'Ilm al-Ūṣūl* (Bulaque: al-Matba'at al-Amiriyah, 1322 AH), vol. 1.

al-Ghazali, Abu Hamid, *Shifā al-Ghalīl* (Baghdad, Al-Irshad Press, 1971).

al-Ghazali, Abu Hamid, *Mīzān al-'Amal*, Sulaiman Dunya (ed.) (Cairo: Dar al Ma'arif, 1964).

Hasani, Abd al-Ha'i, *Nuzhat al-Khawāṭir wa Bahjat al-Masāmi' wa'l-Nawāẓir*, (Hyderabad: Daerah al Ma'arif al-Uthmaniah, 1962), 7 vols. in 3 collections.

al-Hasani, Abd al-Hayy, *al-I'lām bi man fi al-Hind min al-A'lām* known as *Nuzhat al-Khawāṭir* (Beirut: Dar Ibn Hazm,1999).

al-Haytami, Ibn Hajar, *al-Fatāwā al-Kubrā al-Fiqhiyyah*, (n.p. Dar Sadir, n.d.), vol. 2.

Ibn Bishr, Uthman, *'Unwān al-Majd fi Tārīkh Najd* (the Sign of Honour in the History of Najd), (Riyadh: Wazarat al-Ma'arif al-Saudiyah, 1391 AH).

Ibn Abidin, *Radd al-Muhtar ala al-Durr al-Mukhtar* (Beirut: Dar al-Fikr, 2000).

Ibn Jama'ah, *Taḥrīr al-Aḥkām fi Tadbīr Ahl al-Islām*, ediyed by Fuad Ahmad (Qatar: Presidency of Shari'ah Court and Religious Affairs, 1987), 2nd ed.

Ibn Khaldun, *Muqaddimah* (n.p. Dar al-Fikr, n.d.).

Ibn Kathīr,, *al-Bidāyah wa'l-Nihāyah*, Beirut: Maktabah al-Ma'arif (Riyadh: Maktabah al-Nasr, 1966).

Ibn Nujaym, Zayn al-Abidin b. Ibrahim, *Rasā'il Ibn Nujaym* (Beirut: Dar al-Kutub al-'Ilmiyah, 1980).

Ibn al Qayyim, *I'lām al-Muwaqqi'in* (Cairo: Maktabah al-Sa'adah, 1955).

Ibn al Qayyim, *Zād al-Ma'ād* (Cairo: al-Matba'ah al-Misriyah, n.d.).

Ibn al-Qayyim, *Madārij al-Sālikīn* (Cairo: al-Muhammadiyah Press, 1375 AH).

Ibn Qudamah, *al-Mughnī* (Beirut: Dar al-Kitab al-Arabi, 1972).

Ibn Taymiyyah, *al-Ḥisbah wa Mas'ūliyyah al-Ḥukūmah al-Islāmiyah* or *al-Ḥisbah fi'l-Islām* edited by Salah Azzam (Cairo: Dar al-Sha'b, 1976).

Ibn Taymiyyah, *Iqtidā' al-Ṣirāt al-Mustaqim* (Makkah al-Mukarramah: al-Majd Commercial Press, n.d.).

Ibn Taymiyyah, *Majmū' fatāwā Ibn Taymiyyah* (Riyadh: al-Riyad Press, 1963), vols. 19, 29.

Ibn Taymiyyah, *al-Siyāsah al-Shar'iyyah* (Cairo: Dar al-Sha'b, 1971).

Ibn Zanjawayh, Humayd, *Kitāb al-Amwāl*, Dr. Shakir Deib (ed.), 3 volumes, (Riyadh: Faisal Centre, 1986).

Ihsanoglu, E. (ed.), *al-Dawlat al-'Uthmāniyah-Tārikh wa Hadārah* (Ottoman State – History and Civilization) (Istanbul: IRCICA, 1999).

al-Juwayni, Abd al-Malik, *al-Ghayāthī*, edited by Abd al-Azim al-Deib (Cairo: Matba'ah Nahdah Misr, 1981).

al-Makhzumi, Abu'l-Hasan Ali b. Uthman, *al-Muntaqā min Kitāb al-Minhāj fi Kharāj Miṣr* (Cairo: *Supplement aux Annales, Islamologiques*, 1986).

Malik b. Anas, imām, *al-Mudawwant al-Kubrā*, part 3 (Beirut: Dar al-Fikr, 1978).

al-Maqrizi, Muhammad Ali, *Kitab Shudhur al-'Uqud fi Dhikr al-Nuqud*, edited by Bahr al-Ulum and published as the fourth edition under the titles *al-Nuqud al-Islamiyah* (Najaf: al-Maktabat al-Haydariyah, 1967).

al-Mawardi, Ali, *al-Aḥkām al-Sultāniyyah* (Egypt: al-Babi al-Halabi, 1973).

al-Mawardi, *Adab al-Dunyā wa'l-Dīn*, Beirut: Dar Ihya al-Turath al-Arabi, 1979).

al-Mawardi, Ali, *Adāb al-Wazīr* (Egypt, Maktabah al-Khanji, 1929).

al-Mawardi, Ali, *Tas'hīl al-Naẓar wa Ta'jīl al-Ẓafar* (Beirut: Dar al-Nahdah al-Arabiyyah, 1981).

Miskawayh, *Risalah fi Māhiyat al-'Adl*, edited and translated by M. S. Khan, (Leiden: Brill, 1964).

Miskawayh, *Tahdhīb al-Akhlāq* (Cairo: al-Matba'ah al-Misriyyah, n.d.).

al-Tirmidh, Muhammad b. Isa, *Sunan al-Tirmidhī* (Beirut: Dar Ihya al-Turath al-Arabi, n.d.).

al-Muhibbi, *Khulāṣat al-Athār fi a'yān al-Qarn al-Hādī 'Ashar* (Summary of History of the Eleventh Century), (Cairo: Dar al-Kitab al-Islami, n.d.), V 4 vols.

Muslim, *al-Jāmi' al-Ṣaḥīḥ* (Beirut: Dar al-Jil and Dar al-Afaq al-Jadidah, n.d.).

al-Tusi, Nizam al-Mulk, *Siyāsat-nāmah* translated by Hubert Darke (London, 1961).

al-Qurashi, Yahya b. Adam, *Kitāb al-Kharāj* (Cairo and Beirut: Dar al- Shuruq, 1987).

al-Razi, Fakhr al-Din, *al-Tafsīr al-Kabīr* (Cairo: al-Bahi'ah press,1938), vol. 5

al-Shāṭibi, Ibrahim, *al-I'tiṣām* (Beirut: Dar al-Ma'rifah, n.d.).

al-Shaybani, Muhammad b. Hasan, *al-Iktisāb fi'l-Rizq al-Mustaṭāb*, Beirut: Dar al-Kutub al-Ilmiyyah, 1986).

Shaykhu, Louis, *Kitāb Tadbīr al-Manzil*, in: *al-Mashriq* (Beirut), vol. 19, no. 3, (1921), pp. 161–181.

al-Siyalkoti, Muhammad Bashir, *al-Shāh Walī-Allāh al-Dihlawī* (Beirut: Dar Ibn Hazm, 1999).

al-Tunji, Muhammad (ed.), *Tarājim A'yān al-Madīnat al-Munawwarah fi'l-Qarn al-Thānī 'Ashar al-Hijrī* (Biographies of the Elites of Madinah in the 12th Century Hijrah), (Jeddah, Dar al- Shuruq, 1984).

Other Languages

Abdel-'Aal, Khalil Abdel-Hamid, *God, the Universe, and Man in Islamic Thought: The Contribution of Shah Waliullah of Delhi (1702-1762)*, PhD. Dissertation (London: University of London, 1970).

Ahmad, Aziz, *Studies in Islamic Culture in the Indian Environment*, Oxford, O.U. Press, 1964).

Ahmad, Bashir al-Din, *Waqiat-e Dar al-Hukumat-e Dihli* (Agra: Shamsi Press, 1919), 3 vols.

Baeck, Louis, *The Mediterranean Tradition in Economic Thought* (London and New York: Routledge, 1994).

Baljon, J.M.S., *A Mystical Interpretation of Prophetic Tales by an Indian Muslim*. (The translation of Dihlawi's treatise *Tawil al-Aḥādīth*) (Leiden: E. J. Brill, 1973).

Baljon, J.M.S., *Religion and Thought of Shah Wali-Allah Dihlawi* (Leiden: E. J. Brill, 1986).

Baloglou, Christos P., 'The Tradition of Economic Thought in the Mediterranean World from the Ancient Classical Times Through the Hellenistic Times Until the Byzantine Times and Arab-Islamic World' in J.G. Backhaus (ed.), *Handbook of the History of Economic Thought*,

The European Heritage in Economics and the Social Sciences (Switzerland: Springer, 2012), pp. 9–91.

Berque, Jacques, 'Un contemporarian islamo-indien de Jean- Jacques Rousseau.' *L'Islam au temps du monde* (Paris: Sindbad, 1984), pp. 113–146.

Bhatnagar, Ram Ratan, *Rise and Growth of Hindi Journalism 1826–1945* (Allahabad: Kitab Mahal, 1947).

Bhatt, S. C. and Gopal K. Bhargava (eds,), *Land and people - Karnataka,* (Delhi: Kalpaz Publications, 2006), vol. 13.

Chapra, Umer, 'Mawlana Mawdudi's Contribution to Islamic Economics' in the *Muslim World* (Hartford Seminary), vol. 94, no. 2, April 2004, pp.163–180.

Crowther, Geoffrey, *An Outline of Money* (Rev. ed., London: Reprint Nelson, 1967 [1958]).

Dalton, Hugh, *Principles of Public Finance,* (London: Routledg and Kegan Paul Ltd. 1964).

al-Dawwani, Jalal al-Din, *Practical Philosophy of the Muhammadan People* (A Translation of the *Akhlāq-i Jalaly*), trans. from Persian by W. F. Thompson (Karachi: Karimson, 1977), (First published in London: The Oriental Translation Fund, M.DCCC.XXXIX).

Day, A.C.L., *Outline of Monetary Economics* (Oxford: Clarendon, 1957).

Dihlawi, *Anfās al-ʿĀrifin,* (Delhi, Matbaʿ Mujtaba'I, 1917).

Durant, Frederick C. 'Rocket and missile system', Britannica [Website] https://www.britannica.com/technology/rocket-and-missile-system accessed 31 July 2021

El-Ashker, Ahmad A. F. and Wilson, Rodney, *Islamic Economics: A Short History,* (Leiden and Boston, Brill. 2006).

Essid, Yassine. *A Critique of the Origins of Islamic Economic Thought* (Leiden. New York. Koln: E.J. Brill. 1995).

Fahd, Obaidullah, *Islami Umraniyat – Shah Wali-Allah Dihlawi ka Mutalaʿah* (Islamic Sociology – A study of Shah Wali-Allah Dihlawi), (New Delhi, Urdu Book Review, 2011).

Faridi, Nasim Ahmad, *Nadir Maktubat Shah Waliullah* (Phulat, Muzaffar Nagar, India: 1998).

Flinn, M. W., *An Economic and Social History of Britain 1066-1939* (London: Macmillan & Co. Ltd. 1965)

Gardet, Louis, *La Cite' Musulmane* (Paris : Vrin 1969).

al-Ghazali, Abu Hamid, *Counsel for Kings*, tr. by Bagley, F.R.C. (London: Oxford University Press, 1964).

al-Ghazali, Muhammad, *The Socio-Political Thought of Shah Wali-Allah* (New Delhi: Adam Publishers and Distributors, 2004).

Ghazanfar, S.M. and Islahi, A.A., *Economic Thought of al-Ghazali* (Jeddah: Scientific Publishing Center, KAU, 2012).

Ghazi, Mahmood Ahmad, *Islamic Renaissance in South Asia 1707-1867* (Islamabad: Islamic Research Institute, 2009) (1st ed., 2002).

Green, David I., 'Pain-Cost and Opportunity-Cost,' *The Quarterly Journal of Economics*, Oxford University Press, vol. 8/2 (1894), pp. 218–229.

Greyling, Chris, 'Schech Yusuf, the founder of Islam in South Africa', *Religion in South Africa*, 1/1 (1980), pp. 9–22.

Grice-Hutchinson, Marjorie, *Early Economic Thought in Spain, 1177-1740* (London: George Allen & Unwin, 1978).

Halepota's thesis, '*Practical Theology and Ethics of Shah Wali-Allah*' cited by Abdel-'Aal, Khalil Abdel Hamid (1970), 'God, the Universe, and Man in Islamic Thought: The Contribution of Shah Waliullah of Delhi (1702–1762)', (University of London: 1970) pp. 392–397. PhD Dissertation

Heffening, W., "*Tadbīr*' in *The Encyclopaedia of Islam*, Old Edition, Leyden E.J. Brill & London, Luzac and Co., 1934), vol. 4, p. 595.

Heilbroner, Rober L. and Thurow, Lester C., *The Economic Problem* (New Jersey: Prentice Hall, Inc. 1975), Fourth Edition.

Hermansen, Marcia K., *The Conclusive Argument from God* (Translation of Shah Wali-Allah's *Ḥujjat-Allāh al-Bālighah* (Leiden: E. J. Brill, 1996).

Hodgson, Marshall G. S., *The Venture of Islam* (Chicago: The University of Chicago Press, 1974), Vol. 3.

Hunter, M.H. and H.K. Allen, *Principles of Public Finance* (New York: Harper and Brother, 1940).

Iqbal, Mohahammad, *The Reconstruction of Religious Thought in Islam* (New Delhi: Kitab Bhavan, 2006).

Islahi, Abdul Azim, *Economic thought of Ibn al-Qayyim* (Jeddah: International Centre for Research in Islamic Economics, King Abdulaziz University, 1984).

Islahi, Abdul Azim, *Economic Concepts of Ibn Taimiyah* (Leiscester: Islamic Foundation, U.K., 1988).

Islahi, Abdul Azim, An Analytical Analysis of Al-Ghazali's Thought on Money and Interest, Paper presented to *the International Conference on Legacy of Al-Ghazali, organized by ISTAC, Kuala Lumpur,* during Oct. 24-27, 2001).

Islahi, Abdul Azim, *Contributions of Muslim Scholars to Economic Thought and Analysis* (Jeddah: Scientific Publishing Centre, KAU, 2005).

Islahi, Abdul Azim, *Muslim Economic Thinking and Institutions in the 10th AH/16th AD Century*, (Jeddah: Scientific Publishing Centre, King Abdulaziz University, 2009)

Islahi, Abdul Azim, *A Study of Muslim Economic Thinking in the 11th AH / 17th CE Century* (Jeddah: K.A.U. Deanship of Scientific Research, 2011a).

Islahi, Abdul Azim, 'The Myth of Bryson and Economic Thought in Islam' in: *Journal of King Abdulaziz University: Islamic Economics*, 21/1 (2008), pp. 57–64.

Islahi, Abdul Azim, *Muslim Economic Thinking and Institutions in the 10th AH/16th CE Century* (Jeddah: Scientific Publishing Center, King Abdulaziz University, 2009).

Islahi, Abdul Azim, *Islamic Economic Thinking in the 12th AH and 18th CE Century*, (Jeddah: Scientific Publishing Center, King Abdulaziz University, 2011b).

Islahi, Abdul Azim, *History of Islamic Economic Thought* (Cheltenham, UK and Northampton, USA: Edward Elgar, 2014).

Islahi, Muhammad Ajmal, 'Tasānīf-e Farāhi Kā Ghair Matbuah Sarmāyah' (Farahi's unpublished works) in *Allāmah Hamduddin Farāhi: Hayāt -o-Afkār* (Allamah Hamid al-Din – Life and thought), Proceeding of Farahi Seminar (Sarai Mir, Azamgarh: Dairah Hamidiyah, 1992) pp. 57–96.

Itzkowitz, Norman, *Ottoman Empire and Islamic Tradition,* First published 1972, Reprint. (Chicago and London: the University of Chicago Press, 1980) Phoenix Edition.

Jalbani, G. N., *Teaching of Shah Waliullah of Delhi,* New Delhi: Islamic Book Service, 1998).

Jalbani, G. N., *An English Translation of Sata'at* (Hyderabad (W.P.): Shah Waliyullah Academy, 1970).

Jalbani, G. N., *Life of Shah Wali-Allah* (Lahore: Ashraf, 1978).

Jalbani, G. N., Shah Waliyullah of Delhi, in *The Muslim Luminaries,* Islamabad, National Hijra Council, 1988), pp. 15–56.

Jamil, Ahmad, Kh., Shah Waliullah, in Jamil, A. K. *Hundred Great Muslims* (Des Plaines, IL (U.S.A.), Library of Islam, 1987), pp. 297–303.

Kamali, Sabih Ahmad, *Type of Islamic Thought* (Aligarh: Aligarh Muslim University Press, 1966).

Keynes, *J.M., The General Theory of Employment, Interest and Money,* (London: Macmillan and Co. 1936).

Khan, Iqbal Ghani, 'The Awadh Scientific Renaissance and the Role of the French: C. 1750-1820', *Indian Journal of History of Science,* vol. 38/3 (2003), pp. 273–301.

Khan, Nawab Siddiq Hasan, *Ithāf al-Nubalā al-Muttaqīn bi-Akhbār Ma'āthir al-Fuqahā wa'l-Muḥaddithīn* (Kanpur: Matba Nizami, 1288 AH).

Kuran, Timur, 'Continuity and Change in Islamic Economic Thought', in: Lowry, S. Todd (ed.), *Pre-Classical Economic Thought,* Boston, Kluwer Academic Publisher, (1987), pp. 103–113.

Laffer, Arthur B., 'The Laffer Curve: Past, Present, and Future', (2004), http://www.heritage.org/Research/Taxes/bg1765.cfm, accessed 15 June 2006.

Lane, E. W., *An Arabic-English lexicon*, (Cambridge: Islamic Texts Society, 3: (1984), 1125–1126.

Leshem, Dotan, 'Oikonomia Redefined.' *Journal of the History of Economic Thought*, vol. 35/1(2013), pp. 43–61.

Leshem, Dotan, What Did the Ancient Greeks Mean by *Oikonomia*? *Journal of Economic Perspectives*, 30/1 (2016), Winter, pp. 225–231.

Lewis, Bernard, *The Muslim Discovery of Europe*, London, Weidenfeld and Nicolson, 1982).

Lewis, Geoffrey, *Turkey* (London: Ernest Benn Ltd. 1965). 3rd Revised ed. First published in 1955.

Lipsey, Richard G., and Streiner, Peter O., *Economics* (New York: Harper International, 1981).

Mawdudi, S. Abul A 'la, *Tajdīd -o- Ihyā'-i Dīn* (A Short History of Revivalist Movement in Islam) (Delhi, Markazi Maktabah Islami, 1986 [1978]).

Mawdudi, S. Abul A 'la, *Pardah* (the Veil) (Lahore: Islamic Publications, 1987 [1940]).

Moinul-Haq, S., *Islamic Thought and Movements* (Karachi: Pakistan Historical Society, 1979).

Muḥibbul-Hasan (ed.), *Waqā'i'-i Manāzil-i Rūm: Diary of a Journey to Constantinople* by Khwaja Abdul-Qadir (Aligarh: Department of History, Aligarh Muslim University, 1968).

Nadwi, Mujibullah, *Fatāwā-i Ālamgirī aur uske Mu'allifin* (*Fatāwā-i Alamgirī* and its Editors) (New Delhi: Taj Company, 2001).

Nadwi, Syed Abul Hasan Ali Hasani, *Tārīkh-i Dāwat -o- Azīmat* (*Saviours of Islamic Spirit*), (Lucknow, India: Majlis-i Tahqiaqat -o- Nashriyat-i Islam, 2006).

Nagrami, Muhammad Uwais, 'Shah saheb ka yek Ilmī mākhaz' (A source of Shah Wali-Allah's thought), *Shah Wali-Allah Number, Al-Furqan* (Breily), (1359/1941), pp. 347–351.

Nizami, Khaliq Ahmad, *Shāh Wali-Allāh ke Siyāsī Maktūbāt (the Political Letters of Shah Wali-Allah)* ed. and tr. by K.A. Nizami (Aligarh, unkown publisher, 1955).

Nizami, Khaliq Ahmad, *Some Aspect of Religion and Politics in India during the Thirteenth Century* (Delhi: Idara-i-Adbiyat-i-Delhi, 1971), 2nd ed.

Numani, Shibli, *Ilm al-kalam* (Azamgarh, Dar al-Musannefin, Shibli Academy, 2017).

Olson, Mancur, *Rise and Decline of Nations* (New Haven: Yale University Press, 1982).

Orman, Sabri, 'From Oikonomia to 'IlmTadbīraI-Manzil - Intercivilizational Exchange of Knowledge', in: Recep Şentürk (ed.), *the Intellectual Tradition of Islam, Civilization and Values* (Istanbul: Istanbul Chamber of Commerce, 2013), pp. 170–202.

Oser, Jacob, *The Evolution of Economic Thought* (New York: Harcourt Brace, 1970).

Oser, Jacob and Blanchfield, W.C., *The Evolution of Economic Thought* (New York: Harcourt Brace, 1975), Third Edition.

Plessner, Martin, *Der Oikonomikos des Neupythagoreers 'Bryson' und sein Einflus auf die Islamiche Wissenshaf* (Heidelberg: C. Winter, 1828).

Ritter, Helmut, 'Ein Arabiches Handbuch Der Handelswissenshaf", *Der Islam*, 1917), VII: 1–91.

Rizvi, Saiyid Athar Abbas, *Shah Wali-Allah and his Times* (Canberra, Ma'rifat Publishing House, 1980).

Rosenthal, E. I., *Averroes' Commentary on Plato's Republic* (Cambridge: Cambridge University Press, 1965).

Rosenthal, F., *Muqaddimah of Ibn Khaldun*, (An Introduction to History) Translated by (New York: Princeton University Press, 1967).

Schimmel, Annemarie, *Islam in the Indian Subcontinent* (Leiden: E J Brill, 1980).

Schumpeter, Joseph A., *History of Economic Analysis* (London: Routledge, 1997).

Shaykhu, Louis, *KitābTadbīr al-Manzil* in: *al-Mashriq* (Beirut), (1921), 19/ 3, pp. 161–181.

Shemesh, A. Ben (Tr.), *Taxation in Islam*, (vol. I), Yahya ben Adam's *Kitāb al-Kharāj*, Revised Edition (Leiden: E.J. Brill, 1967).

Shemesh, A. Ben (Tr.), *Taxation in Islam*, vol. II (Leiden: E.J. Brill, 1965).

Shemesh, A. Ben (Tr.), *Taxation in Islam*, vol. III, Abu Yusuf's *Kitāb al-Kharāj* (Leiden: E.J. Brill and London: Luzac & Co, 1969).

Sialkoti, Hafiz Ibrahim Mir, *Tārikh Ahl-i Ḥadīth* (History of Hadith Followers) (Lahore: Maktabah Quddusiah, n.d).

Siddiqi, Abdul Hamid, 'Renaissance in Indo-Pakistan: Shah Wali-Allah Dihlawi' in: M. M. Sharif (ed.), *A History of Muslim Philosophy* (Karachi: Royal Book Company, 1983), vol. 2, pp. 1557–1579.

Siddiqi, Muhammad Nejatullah, *Rationales of Islamic Banking* (Jeddah: International Centre for Research in Islamic Economics, King Abdulaziz University, 1981).

Sindhi, Ubaidullah, *Shāh Waliullāh aur unki Siyāsi Tahrik* (Shah Wali-Allah and his Political Movement) (Lahore: Kitab khanah Punjab, 1942).

Sindhi, Ubaidullah, Imām Wali-Allah ki *ḥ*ikmat ka ijmali ta'aruf (A concise introduction of imām Wali-Allah's philosophy), *Shah Wali-Allah Number, al-Furqan* (Bareily) (1359/1941), pp. 235–287.

Smith, Adam, *Wealth of Nations* (New York: Modern Library Edition, 1937), (originally published in 1776).

Spengler, Joseph J., 'Economic Thought of Islam: Ibn Khaldun', *Comparative Studies in Society and History*, (The Hague), (1964), vol. VI, pp. 268–306.

Spiegel, H. W., *The Growth of Economic Thought*, (Durham: Duke Univ. Press, 1983).

Tabatabai, Ghulam Husayn Khan, *Siyar al-Muta'akhkhirin* (the biographies of scholars in the later centuries) (Lucknow, India: 1866).

Tusi, Nasir ad-Din, The Nasirean Ethics, trans. from Persian by G. M. Wickens (London: G. Alien and Unwin Ltd. 1964).

Voll, J., 'Muhammad Hayya al-Sindi and Muhammad Ibn Abd al-Wahhab: an Analysis of an Intellectual Group in Eighteenth Century Madina', *Bulletin of the School of Oriental and African Studies* (1975), vol. 38, pp 32–39.

Whittaker, Edmund, *Schools and Streams of Economic Thought* (London, John Murray, 1960).

Woelfel, Charles J., *Encyclopedia of Banking and Finance* (Chicago and Cambridge: Probus Publishing Company, 1994).

Zwemer, S.M., 'The Wahabis: Their Origin, History, Tenets, and Influence', *Journal of the Transaction of the Victoria Institute*, (1901), vol. 33, pp. 311–30.

Index

B

D

E

F

G

J

K

N

O

P

Q

R

S

T

U

W

Y

Z